Stan Without Ollie

Stan Without Ollie
The Stan Laurel Solo Films, 1917–1927

TED OKUDA *and*
JAMES L. NEIBAUR

Foreword *by* JERRY LEWIS

McFarland & Company, Inc., Publishers
Jefferson, North Carolina, and London

OTHER NEIBAUR AND OKUDA WORKS FROM MCFARLAND

Chaplin at Essanay: A Film Artist in Transition, 1915–1916, by James L. Neibaur (2008); *Arbuckle and Keaton: Their 14 Film Collaborations*, by James L. Neibaur (2007); *The Bob Hope Films*, by James L. Neibaur (2005); *The Jerry Lewis Films: An Analytical Filmography of the Innovative Comic*, by James L. Neibaur and Ted Okuda (1994); *The RKO Features: A Complete Filmography of the Feature Films Released or Produced by RKO Radio Pictures, 1929–1960*, by James L. Neibaur (1994; paperback 2005); *Grand National, Producers Releasing Corporation, and Screen Guild/Lippert: Complete Filmographies with Studio Histories*, by Ted Okuda (1989; paperback 2012); *Tough Guy: The American Movie Macho*, by James L. Neibaur (1989); *The Monogram Checklist: The Films of Monogram Pictures Corporation, 1931–1952* by Ted Okuda (1987; paperback 1999); *The Columbia Comedy Shorts: Two-Reel Hollywood Film Comedies, 1933–1958*, by Ted Okuda *with* Edward Watz (1986; paperback 1998); *Movie Comedians: The Complete Guide*, by James L. Neibaur (1986)

LIBRARY OF CONGRESS CATALOGUING-IN-PUBLICATION DATA

Okuda, Ted, 1953–
    Stan without Ollie : the Stan Laurel solo films, 1917–1927 / Ted Okuda and James L. Neibaur ; foreword by Jerry Lewis.
       p. cm.
    Includes bibliographical references and index.
    Includes filmography

    ISBN 978-0-7864-4781-7
    softcover : acid free paper ∞

    1. Laurel, Stan — Criticism and interpretation. I. Neibaur, James L., 1958– II. Title.
PN2287.L285O38 2012
791.4302'8092 — dc23   2012022489

BRITISH LIBRARY CATALOGUING DATA ARE AVAILABLE

© 2012 Ted Okuda and James L. Neibaur. All rights reserved

No part of this book may be reproduced or transmitted in any form or by any means, electronic or mechanical, including photocopying or recording, or by any information storage and retrieval system, without permission in writing from the publisher.

Front cover photograph: Stan Laurel, circa 1920s (Photofest); cover design by David K. Landis (Shake It Loose Graphics)

Manufactured in the United States of America

McFarland & Company, Inc., Publishers
  Box 611, Jefferson, North Carolina 28640
    www.mcfarlandpub.com

To the Sons of the Desert,
the international fraternal organization
dedicated to the appreciation
and preservation of the legacy
of Stan Laurel and Oliver Hardy

Table of Contents

Acknowledgments — viii
Foreword by Jerry Lewis — 1
Introduction — 4

1. Stan Laurel — 7
2. Laurel at Universal — 11
3. Stan Laurel Meets Hal Roach — 16
4. Stan Laurel at Vitagraph — 30
5. Stan and Broncho Billy — 38
6. Stan Returns to Hal Roach — 60
7. Stan Laurel and Joe Rock — 129
8. Stan Returns to Hal Roach Again — 166
9. Laurel with Hardy — 180
10. Laurel and Hardy — 216

Epilogue — 226
Appendix: Compilations, Television Syndication, 8mm Movies and the Home-Video Market — 229
Bibliography — 234
Index — 235

ACKNOWLEDGMENTS

Every book dealing with the lives and careers of Stan Laurel and Oliver Hardy (including this one) owes a debt to John McCabe's pioneering *Mr. Laurel and Mr. Hardy* and William K. Everson's *The Films of Laurel & Hardy*. Randy Skretvedt's *Laurel and Hardy: The Magic Behind the Movies* and Scott MacGillivray's *Laurel & Hardy: From the Forties Forward* broke new ground with their illuminating critical assessments and production histories. Rob Stone added to this sterling scholarship with his landmark *Laurel or Hardy: The Solo Films of Stan Laurel and Oliver "Babe" Hardy*, which chronicles their pre-teaming output. Our sincere thanks to all of these authors (and others we've failed to mention) for their influence on this book, and for influencing the way we look at Stan and Ollie in general.

We extend our deepest gratitude to the generous folks who provided us with research materials, information, and advice: Dave and Ali Stevenson, Serge Bromberg, Paul E. Gierucki, Alex Bartosh, Bill Cappello, Mark A. Miller, Michelle Vogel, David Maska, and David J. Hogan.

Years ago, when veteran comedians Clyde Cook and Emil Sitka graciously shared their memories of Stan Laurel and his films, we didn't expect we would be utilizing these quotes one day. We're glad to have the opportunity to do so now.

For encouragement and support, our heartfelt thanks to Jamie Brotherton, John Cavallo, Mary and Steve Cooper, Jan MacGillivray, Dave Kehr, Sam Mastromauro, Henry and Karen Ottinger, Ralph and Kathy Schiller, Terri Niemi, Leonard J. Kohl, Jim Mueller, Bob Furmanek, Eddie Deezen, Steve Randisi and members of the Chicago chapter ("tent") of the Sons of the Desert, the Bacon Grabbers (including Mark Yurkiw, Marcia Opal, Mike Tynus, Lee and Dee McBeath, Laura Roman, Gary Cohen, and Laura LaRocca).

We are greatly indebted to Jerry Lewis for providing us with an affectionate and eloquent foreword.

Foreword by Jerry Lewis

I welcome this opportunity to say a few words about Stan Laurel, who was an idol, mentor and friend. My friendship with Stan was so meaningful to me because I had — and *have*— such a deep adoration for him. I grew up loving his movies and I would later discover, to my delight, that this great artist was also a beautiful human being. He was always encouraging and supportive. He was a comic genius and an authority on what makes people laugh, yet he was modest about his own achievements. He was a kind and thoughtful man. I saw Stan do things that I've never seen anyone else do. He would get fan mail from all over the world and I watched him sit down and type individual responses to his fan letters. That's just one example of his humanity.

Stan was not only a great comedian, he was an amazing writer and creator of comedy. Like Charlie Chaplin, Stan had been part of the Fred Karno troupe in England. That experience taught him how to hold an audience by doing pratfalls and other physical bits of business. Stan loved working in an ensemble, playing off of the human element. It stirred his creative energy. When he was making movies, I think he was looking for what he had missed from the ensemble because he surrounded himself with funny people. Stan was very much a team player. He worked hard to create comedy but he didn't feel he always had to be the one who delivered the gag. That's why he was just as happy to work behind the camera as well as in front of it. That's why he gave some of the best material to Ollie or someone else. Stan wanted to create laughter but he wasn't concerned about who got the laughs. That generosity of spirit is what made him special.

Stan was the creative force behind his movies, regardless of who received directorial credit. It's not that those directors were inept or ineffectual, but it was Stan who set the ground rules. In his early films, Stan experimented with ideas and characters, learning through trial and error what worked for him and what didn't. Every comedian needs to find out who he is and what his strengths are. He also schooled himself in the filmmaking process and became one of the finest technicians in Hollywood. By the time he was working with Oliver Hardy, Stan knew how to create gags, how they should be performed and the best way to film them. Stan drew upon his collective experience and created masterpieces that are just as funny today as they were all those years ago.

In the later Laurel and Hardy movies, Stan was not allowed the same creative control he had at the Hal Roach Studio, so those later films are below his usual high standards, which is not surprising. Without a comedian's input, any comedy film will suffer.

This book contends that Stan might have been quite a formidable presence as a comedy star even if he had remained a solo performer. I respectfully disagree with that and I believe Stan would have disagreed too. Stan became what he became because his partnership with Oliver Hardy boosted him to the level of greatness. Alone, Stan wouldn't have gotten that far because he would have missed that support, the "wall" that Ollie provided in order for their comedy to work as well as it did. Ollie provided that wall for Stan, just as Dean did for me. That wall is filled with love, compassion and respect, and I know how much a team needs it. With Ollie as his partner, Stan came up with ideas that took them to magnificent places — places that Stan would not have gone if he had been on his own. Ollie was a great exponent of Stan's ideas, and I know that Stan loved how Ollie would take the material and turn it into something beautiful, something beyond expectations. So when you talk about what Stan would have been without Ollie, I would have to acknowledge that Stan would have probably been a body in motion with an inventive mind but without that extra layer of genius. And Stan would have been the first to say so.

I paid tribute to Stan in *The Bellboy* (1960), the first film I directed. My character was named Stanley, and when the bell captain refers to me as "the only Stanley in the world," out comes Bill Richmond doing a terrific impersonation of Stan Laurel. Bill, who's been my collaborator on numerous projects, is also a great admirer of Stan and as far as we're both concerned, Stan truly was the only Stanley in the world.

Normally I'm a little skeptical about books like this because I don't think everyone is qualified to discuss another person's credits, especially if they're not filmmakers themselves. But the authors did such a marvelous job of examining my own film career — they were insightful and fair-minded in dishing out praise and criticism — that I am confident my dear friend Stan is in good hands.

Jerry Lewis paid tribute to Stan Laurel in *The Bellboy* (1960).

Postscript: During a visit to Stan's home, Jerry was presented with one of Stan's employee passes (dating back to the 1920s) to the Hal Roach Studios. To this day, Jerry keeps Stan's pass in his wallet.

Jerry Lewis, best known for his slapstick brand of humor, is a comedian, actor, film producer, screenwriter and film director.

INTRODUCTION

Stan Laurel and Oliver Hardy represent perhaps the greatest pairing of actors in motion picture history. The beloved duo continues to delight their fans, old and new, with their warmly human characters and the relaxed, methodical style that defined their special brand of humor. Above all, their unshakeable bond of friendship distinguishes them from most other comedians and has served as an inspiration for countless double-acts that have come in their wake.

Unlike Abbott and Costello or Martin and Lewis, Laurel and Hardy did not enter films as an established team. They worked as solo artists for years, with Hardy cast in bit parts and supporting roles (and as an occasional lead) as far back as 1913, and Laurel alternating between acting, writing and directing assignments (sometimes a combination of all three) since 1917. While Hardy worked mostly as a character actor and comic foil, Laurel was usually the lead comedian who more often than not received top billing.

During his nearly ten years of solo work, Laurel did not fully establish his familiar "Stanley" persona until after he teamed with Hardy. In his early films, Laurel displayed certain Stanley-esque qualities and there were clear indications of what lay in the future. Yet Laurel would discover, through trial and error, what was best suited to his talents and, ultimately, that working opposite a strong comic figure like Ollie would define and enhance his own character. While we can see the rudiments of Stanley in his solo films, it's hard to dispute that Laurel would have taken a different path had he not become part of a team.

Immersed in the filmmaking process, Laurel eventually supervised the writing and direction of his movies (and wrote and directed comedies in which he didn't appear). It is interesting to speculate what Laurel would have accomplished had he maintained a solo career. He may have achieved the same *auteur* status as Charlie Chaplin and Buster Keaton. It can be argued that

Laurel might have become a formidable comedy star on his own, at least on the same level as Charley Chase or Larry Semon. If Laurel had been allowed to graduate to feature-length films, he may have even rivaled Chaplin, Keaton, Harold Lloyd and Harry Langdon. As it turned out, he *did* rival them — but with Oliver Hardy at his side.

While there have been numerous studies of the Laurel and Hardy canon, relatively little has been written about Laurel's solo efforts. Rob Stone's ground-breaking *Laurel or Hardy: The Solo Films of Stan Laurel and Oliver "Babe" Hardy* was the first book to offer an extensive examination of the subject, and we owe him a great debt of thanks. Placed within the context of Laurel's overall output, these early efforts are frequently referred to as intriguing curios or outright failures, and a number of them fall neatly into these categories. But many of these films are surprisingly good, even when parts are better than the whole.

The main hurdle facing Laurel's solo work, in terms of general acceptance or reevaluation, is the inevitable comparison to the prime Laurel and Hardy output, which is undeniably superior on every level. Yet without the lessons Laurel learned during his solo years, the team of Laurel and Hardy as we know it would have never existed, and for this reason alone, Laurel's early films have earned the right to be acknowledged and appreciated. That many of these films are quite entertaining on their own terms is an added plus.

Stan Laurel was not an investigative filmmaker. He explored how the cinema could enhance gags and routines, but he did not aspire to the technical wizardry that came so instinctively to Buster Keaton. This is not to imply that Laurel's movies were not *cinematic*. Laurel quickly learned that through cinematography and editing he could create comedy of a type that would have been impossible to replicate on stage in a live performance. In time, Laurel's skills as a "total filmmaker," as Jerry Lewis calls it, became second to none.

Basic questions arise when discussing Laurel's solo films, especially since they are usually looked upon as a mere training ground for his brilliant work with Hardy. Is there anything in Laurel's performances and creative abilities as a writer and director that offer a portent to what lay ahead — or what might have been? Was his artistic growth significant enough to warrant a reassessment of these embryonic efforts? Do these films remain amusing a century after the fact and do they possess the timeless quality of his comedies with Hardy? What about his development as an actor? As a director? As a writer? What are parallels between "solo Stan" and "Stanley"? Hopefully, we have addressed all of these issues.

Our text examines Laurel's solo efforts in the order they were made, not in the order they were released, because a number of them were not distributed or copyrighted chronologically. So we felt the best (and only) way to properly assess Laurel's artistic growth and development was to look at the films in the order of production.

Also, unlike similar studies, we do not end the coverage once Laurel is paired with Hardy. Most of the initial Laurel and Hardy comedies were, in spirit if not content, actually solo Laurel comedies that Hardy just happened to appear in. Further experimentation was still required before they truly became Laurel *and* Hardy, so we've included the entries that best illustrate this point.

The Laurel and Hardy films were the culmination of everything Stan Laurel had learned during his formative solo years. These early efforts deserve to be examined and defended, not only for their historical significance but for the opportunity to see a bona fide comic genius in action.

1

STAN LAUREL

The team of Stan Laurel and Oliver Hardy achieved legendary status as early as the 1950s, when TV broadcasts of their classic comedies won them a new generation of fans. These viewers, like moviegoers before them, were unaffected by the long-held beliefs of "professional" critics who deemed Stan and Ollie unworthy of ranking alongside great comedians such as Charlie Chaplin or Buster Keaton. Laurel and Hardy made some of the funniest movies ever made, a fact that was abundantly clear in spite of the occasionally ruthless treatment on the part of a station editor or an endless series of commercial interruptions.

Fortunately, this new exposure would lead to a general reappraisal of the team and their work, resulting in a number of biographies, filmographies, and other discourses written by the very same people who came to cherish Laurel and Hardy comedies through television (and later, 8mm movies and various home-movie formats).

Yet relatively little attention has been paid to their pre-team solo films, the conventional wisdom being that what they accomplished as a team eclipsed either man's earlier work. The Stan Laurel films in particular are dismissed as rehearsals for the cinematic magic that lay ahead. While Laurel would not achieve true greatness until he partnered with Hardy, his best solo efforts are clever, high-spirited comedies that are funny in a different style from later output. In many instances, the similarities between his solo films and the Laurel and Hardy films are unmistakable and surprising.

Stan Laurel was born Arthur Stanley Jefferson on June 16, 1890, in Ulverston, Lancashire, England, to parents who were heavily involved in the theater. His father, Arthur Jefferson, was an actor, playwright, and theater manager, so it was natural that his son would eventually be bitten by the theater bug.

Young Jefferson first performed on stage at the age of 16 in 1906, toiling as a single act before joining Fred Karno's famed acting troupe in 1910. Another

As a member of The Stan Jefferson Trio, Stan imitated Charlie Chaplin (1916) (courtesy Paul Gierucki).

comedian, Charles Spencer Chaplin, was already established in the Karno troupe, and Arthur Stanley Jefferson became his understudy. On a tour of the United States, Chaplin found his way into American films by signing with Mack Sennett's Keystone Studio. Chaplin's departure elevated Stan's position in the troupe.

After a degree of success on the vaudeville circuit with The Keystone Trio and The Stan Jefferson Trio, an act with Alice and Baldwin Cooke, he changed his name to Stan Laurel at the suggestion of his onstage (and offstage) partner, Mae Charlotte Dahlberg (1888–1969). Mae saw a drawing of a Roman general wearing a laurel wreath and suggested "Laurel" as a surname.

A 1913 portrait of Stan Laurel, who was then billing himself as "Stan Jefferson."

In 1917, while performing in a double act with Mae (who had also adopted the name Laurel), Stan was offered $75 per week to star in two-reel short comedies. Charlie Chaplin had achieved international stardom almost overnight, so Stan decided to investigate his potential in motion pictures.

Nuts in May

Cast

Stan Jefferson .... Mental patient
With
Mae Dahlberg, Lucille Arnold, Owen Evans, Charles Arling.

Credits

Robin E. (Bobby) Williamson .... Director
Harry Fowler .... Cinematographer

No copyright registered.
Production dates: Late June–early July 1917.
Released in 1917 (?), by Isadore Bernstein Productions, Inc. Two reels.

It is unfortunate that so little is known about Stan Laurel's screen debut, *Nuts in May*, one of the many lost films of the silent era. While other lost films at least received documented theatrical releases, there is no confirmation that *Nuts in May* was ever distributed, which further compounds the lack of available data.

In 1917, Isadore Bernstein, formerly the general manger of Universal Studios, went into independent film production. After some success with feature-length melodramas, Bernstein decided to form a comedy shorts unit and signed Stan for a series of "Stanley Comedies." Based on a surviving trade announcement, Stan was supposedly billed as Stan Jefferson in the first series entry, *Nuts in May*, though he had already changed his stage name to Stan Laurel. In the film, he appeared opposite his vaudeville partner Mae Dahlberg, who had also adopted the Laurel surname despite the fact they were never legally married.

Filmed in Boyle Heights, California, *Nuts in May* reportedly dealt with the exploits of an escaped mental patient (Stan) who has a Napoleon Bonaparte complex, to the point where he runs around town wearing a very conspicuous Napoleon hat. The completed two-reeler was previewed at the Hippodrome Theater in Los Angeles, with Charlie Chaplin and Carl Laemmle, the head of Universal, in attendance. Then Bernstein scrapped his plans to produce comedy shorts and *Nuts in May* apparently languished. Bernstein marketed his movies on a "states' rights" basis, which meant selling them on a territorial basis to regional film exchanges. It is a possibility that *Nuts in May* also received the states'-rights treatment, but since independently made movies marketed in this manner rarely played major, studio-controlled theatrical circuits, it would have gone unnoticed by reviewers. On the other hand, it was never registered for copyright, nor are there any censor-board records or trade advertisements, so the question remains as to whether it saw any kind of distribution.

Although no prints of *Nuts in May* are known to exist, a copy was still available in the mid–1920s when Laurel and G. M. Anderson lifted scenes from it to insert into *Mixed Nuts*, which was largely comprised of unused footage from *The Pest* (1922). Like *Nuts in May*, *Mixed Nuts* was marketed on a states'-rights basis, making an exact release date impossible to confirm. (It is generally assumed it was sometime in 1925.) Unlike *Nuts in May*, however, a print of *Mixed Nuts* has survived.

2

LAUREL AT UNIVERSAL

Charlie Chaplin and Carl Laemmle attended the preview of *Nuts in May* and both saw Laurel's potential as a movie comedian. Chaplin expressed interest in making him a member of his stock company, but Chaplin didn't follow through with a concrete offer, so Laurel signed a contract with Laemmle.

Carl Laemmle was the president of Universal Studios, and under his guidance Universal produced some of the most successful feature-length films of the silent era, including *Traffic in Souls* (1913), *Blind Husbands* (1919), *Foolish Wives* (1922), *The Hunchback of Notre Dame* (1923), *The Phantom of the Opera* (1925) and *The Cat and the Canary* (1927). With the advent of talking pictures, Universal would inaugurate the horror-movie genre with such classics as *Dracula* (1931) and *Frankenstein* (1931).

In 1917, Laemmle hired new performers and increased film production to build up a reserve of titles, so the studio could avoid paying a war tax on new product that was about to go into effect. When Stan Laurel signed with the Universal Film Manufacturing Company in mid–September 1917, the studio had separate units that produced films under the studio banner, among them two comedy units: the L-KO Motion Picture Kompany and Nestor Comedies. L-KO (which stood for "Lehrman-Knockout" comedies) was originally started by director Henry Lehrman, who worked on some of Chaplin's early Keystone efforts, but now run by the Stern Brothers from a studio at Sunset and Gower in Hollywood. Nestor, started by David Horsley, shot their films on the Universal lot. Laurel would recall in later interviews that the atmosphere at Universal was very tense, and that the established comics looked upon newcomers with suspicion and jealousy.

Laurel completed four films for Universal (two for L-KO, two for Nestor) but his stay there came to an end on November 1, 1917, after Laemmle decided the studio had enough titles stockpiled. The Laurel comedies were released over the course of a year, and as is the case with his first film, *Nuts in May*, there are no surviving prints.

Period reviews indicate that these films were received as average, pleasant vehicles, but it is obvious that Laurel was still working from his stage roots and did little to establish a motion picture persona during his brief tenure at Universal. The title of one of Universal films, *Hickory Hiram*, subsequently led to speculation that Laurel made several comedies playing this character, similar to Harold Lloyd's Willie Work or Lonesome Luke pictures. However, historian Rob Stone clarifies that there never was a Hickory Hiram series.

Because the films are lost, no assessment can be made of Stan Laurel's Universal output. The credit and plot information, referenced from Rob Stone's *Laurel or Hardy* book, is provided. The films are listed in the order that they were made, despite being released in a different order. In all of his Universal comedies, Stan was billed as "Stanley Laurel."

(This would not be Laurel's last association with Universal. Some of his later comedies for producer Joe Rock — most notably *Dr. Pyckle and Mr. Pride* [1925] — were shot on the Universal lot.)

Phoney Photos

Cast

Stanley Laurel .... Swift
Rena Rogers .... Grace Grouch
Neal Burns .... Jules
Walter Belasco .... Mr. Grouch
Lydia Yeamans Titus .... Mrs. Grouch

Credits

Edwin Frazee .... Director, writer
Henry McRae .... Supervisor
Working titles: "The Photographer's Story" and "Skidding Hearts."
A Carl Laemmle production. Copyrighted June 24, 1918.
Production dates: late September–early October 1917.
Released July 3, 1918, by the L-KO Motion Picture Kompany.
Two reels.

Phoney Photos was Laurel's first film for Universal, though not the first one released. Series films were not always released in the order they were made, and this practice would occur throughout Laurel's movie career.

The plot centers around Grace, who loves Swift, though her parents want her to marry Jules instead. Grace and Swift make plans to elope, but Mrs. Grouch dresses her maid to resemble Grace in order to fool Swift. But

Jules is the one who gets confused and ends up with the maid, while Grace runs off to the minister with the man of her choice.

Of *Phoney Photos*, *Moving Picture World* noted, "The action is of the nonsensical, farcical sort and while not extremely laughable has numerous funny spots. The number is one of about average strength."

Hickory Hiram

Cast

Stanley Laurel	Hiram
Teddie Sampson	Trixie
Neal Burns	Neal

With Bartine Burkett

Credits

Edwin Frazee .... Director, writer

Working title: "Doing His Bit."
A Carl Laemmle production. Copyrighted March 27, 1918.
Production date: circa October 1917.
Released April 8, 1918, by Nestor Comedies/Universal Film Manufacturing Company. One reel.

Despite its lost-film status, this is perhaps the best-known entry in Laurel's Universal output, if only for the references to the title character Stan would make in later interviews.

Hiram is a farm worker who longs to live in the big city. He and his girl, Trixie, run off to experience city life, with $1.98 to cover their expenses. They go to a burlesque show, but when Neal steals Hiram's wallet, Hiram and Trixie land in jail when they're unable to pay their bill. Hiram later wakes up, realizing that his excursion with Trixie was merely a dream.

Neal Burns, who played Laurel's rival, later signed with producer Al Christie and starred in his own series of comedy shorts. Leading lady Teddie Sampson was, at the time, married to popular screen comedian Ford Sterling.

Although *Hickory Hiram* was made after *Phoney Photos*, it was released three months ahead of it. *Bioscope* found *Hickory Hiram* to be "quite funny and unusually well acted."

Whose Zoo?

Cast

Kathleen O'Connor	Katherine
Rube Miller	Rube
Stanley Laurel	Stanley
Eddie the Ellfa-Nut	Charlie the elephant

Credits

Craig Hutchinson . . . . Director, writer
Also known as *Who's Zoo?*
A Julius Stern production. Copyrighted May 14, 1918.
Released May 22, 1918, by the L-KO Motion Picture Kompany.
Two reels.

Stanley, a head waiter at a posh hotel, decides to have fun at the expense of Rube, a tourist. Both get mixed up with Katherine, the pretty wife of a jealous husband, resulting in a slapstick bedroom farce with a lot of running in and out of rooms, and leaping from windows. At one point, Rube, who has gotten a job at a zoo, releases the animals from their cages, including a bear and an elephant which chase him into the hotel.

There's a possibility that two versions of *Whose Zoo?* were released, as it was originally slated for release as a one-reel short in March 1918 and was even reviewed at that length by *Moving Picture World* ("entertaining and will go over with children"). Yet historian Rob Stone discovered that the film was officially released as a two-reeler on May 22, 1918. To add to the confusion, the longer edition was sometimes referred to in reviews as *Who's Zoo?* Press materials indicate Rube Miller was the dominant male lead in the picture, with Stan second-in-command.

Bioscope called *Whose Zoo?* "a diverting extravaganza ... an L-KO farce of especial merit."

O, It's Great to Be Crazy

Cast

Stanley Laurel . . . . Sam Squirrel

Credits

Leslie T. Peacocke . . . . Director, writer
A Carl Laemmle production. Copyrighted December 23, 1918.
Released December 30, 1918, by Nestor Comedies/Universal Film
Manufacturing Company. One reel.

In his final Universal release, Laurel plays Sam Squirrel, who gets a job as a supervisor at an insane asylum. The sanitarium director informs Sam that all of the inmates had escaped due to the negligence of the previous supervisor. Hoping to impress the director—and the director's daughter in particular—Sam manages to recapture the errant inmates. Despite Sam's accomplishment, the daughter rejects him anyway, so Sam joins the inmates as a fellow lunatic.

There are no production dates given for *O, It's Great to Be Crazy*, although he left the studio after November 1, 1917, which means it was released more than a full year after it was made.

Moving Picture World was unenthusiastic about the results: "This is full of knockabout situations, but there is no very definite trend to the various happenings and much of the action is lacking in point. Number is only fairly interesting." (*Moving World Picture* referred to the film as a two-reel comedy. This discrepancy may have been an error on the part of the reviewer since the picture was copyrighted as a one-reeler.)

3

STAN LAUREL MEETS HAL ROACH

Hal Eugene Roach (1892–1992) would be a very key figure in Laurel's cinematic career, especially during the 1920s when Laurel would excel as a writer, director, actor and, eventually, one half of the greatest comedy team in movie history.

The New York–born Roach held a variety of odd jobs before arriving in Los Angeles, where he found work as a movie extra and soon worked his way up to bit player and assistant director. In 1914, Roach produced nine short films, six of which starred his friend (and fellow extra) Harold Lloyd. Although this initial stab at producing failed, Roach formed the Rolin Film Company with his business partner Dan Linthicum and turned out a series of "Lonesome Luke" comedies starring Lloyd. The Lonesome Luke character was a Chaplin knockoff, but these early films allowed Lloyd to investigate gags ideas and hone his comic style. (Like Laurel, Lloyd would eventually develop his own unique screen persona.)

With the success of Lonesome Luke, Roach struck a deal with the Pathé Exchange to turn out additional comedy shorts. To meet his new quota, Roach signed famed clown Toto (real name: Arnold Novello), but the performer proved to be difficult to work with. (Rob Stone noted that Toto had a clause in his contract stating he would never have to jump into water.) Toto soon parted company with Roach, who owed Pathé five more shorts. Alf Goulding, who would later direct the Laurel and Hardy feature *A Chump at Oxford* (1940), suggested Stan Laurel as an ideal candidate to fill the void left by Toto. The replacement was contingent on Pathé's approval, so on or about May 25, 1918, a short test film was made, featuring Stan (as a slapstick waiter) and Roach contract comedian Harry "Snub" Pollard. Pathé liked what they saw, and on June 11 Laurel began work on his first Hal Roach production, *Do You Love Your Wife?*

3. Stan Laurel Meets Hal Roach

Do You Love Your Wife?

Cast

Stan Laurel .... Toby, the janitor
Marie Mosquini .... First class vampire
William Gillespie .... Elmer, the faithless husband
Bud Jamison .... Henpecked husband
Charles Stevenson .... Detective
Noah Young .... Policeman
James Parrott .... Hotel Patron

With

Dorothy Wolbert, Arbutus "Bunny" Bixby, Gus Leonard, Lois Neilson, Mildred Forbes, Belle Mitchell, William Peterson, May Burns

Credits

Hal Roach .... Director
Robb Doran .... Cinematographer
T. J. Crizer .... Editor

A Hal Roach production. Copyrighted November 21, 1918.
Production dates: June 11–15, 1918.
Released January 5, 1919, by Rolin Film Company/Pathé Exchange.
One reel.

"A vivid, gripping, gosh-awful story of intrigue, devotion and indigestion" was the introductory title to *Do You Love Your Wife?*

This is the earliest surviving Stan Laurel film and was made after he had already established himself as a screen comedian at Universal. Since none of Laurel's Universal output is known to exist, it is impossible to gauge his cinematic development up to this point. (However, no one knows what the future holds. For years, *Do You Love Your Wife?* was a lost film; now, it's available on DVD.) Nevertheless, Laurel's first film for Hal Roach is a tight little one-reel comedy filled with clever gags and situations. Laurel turns in a formidable performance (it's easy to see why Pathé approved him) and his creative input is evident throughout.

Stan plays Toby (the name is similar to Toto, and perhaps this was a project intended for the departed clown), a janitor at a posh hotel where assorted marital situations are taking place. Elmer (Charles Stevenson), an unfaithful husband, is having a rendezvous with a "strictly first class vampire" (Marie Mosquini, parodying screen vamp Theda Bara), while the henpecked husband (Bud Jamison) across the hall tends to his wife's French poodle.

Toby is blissfully unaware of all this as he enters the lobby from an elevator, pushing a broom along the floor and getting in the way of the patrons. When Toby is asked to mail a letter, he finds that the mailbox is stuffed with envelopes. He opens up the box, tosses out the contents, then locks it back up and inserts the letter with which he was entrusted. He then starts pushing his broom across the floor, attempting to sweep up all the envelopes he's discarded.

With these opening sequences, Stan establishes his character and effectively stands out among the other cast members. There are comedians whose appearance is so benign that they hardly distinguish themselves from the supporting players, especially in early one-reel comedies where garish makeup was something of the norm for everyone onscreen. But Stan possesses the discernible charisma necessary to be noticed.

Laurel immediately employs objects for his comedy. The broom, the mailbox, and the resulting attempt to sweep up the letters that he himself discarded, all dovetail into one another effortlessly. Even at this early date, Laurel's penchant for flowing, interconnected gag sequences was already evident. When Toby eschews the broom and brings out a vacuum cleaner to pick up the letters, Laurel explores additional gag possibilities with the machine. The suction from the vacuum causes the hose to stick to his chin, and to other patrons, but does little to pick up the envelopes. Laurel gets a lot of mileage out of these simple tasks, and it is fascinating to see what an adept movie comedian he is in only his sixth film. His physical agility is already on display, as he does the "rubber legs" bit he would repeat in the Laurel and Hardy comedies *You're Darn Tootin'* (1928), *Bonnie Scotland* (1935) and *The Flying Deuces* (1939).

Toby finds himself at the epicenter of marital discord when he leaves the hotel lobby to work upstairs, closer to the apartments. Vermicelli, Elmer's devoted wife, arrives to confront her cheating husband, whom she catches canoodling with the vamp. As Toby and the henpecked husband (Bud Jamison) flirt with the vamp's distraught maid from across the hall, Vermicelli pulls out a gun and shoots. The sound of gunfire startles Toby, who throws the milk bottle he's holding into the air. The bottle shatters over the henpecked hubby's head, so Toby hops on the man's back, reaches for a ceiling sprinkler, and cleans him off.

It is the timing of these gags that makes them succeed. When Stan throws the milk bottle in reaction to the gunshot, there is a three-second delay before it comes crashing down on Bud's head. During that delay—a clever and unexpected touch—none of the actors are looking upward. (Stan and the maid are too occupied reacting to the gunplay, while Bud is oblivious to both the gunfire and the tossing of the bottle.) The shattering bottle splatters milk all over the top of Bud's head, a (literally) striking visual gag. Stan's dragging a dazed Bud to the sprinkler (and resourcefully hopping onto his back) to rinse the milk out of his hair is a funny wrap-up to this series of interconnected gags, all neatly constructed for cohesive, cumulative effect.

After this point, *Do You Love Your Wife?* becomes surreal, a style of humor that Laurel would continue to indulge in for the remainder of his career. As Vermicelli continues firing her gun at Elmer, Toby steps in — to assist Vermicelli! He tells her, "Lady, you are wild, you have no control!," then helpfully draws a bull's-eye target on Elmer's back. When the gun runs out of bullets, Toby instructs Vermicelli, Elmer and the vamp to "wait here a minute," while he scurries out of the hotel and down the street. He takes a gun from a policeman (Noah Young) who, with a detective (Charles Stevenson), is apprehending a criminal. Returning to the hotel, Toby hands the cop's gun to Vermicelli, who, along with her husband and the vamp, has been waiting patiently. Toby positions both Vermicelli and Elmer for maximum impact, so the next shot strikes Elmer.

Things are wrapped up in an equally surreal manner. Vermicelli hands the gun to Toby and exits, just as the detective and policeman arrive to find Toby brandishing the weapon. As the cop drags Toby away, Elmer regains consciousness, only to discover the vamp has found another man — the detective, no less. Out in the hallway, Elmer reconciles with Vermicelli ("Darling, you're a good wife, but a bum shot," he tells her). Meanwhile, Toby knocks out the cop and switches uniforms with him, so the backup officers wind up dragging the cop away instead. But when Toby sees Vermicelli and Elmer acting lovey-dovey, he checks his pulse then grabs his own collar and drags himself off to jail.

Do You Love Your Wife? is filled with interesting ideas and is packed with more layers than one would expect to find in an early one-reel comedy, especially one starring a relative newcomer like Laurel. Balancing marital farce, outlandish visual gags (at one point, Laurel effortlessly lifts a marble pillar), and surrealism within the structure of a melodramatic parody is a lot for a one-reeler to take on. While the surrealism of the film's second half differs from the gag-driven comedy of the first half, the styles blend effectively to form a unified whole. There is nothing clumsy or awkward about the structure. Hal Roach was the credited director, but one has to wonder how much Laurel might have contributed to the film, even at this embryonic stage of his movie career, since concepts and themes that would become Laurel hallmarks are quite evident here.

Laurel's appearance is galvanizing. Even in a sequence where a young couple, in the foreground, is trying to mail a letter, it is Stan, standing in the background, who catches the viewer's eye, though he is making no attempt to steal the scene. When he gets the vacuum hose stuck to a lady's hat or his own chin, Laurel never blatantly calls attention to the gag. It all unfolds in a very natural fashion.

In Stan's brief scenes with burly Bud Jamison, the dynamics of a big guy contrasting the slightly built Stan are a portent to Laurel's later work with Oliver Hardy. Even by 1918, William "Bud" Jamison (1894–1944) was an experienced comic foil, having co-starred in the majority of Charlie Chaplin's films for Essanay. Jamison would have an extensive career in comedy, lending fine support to The Three Stooges, Buster Keaton, Harold Lloyd, W. C. Fields, Charley Chase, Andy Clyde, Bing Crosby, Edgar Kennedy, and Clark and McCullough. In *Do You Love Your Wife?*, Jamison earns laughs of his own when he is ordered by his domineering wife to exercise her pampered dog. As Jamison runs back and forth in the living room with the dog on a leash, the animal barely bothers to move at all.

Although Bud Jamison never appeared in any Laurel and Hardy films, two other supporting players in *Do You Love Your Wife?* would have connections with the team. James Parrott (1897–1939), seen in this film as the man whose wife (or girlfriend?) hands Stan a letter to mail, would later direct some of the finest Laurel and Hardy comedies, including *Two Tars* (1928), *Perfect Day* (1929), *Brats* (1930), *Hog Wild* (1930), *Helpmates* (1932) and *The Music Box* (1932), as well as co-writing the screenplays for *Way Out West* (1937), *Swiss Miss* (1938) and *Block-Heads* (1938). During the 1920s, Parrott, the younger brother of Charley Chase, also starred in a series of shorts (as "Paul Parrott") produced by Hal Roach.

Noah Young (1887–1958), a former champion weightlifter, co-starred with Stan and Ollie in *Do Detectives Think?* (1927), *Sugar Daddies* (1927), *The Fixer Uppers* (1935) and *Bonnie Scotland* (1935).

Lois Neilson, an extra in *Do You Love Your Wife?*, would later become Stan's first wife (they married in 1926 and divorced in 1933). The union produced two children, Lois Jr. and Stanley Robert Jefferson (born two months premature, he died nine days after birth).

Parody and satire were staples of silent comedy during this period. Even at Keystone, producer Mack Sennett was actually presenting satirical material at a slower pace (most of the wild, gag-filled comedies he is noted for came earlier in the decade). Hal Roach was just following suit, and Laurel's surrealistic touches provided a welcome and effective variation on the format. The sheer outrageousness of this material makes it every bit as amusing now as it was nearly a century ago.

(Although *Do You Love Your Wife?* was Laurel's debut for Roach, it was released two months after the second effort, *Just Rambling Along*, which was produced one week after this film.)

Just Rambling Along

Cast

Stan Laurel . . . . Drifter
Bud Jamison . . . . French chef

Noah Young .... Policeman
James Parrott .... Cook
Marie Mosquini .... Diner patron
Clarine Seymour .... Girl at register
With
Belle Mitchell, Wallace Howe, Max Hamburger, Hazel Powell, Dorothea Wolbert, Arbutus "Bunny" Bixby, Adu Sanders, Lillian Rothchild, Helen Fletcher, Alma Maxim, May Burns, William Peterson, M. Fitzgerald, Herb Morris, Bert Jefferson, A. Sanburg, G. Hutchins, Harry Clifton, E. Pearson, Emmy (Emmylou) Wallace.

Credits

Hal Roach .... Director
Robb Doran .... Cinematographer
T. J. Crizer .... Editor
A Hal Roach production. Copyrighted September 27, 1918.
Production dates: June 18–22, 1918.
Released November 3, 1918, by Rolin Film Company/Pathé Exchange.
One reel.

For decades, *Just Rambling Along* was the earliest surviving example of Stan Laurel's film work—aside from the footage of *Nuts in May* (1917) that was incorporated into *Mixed Nuts* (allegedly released in 1925)—until the rediscovery of *Do You Love Your Wife?*, which was produced a week before *Just Rambling Along*, though released two months after it. Four of the five one-reelers Laurel made for the Rolin Film Company were directed by Hal Roach, who would later remark that he was impressed by the young English comedian but could not have realized the impact each would have on the other's career.

In *Just Rambling Along*, Stan is on the boardwalk at Venice Beach when he notices a billfold on the ground. He points it out to a young boy, who picks it up and finds it is stuffed with money. Realizing his mistake, Stan tries to grab the billfold away from the kid, but the boy's father, who happens to be a policeman, intercedes. A pretty sunbather woos a group of male admirers, including Stan, and cunningly lures them into a nearby diner. The diner hostess/cashier can immediately tell Stan has no money and she literally tosses him out of the place.

The policeman gives his son a dime as a reward for recovering the billfold. Stan steals the dime from the boy and re-enters the diner, making it a point to show the stern hostess that "I am with money." After conniving free samples out of the French chef, Stan orders a ten-cent cup of coffee. He sits down next to the sunbather and, when he isn't looking, she grabs his check and swaps it with her $1.25 check. As she leaves, Stan attempts to follow her, but notices he doesn't have enough to cover the suddenly inflated amount of the check. He sneakily crawls out of the diner and runs smack into the cop and his son. Crawling back into the diner, he is roughed up by the angry chef and cook, who toss him out again. The cop beats Stan with a nightstick while the son cheers.

The title *Just Rambling Along* describes the structure of the film itself. There's no real plot, just a loose framework upon which to hang the gags. While the gags are amusing, it is Laurel's nimble performance that makes this one-reeler exceptional.

The initial setup involving the lost billfold instantly establishes the nature of Stan's character (he's polite enough to point the billfold out to the young boy, but aggressive enough when he sees the money and realizes it doesn't belong to the kid) and his situation in life (he's obviously destitute, living hand-to-mouth). His desperation leads him to fight a child, but he stops short of fighting a grown man, especially a policeman who looks as if he could break Stan in two with very little effort. Casting Noah Young as the menacing cop was a good move (a decision that was mostly likely made by Hal Roach in his capacity as producer and director) since the brutish-looking Young provides a sharp counterpoint to Stan's scrawny build. The contrast of their appearances further enhances the comic effect of their conflict.

Throughout *Just Rambling Along*, Laurel creatively embellishes rudimentary comedy material and situations. When he steals the dime from the young boy, Stan does not simply snatch it. Instead, he covers the boy's eyes with his left hand, presses his right index finger against the child's back and plucks the coin from his boy's hand. Stan executes this brief, impromptu hold-up with effortless grace, and the quick rhythm of his sleight-of-hand makes this throwaway bit seem funnier and more charming. (Stealing money from a child might be a dubious subject for humor, but the kid is so obnoxious that our sympathy is with Stan.)

Back inside the diner and on his way to the serving line, Stan spots the pretty sunbather. He flirts with her and she throws a glass of water in his face. Stan doesn't respond as other, lesser comedians would by making exaggerated gestures. He simply looks dazed, then makes swimming motions with his arms, and moves along without further incident. It is an inventive and surprisingly restrained piece of pantomime.

Hal Roach's perfunctory direction permits the actors to flesh out the comic setups with various bits of seemingly improvised business. Bud Jamison is especially amusing as the French chef who is so eager to impress Stan with his cooking that he allows Stan to freely sample the selections. Nothing appears to have been written specifically for Jamison. Roach, who may have known Jamison when both were working for Essanay, just lets Bud take control of the scene. With little screen time, Jamison offers a detailed picture of a big man working in cramped quarters, filling all orders in a timely fashion. In his encounter with Stan, Jamison goes through a wide range of facial expressions, from an anxious smile as he eagerly awaits Stan's assessment of the cuisine, to a disgusted snarl after Stan says he just wants "*ze* cup of coffee."

While Stan waits to get his check from the girl at the register, the cook (James Parrott, misidentified in filmographies as his older brother Charley Chase) absent-mindedly flips pancakes into Stan's hat, which Stan is holding behind his back. Stan puts the hat back on his head, unaware of its new contents. He sits down next to the sunbather, who instructs him to remove his hat, and then tries to point out the pancakes that are now perched on top of his head. But Stan doesn't get the hint and thinks she's pointing to someone seated at an adjoining table. She gestures again, and Stan scans the room, using the salt-and-pepper shakers as a makeshift pair of binoculars. Frustrated, she points to her head, indicating that he should check his own, but instead, Stan examines *her* scalp. Finally, Stan realizes what she's been trying to tell him and removes the pancakes. As the girl begins touching up her face with a powder puff, Stan uses one pancake as though it were a compact mirror and dips the another pancake into a sugar bowl, and touches up his own face. Again, Stan's impeccable timing makes this set-piece seem all the more funny. (Some of the diner gags in *Just Rambling Along* were repeated in a later Laurel solo effort *Mixed Nuts* [allegedly released in 1925, though the date is unconfirmed].)

James Parrott performs an amusing bit with Stan earlier in the film, when Laurel refuses to take off his hat. Parrott snatches Laurel's hat and hangs it on a hat rack. Stan grabs it and puts it back on. Parrott removes it again, so when Stan retrieves it, he also grabs another hat from the rack and puts that one on his head. This time, Parrott winds up snatching the wrong hat as Stan puts his own hat back on and moves along. As with most gag sequences that are purely visual, printed words can't convey the expert physical timing of this seconds-long sequence, but it is one of the highlights of the film.

Parrott would later direct some of the Laurel and Hardy comedies. Of course, these films sprang primarily from Stan's creative vision, but Parrott's contributions should not be summarily dismissed, as he was the credited director on several of the team's best efforts — including *Two Tars* (1928), *Helpmates* (1932) and the Oscar-winning *The Music Box* (1932) — and that's an achievement not to be taken lightly.

Nineteen-year-old Clarine Seymour (born December 9, 1898) has a bit part as the girl who hands Stan his ten-cent check. Seymour appeared in *Just Rambling Along* fresh from her stint in the Rolin Film Company's ill-fated Toto (the clown) series. The following year, Seymour became a member of

D.W. Griffith's stock company, with prominent roles in *True Heart Susie*, *Scarlet Days* and *The Girl Who Stayed Home* (all 1919 releases). Griffith gave her the female lead in *The Idol Dancer* (1920), her biggest opportunity to date and, tragically, her final film. Seymour died on April 25, 1920, at the age of 21, after an operation for strangulation of the intestines.

In his book *Laurel or Hardy: The Solo Films of Stan Laurel and Oliver "Babe" Hardy*, Rob Stone accurately notes that "Stan is relatively calm compared to the hyperactive characteristics that he displayed so frequently in his early comedies. The film has no chase, Stan doesn't do a single scissors kick, and the film works."

As in many of his early comedies, Stan wears heavy makeup around his eyes because the orthochromatic film stock used during this period could not properly photograph his pale blue eyes. Later, with the advent of panchromatic film stock, Stan was able to abandon this requirement.

Just Rambling Along is a tight, funny, and very interesting one-reel comedy. It shows the intuitive comic creativity of Stan Laurel, who manages to elevate the humor to a much higher level with just the slightest nuance in his expressions.

The critical response to *Just Rambling Along* is typified by this *Bioscope* review:

> This is quite a bright little slapstick comedy. It is not too ambitious, but relies, much more on the acting of its leading artiste than on the fooling itself.... Stan Laurel appears to be above the average slapstick comedy star, and has many little tricks of his own and good facial expression which appear to have been modeled on Charlie Chaplin's. They are, of course, not nearly as good, but are amusing all the same.

Chaplin cast such a large shadow that comparisons were inevitable and unavoidable. In time, however, Laurel would step out from behind that shadow and establish himself as one of the greatest comedians of all time.

Hoot Mon!

Cast
Stan Laurel, Bud Jamison, Margaret Joslyn, Marie Mosquini, Noah Young, James Parrott, W. Howe, Belle Mitchell, Dorothea Wolbert, Bunny Bixby, Lillian Rothchild, William Peterson, M. Fitzgerald, Harry Clifton, Emmy Wallace, Gus Leonard, Jerome Laplauch, D. Coburn, D. Alberts, Carrie Fowler

Credits
Hal Roach .... Director
T. J. Crizer .... Editor
Robb Doran .... Cinematographer

A Hal Roach production. Copyrighted January 23, 1919.
Production dates: June 24–29, 1918.
Released March 1, 1919, by Rolin Film Company/Pathé Exchange.
One reel.

Another intriguing lost item in the early Laurel filmography, *Hoot Mon!* cast Stan as an American who journeys to Scotland. There he purchases a tavern called the Ye Blue Coo Inn and tries to adapt to the culture by wearing kilts and playing golf. The Scottish setting foreshadows *Short Kilts* (1924), and the America-to-Scotland premise would be reversed for the Laurel and Hardy comedy *Putting Pants on Philip* (1927), in which Stan played a kilt-clad Scotsman. (Hal Roach evidently had a fondness for this theme, since he would later refer to *Putting Pants on Philip* as the funniest short comedy his studio ever produced.) The golf angle would also seem to predate *Should Married Men Go Home?* (1928), one of Laurel and Hardy's best silent-era two-reelers.

We have access to the films that immediately precede *Hoot Mon!*, allowing us to understand Laurel's status of comic development at this point in his film career. Reviews indicated that *Hoot Mon!* did not have a great deal of plot but did contain strong characterizations and a number of amusing gags. The *Exhibitors Trade Review* noted, "Stan Laurel, the English comedian who has acted in a series of comedies for the Rolin Company, keeps the gait rapid, though it might be a bit unsteady at times." *Hoot Mon!* appears to have been on the same artistic level as previous Laurel efforts, as Stan continued to refine his comedic style.

No Place Like Jail

Cast

Stan Laurel . . . . Convict

With

Bud Jamison, Marie Mosquini, Noah Young, James Parrott, W. Howe, Belle Mitchell, Dorothea Wolbert, William Peterson, Gus Leonard, Dorothy Coburn, Dan Alberts, Cris Lynton, Herb Morris, Estelle Harrison, Hazel Powell, Alice Renze, Vivienne Plaza, Edna Renze, Dorothy Terry, Margaret Hansen, Sherman P. McIntyre

Credits

Frank Terry . . . . Director
T. J. Crizer . . . . Editor
Robb Doran . . . . Cinematographer

A Hal Roach production. Copyrighted September 27, 1918.
Production dates: July 1–5, 1918.
Retakes: July 12, 1918.
Released October 7, 1918, by Rolin Film Company/Pathé Exchange.
One reel.

A lost film, *No Place Like Jail* was the first of Stan Laurel's five Hal Roach–produced Rolin comedies to receive theatrical release, although it was not the first one made. (The initial effort, *Do You Love Your Wife?*, was not released until January 1919.) Its jail setting suggests this is a forerunner of Laurel's later solo effort *Detained* (1924) as well as the Laurel and Hardy prison-themed comedies *The Second Hundred Years* (1927), *The Hoose-Gow* (1929) and *Pardon Us* (1931), but this is just speculation.

Stan Laurel and his pal (presumably Bud Jamison, though unconfirmed) are inmates being released from prison after first having to serve an extra six-month sentence for bad behavior. When they finally get out, a man hires them to kidnap his former lover, who is a student at an all-girls school, and the ex-cons wind up abducting the school's headmistress instead. Fearing the wrath of the spurned man, the bumbling duo turn themselves in to the police and are once again safe behind bars.

Contemporary reviewers dismissed *No Place Like Jail* as a conventional effort. *Moving Picture World* found "the scenes in the girls school are most amusing, the number on the whole is of average interest." But *Bioscope* observed, "There is nothing in it to approach the humor of Charlie Chaplin or the ingenuity and imagination of the Harold Lloyd comedies.... Stan Laurel shows signs of talent which may possibility be developed later on, but at present there is nothing to warrant an eager expectancy of something startling good to come."

By 1918, Chaplin had established himself as the screen's premier comic artist, and the *Bioscope* review attests that Lloyd's popularity had solidified long before his later, more acclaimed films. Stan was perceived as a promising rookie, but time would prove that something "startling good" was indeed to come from Mr. Laurel.

(This lost film should not be confused with a home-movie edition of *Detained* that was retitled *No Place Like Jail*.)

Hustling for Health

Cast

Stan Laurel	Houseguest
Frank Terry	Friend
Marie Mosquini	Friend's wife
Bud Jamison	Mr. Spotless
Noah Young	Train conductor, garden inspector

With

Margaret Joslyn, Belle Mitchell, Dorothea Wolbert, James Parrott, D. Coburn, Hazel Powell, Sadie Gordon, Catherine Proudfit, Rose Gore, Pearl Elmore, Mrs. Fleming, J. LaPlouch.

Credits

Frank Terry . . . . Director
T. J. Crizer . . . . Editor
Robb Doran . . . . Cinematographer
Working title: "The Rest Cure."
A Hal Roach production. Copyrighted December 17, 1918.
Production dates: July 6–11, and July 13, 1918.
Released February 2, 1919, by Rolin Film Company/Pathé Exchange.
One reel.

Coming as early as it does in Laurel's screen career, his performance in *Hustling for Health* reveals a surprising subtlety that would be less evident in many of his subsequent solo films. There are even minor traces of the "Stanley" character that lay nearly a decade in the future.

As the film opens, Stan is off for a quiet vacation ("He longs to smell the salt air of the pine woods," reads an intertitle), but just misses his train. At the station, he runs into an old friend who invites him to his home for a restful stay. ("Nothing to annoy you but mosquitoes and poison ivy," he tells Stan.) The friend has a messy yard and the next-door neighbor, Mr. Spotless, reports the eyesore to the garden inspector. To help out, Stan cleans up the yard — by dumping the debris over the brick fence, onto Mr. Spotless's property. His friend's wife refuses to cook dinner, so Stan once again helps out, by going next door and stealing a meal Mrs. Spotless has prepared. When Mr. and Mrs. Spotless bemoan the theft, the friend's wife invites them over for a snack. But Mrs. Spotless recognizes her own cooking and Stan nervously slips out the door and retreats to the yard, where he flirts with the Spotlesses' daughter.

The predictable formula for a setup like this would have presented the lead comedian as a demanding, sloppy houseguest who indulges in all manner of creature comforts but offers nothing in return and shows no intention of leaving. *Hustling for Health*, however, adopts an entirely different perspective. Immediately upon accepting his friend's invitation, Stan is the patsy. He is handed several packages to carry, stacked so high they cover his face. To pay their train fare, the friend takes money from Stan's pocket. Once they get off the train, the friend hires a horse-drawn wagon and Stan is forced to ride in the back of the cart with all the packages. But the extra weight causes the horse to break free from the harness, so Stan is recruited to pull the wagon all the way to the house. To emphasize Stan's struggle, the camera is tilted to one side, making it appear he's pulling the wagon, which now looks like an oversized rickshaw, up a steep hill. The idea for this bit, and the way it's photographed, derived from Charlie Chaplin's *Work* (1915), in which Charlie is a paperhanger's assistant who has to pull a loaded wagon up a steep incline.

If we are to assume that Laurel was allowed some measure of creative input, even at this early stage of his film career, then it is interesting to see that his character is a patsy, as he would often be in the Laurel and Hardy pictures. The friend is using Stan in the same manner Ollie would contrive to get Stanley to do most of the heavy lifting. Unlike the meek, hapless Stanley, here Stan is put off and disgusted by this treatment, but goes along with it regardless. It is an intriguing parallel to the situations and interactions that would come to define the dynamics of the Laurel-Hardy relationship.

When they arrive home, the humor turns to a then-topical subject as the friend's wife (Marie Mosquini) is presiding over a suffragette meeting (the topic: "Are husbands human beings or microbes?"). *Hustling for Health* was made less than two years before women won the right to vote (on August 26, 1920), so meetings such as this, held in private homes, were quite the norm by 1918, as women discussed their lack of equal rights in a male-dominated society. Reflecting the attitude of most men of the era, the suffragettes are depicted as dour, sexless old biddies. Even the attractive Mosquini, who usually played ingénues, downplays her good looks by wearing glasses and an ultra-conservative wardrobe. Stan enters the house and is roughed up by the suffragettes, who take out their anti-male hostility on him.

The film then shifts gears as Stan's character becomes less of a victim and more of stumblebum whose attempts to be helpful and sociable create havoc. The next-door neighbor, Mr. Spotless (Bud Jamison), is shown meticulously tending to his garden. Stan tries to be friendly, leaning on the brick fence that separates the properties, which causes bricks to loosen and fall into the neighbor's yard, crashing through glass-enclosed structures. As Stan cleans his friend's dirty yard, he throws rubbish over the fence, further ruining Mr. Spotless's carefully cultivated garden. Yet Stan isn't being deliberately aggressive or spiteful. He simply thinks he's being helpful and is puzzled by the neighbor's apoplectic reaction.

Stan's character goes off on another tangent when he steals food from the neighbors and serves it to his friend's family. Now he is neither a victim nor an innocent — he's a rascal who is fully aware of his guilt. This behavioral shift makes little sense, and when he sneaks away after the theft is discovered, he returns to his genial self and flirts with the Spotlesses' daughter, continuing to do so as a rainstorm engulfs them. But the basic conflicts remain unresolved, as the film comes to a sudden and disappointing conclusion.

Although it is inferior to *Do You Love Your Wife?* and *Just Rambling Along, Hustling for Health* is interesting for the themes upon which Laurel would later expand. His "houseguest" status would be repeated in the Laurel and Hardy films *Unaccustomed As We Are* (1929) and its quasi-remake, *Block-*

Heads (1938). In both, Ollie promises Stan that his wife will prepare a sumptuous meal, only to have Mrs. Hardy balk at the idea. (Stan doesn't resort to stealing food on these occasions.) Stan "helping out" Ollie was a recurring premise, one of the prime examples being *Helpmates* (1932), in which Ollie recruits Stan to clean up the house before Mrs. Hardy returns. Ollie is frantically trying to cover up all traces of the wild party he threw the night before, and Stan's "help" only creates a bigger mess, culminating in burning Ollie's house down after pouring gasoline into the fireplace. (Compared to that, Mr. Spotless got off easy.)

English comic Frank Terry, who plays Stan's friend in *Hustling for Health*, also directed the film. Terry, who was also known as "Nat Clifford," would appear with Laurel and Hardy in *The Midnight Patrol* (1933) and *Me and My Pal* (1933), and served as one of Stan's gag writers during those years. Terry's lasting contribution to the Laurel and Hardy legacy was the infectious "We Are the Sons of the Desert" tune he wrote for the team's finest feature-length film, *Sons of the Desert* (1933).

Marie Mosquini (1899–1983) was a fixture of the Hal Roach comedies from 1917 to 1926, co-starring with Stan Laurel, Harold Lloyd, Charley Chase, Snub Pollard and Will Rogers. Although she appeared in a total of seven Laurel solo films, she left Roach in 1926, before she had the opportunity of working with Laurel *and* Hardy.

Noah Young plays two roles in *Hustling for Health*. He appears in the opening scenes as a train conductor; later, he dons a fake mustache for the role of the garden inspector who also serves as a health officer, policeman and city councilman.

The *Moving Picture World* review stated that Stan plays a henpecked husband in *Hustling for Health*, but there's no indication of this in the actual film. But they were on-target when they noted, "There is no very definite connecting plot and the number on the whole is only fairly strong."

4

STAN LAUREL AT VITAGRAPH

After completing *Hustling for Health*, Laurel's contract with the Rolin Film Company was fulfilled and his services were no longer needed. He planned a return to vaudeville, but wound up at Vitagraph, where he appeared in three two-reel comedies starring Larry Semon, one of the most popular movie comedians of the era.

The Vitagraph Company of America was founded in 1896 by J. Stuart Blackton and Albert E. Smith. Originally located on the rooftop of a Manhattan building, Vitagraph was soon occupying production facilities in the Flatbush area of Brooklyn, New York. It was one of the first studios to compete with Thomas Edison's productions, with Edison filing patents and arranging a team of lawyers in an attempt to force rival companies to cease production. Shortly after the turn of the century, however, Vitagraph was among the most vital and successful production companies in the American movie industry. Vitagraph's importance to the evolution of motion-picture comedy began with comic visionary John Bunny, who, perceiving the potential of the infant medium, offered his services to the company in 1910. Rotund, expressive and endearing, Bunny was immediately embraced by moviegoers, who loved his comedies, particularly the domestic farces co-starring Flora Finch as his shrewish wife. In no time, Bunny became the most popular film star in the world.

Larry Semon (1889–1928) went to work for Vitagraph in 1916, the year after John Bunny's death. The son of a vaudeville magician ("Zera the Great"), Semon was originally hired as a gag writer, but soon found himself in front of the camera. Like Bunny, Semon quickly established himself as an audience favorite, and his comedies were among the most popular of the era. Vitagraph, which by this time had a West Coast operation, allowed Semon to graduate from one- to two-reel subjects and gave him complete creative control.

Semon's comedies were action-packed, brimming with breathlessly paced and often ingenious sight gags. But as entertaining as his films were, Semon never developed a tangible comic personality beyond his odd appearance (short, scrawny and horse-faced), so there was a certain sameness that crept into all of his work.

Buster Keaton, in his autobiography *My Wonderful World of Slapstick* (with Charles Samuels; Doubleday, 1960), offered this assessment of Larry Semon:

> [Semon] was an extraordinary silent-pictures comic.... His movies were combinations of cartoon gags, fantastic gags, and farcical plots. Chaplin, Lloyd and myself just couldn't make two-reelers as packed with laughs as Larry's. But when an audience got a half a block from the theatre, after being convulsed by Semon's *whammios*, they couldn't have told you what they laughed at. I would say this was because they were impossible gags.

Without a discernible screen persona, Semon attempted to wow his audiences with bigger and more violent gags, and while many were startlingly funny, others came off as painful and sadistic, with a particularly unpleasant dependence on animal abuse. It's extremely disturbing to watch a monkey nearly suffocate in a barrel of gooey dough in *The Dome Doctor* (Chadwick, 1925).

Under the right circumstances, however, Semon was able to overcome his inherent limitations. When he was funny — and he was funny far more frequently than his detractors are willing to admit — one can easily understand why he was so popular. As Kalton C. Lahue observed in *World of Laughter: The Motion Picture Comedy Short, 1910–1930* (University of Oklahoma Press, 1966):

> Larry was an agile acrobatic clown whose comedy may not have been strikingly original, and he was not enough of a comedian by himself to succeed without the aid of a gimmick, but he became extremely clever in the use of visual mechanical gags and he was a great exponent of the chase.

By any standards, Semon efforts such as *The Sawmill* (Vitagraph, 1922) and *The Cloudhopper* (Chadwick, 1925) are excellent examples of silent-screen comedy. Unfortunately, Semon's penchant for lavish, elaborate gags caused his budgets to rise to astronomical sums. Eventually, the Vitagraph brass insisted he underwrite his own films, and in 1924 the studio refused to renew his contract.

Laurel made three films for Vitagraph during the summer of 1918. Since they were starring vehicles for Larry Semon, Laurel's contributions in the first two (*Huns and Hyphens, Bears and Bad Men*) were negligible. However, by the third film (*Frauds and Frenzies*), he was acting as a veritable comedy partner. Semon's enormous popularity guaranteed Laurel a larger viewing audience than his earlier solo work, which benefited his career significantly.

According to published accounts, Semon was displeased with the amount of attention Laurel was getting and fired him. But Rob Stone cites the influenza epidemic of 1918 as a more likely reason for Stan's departure. Vitagraph and several other film companies shut down during this period, forcing Laurel to return to vaudeville. (Vitagraph didn't reopen until November 4, 1918, months after *Frauds and Frenzies* was completed.)

Interestingly enough, Oliver Hardy would later become one of Semon's favorite supporting players, as well as one of his closest friends (it was Semon who introduced Hardy to the game of golf, a passion Ollie held to the end of his life). Hardy remembered Semon as being benevolent and supportive, while Laurel allegedly recalled Semon as egocentric and demanding. (Hardy did not appear in any of the Larry Semon comedies in which Laurel was featured.)

Assessing Laurel's contributions to these films is a bit tricky in that they are not the product of Stan's comic vision. All we can do is to evaluate Stan's performance from the perspective that he was an actor-for-hire and note any bits of business that might be considered harbingers of later accomplishments.

Huns and Hyphens

Cast

Larry Semon	Larry
Madge Kirby	Vera Bright
Stan Laurel	A serious customer
Frank "Fatty" Alexander	Owner of the American Café
Billy McCall	Customer
Peter Gordon	Waiter
Bill (William C.) Hauber	Waiter
Mae Laurel	Café Patron

Credits

Larry Semon	Director
Larry Semon	Writer

An Albert E. Smith production,
for Big V Comedies/Vitagraph Pictures.
Copyrighted September 10, 1918.
Released September 23, 1918, by Vitagraph Company of America.
Two reels.

Huns and Hyphens was the first two-reel comedy Larry Semon made, after having appeared exclusively in one-reel comedies up to this point. The longer format did not allow for greater depth in Semon's humor — he just added more gags without using the additional time for character or plot development. However, while *Huns and Hyphens* may be nothing more than a loosely structured gag fest, it is a clever and funny gag fest that provides a good showcase for Semon's high-energy comic creativity.

In *Huns and Hyphens*, Vera Bright has invented a new gas mask that has just been approved by the U. S. government. Larry is her rich paramour — or so Vera thinks. He's actually a humble waiter at a beer garden known as the American Café, which, unbeknownst to Larry, is being used as a front by a gang of German sympathizers. Vera's servant is also deceiving her; he's Fritz Nasti, a German spy who informs the café owner about her invention. Vera and her stepfather are invited, under false pretenses, to attend a grand gala ball at the café, where they discover Larry is not the millionaire he pretended to be. When the spies demand that Vera turn over the plans for the gas mask (conveniently for plot exposition, she carries the plans around with her at all times), Larry springs into action and defeats the entire gang single-handedly.

The title *Huns and Hyphens* is in the same vein as the nonsensical couplings that comprised the titles of other Semon comedies of the period, such as *Chumps and Chances* (1917), *Slips and Slackers* (1917), *Spooks and Spasms* (1917), *Guns and Greasers* (1918), *Rummies and Razors* (1918), *Bathing Beauties and Big Boobs* (1918) and *Soapsuds and Sapheads* (1919). In *Huns and Hyphens*, it is interesting, from a historical viewpoint, how Semon incorporated the anti–German propaganda prevalent during World War I, illustrating how even frivolous slapstick shorts touched upon these wartime sentiments.

As the star of the picture, Semon dominates the proceedings with an onslaught of fast-paced, amusing sight gags. After leaving Vera's home, the nattily dressed Larry gets on his ridiculously small car (it's so small, he can't get into it, and he straddles the fenders) and has to lasso a passing automobile in order to depart. He parks his car in a doghouse and enters the café, where he strips down to his overalls (with apron attached) and is handed a platter of beer mugs to serve to waiting customers. Laurel would execute similar changes of wardrobe in his working-class comedies *Pick and Shovel* and *Gas and Air* (both 1923 releases).

The showdown with the gang of saboteurs captures Semon at his best, as he relentlessly piles one gag upon another, giving the audience no time to catch its collective breath. Running, jumping, crashing through brick walls, scampering across rooftops — Semon uses every trick in the book, and it's difficult not to be won over by his boundless energy. The final scenes with Semon and one of the saboteurs clinging to an open umbrella and floating their way back to the café bring the film to a pleasing conclusion.

As a gang member identified as "a serious customer," Laurel isn't given much to do, spending most of his limited footage chomping on a cigar and looking menacing (as menacing as Stan Laurel can look, that is). But he is allowed one of the film's best gags. Stan steals eggs and stuffs them into the back pocket of his trousers. Semon gives Stan a swift kick in the behind, and broken egg shells and five newborn chicks tumble from the inside of Stan's pants leg. One wonders if it was Laurel, and not Semon, who contributed this gag as Stan would use it years later in his film *Somewhere in Wrong* (1925). (It's probably unlikely, but intriguing to ponder nonetheless.) Semon would repeat this gag himself in *The Show* (Vitagraph, 1922) and his notoriously wretched feature-length "adaptation" (we use the term very loosely here) of *The Wizard of Oz* (Chadwick, 1925).

Huns and Hyphens was enthusiastically received by reviewers and the movie-going public. *Bioscope* raved, "This remarkably funny and wonderfully photographed comedy is stuffed with laughs. Lawrence Semon is surpassing himself as the acrobatic hero."

Bears and Bad Men

Cast

Larry Semon	Larry Cutshaw
Madge Kirby	Slawson daughter
Stan Laurel	Pete
Frank "Fatty" Alexander	Paw Slawson
Billy McCall	Stranded actor
Blanche Payson	Maw Cutshaw
Pete Gordon	Paw Cutshaw
Mae Laurel	Scared woman

With
Bill (William C.) Hauber, Bessie the bear, Brownie the bear.

Credits

Larry Semon	Director
Larry Semon	Writer

An Albert E. Smith production, for Big V Comedies/Vitagraph Pictures.
Copyrighted September 28, 1918.
Released October 7, 1918, by Vitagraph Company of America.
Two reels.

Bears and Bad Men is another funny, gag-laden Larry Semon comedy, revolving around the oft-used premise of two feuding hillbilly clans—the Cutshaws and the Slawsons—with all of the stereotypes intact, including the usual *Romeo and Juliet* framework.

Larry Cutshaw is in love with a girl from the Slawson clan but the animosity between their families prevents him from courting her out in the open. When a pair of actors get stranded at the train station, they ask a local rube named Pete to carry their oversized steamer trunks to the cabin where the Slawsons live. Pete empties the two trunks to make them easier to carry, but Larry, fleeing from a bear, climbs into one of the trunks while the bear climbs into the other. At the cabin, Larry has to deal with a ferocious bear and an equally ferocious Paw Slawson.

Laurel has slightly more to do in *Bears and Bad Men* than in the previous *Huns and Hyphens*. His big scene is a fishing bit where, after having no success, he breaks his fishing pole. When Larry comes along and handily clubs a fish, picking it out of the water, Stan buys the club and bait from him. Attempting the same method, Stan merely gets a faceful of water from a belligerent fish. Laurel would perform a similar bit in one of the early Laurel and Hardy comedies, *Flying Elephants* (filmed 1927, released 1928).

Stan remains a part of the action during the bear-chase sequences, and is used effectively by Semon to punctuate the gags. Semon's penchant for wild comedy is perfect for the use of an actual trained bear (although a man in a bear suit doubles in some of the closer shots). Semon's fondness for contrasting types is also evident in his pairing of fearsome Blanche Payson and diminutive Pete Gordon as Maw and Paw Cutshaw.

The *Kinematograph Weekly* reviewer felt Stan and the rest of Semon's co-stars were overshadowed by their four-legged foil: "Lawrence Semon is an excellent comedian and a first rate athlete and he is assisted by a wonderful bear which deserves to be featured as a star."

Frauds and Frenzies

Cast

Larry Semon	Larry
Stan Laurel	Simp
Madge Kirby	Dolly Dare (the warden's daughter)
Billy McCall	Warden
Bill (William C.) Hauber	Prison guard

Credits

Larry Semon	Director
Larry Semon, C. Graham Baker	Writers

An Albert E. Smith production, for Big V Comedies/Vitagraph Pictures. Copyrighted October 14, 1918. Released November 11, 1918, by Vitagraph Company of America. Two reels.

From a glorified bit part in *Huns and Hyphens*, to a clear supporting role in *Bears and Bad Men*, and finally to veritable co-star status in *Frauds and Frenzies*, Stan Laurel's status in the Larry Semon films was certainly growing.

Larry and Simp are escaped two convicts who, when not dodging the police, pursue the same pretty young lady. She encourages the rivalry by giving both of them her address, something they're unaware of until they show up at her house at the same time. Her father turns out to be the warden, who recognizes them. While Simp is apprehended, Larry leads the police on a merry chase before hopping onto a passing car, landing right next to the warden, who is bringing Simp back to prison.

Semon employs his usual lightning-paced, gag-laden approach, but in *Frauds and Frenzies* he gives Laurel nearly equal screen time, and the two are a full-fledged team for most of the picture. The prison scenes foreshadow *Detained* (1924), one of Laurel's solo efforts, and *The Second Hundred Years* (1927), the first official Laurel and Hardy comedy, although Semon and Laurel's onscreen relationship bears no resemblance to Stan and Ollie. Semon and Laurel's characters are sweetly in sync one moment, combative the next, as the situation (and the gag) suits them. During a lunch break, Larry steals the meat from Stan's sandwich and replaces it with a handkerchief. When Stan discovers the theft, he starts beating up Larry and the fight continues until an armed guard comes along. The quarreling cons suddenly join hands and start doing a quick-step dance routine, encouraging applause when they conclude. They even get their hats mixed up — Larry's derby winds up on Stan's head, Stan's straw hat winds up on Larry's head — something that would become a treasured Laurel and Hardy hallmark.

Another Laurel and Hardy parallel is an intertitle describing Larry and Stan as "Two heads each filled with naught," foreshadowing the motto Stan chose in 1964 for the Sons of the Desert, the international fraternal organization devoted to the lives and films of Laurel and Hardy: "Two Minds Without a Single Thought" ("Duae Tabulae Rasae In Quibus Nihil Scriptum Est," which literally means "Two blank slates on which nothing has been written").

During this formative period of his film career, it is fascinating to watch Laurel operating within a two-man team dynamic, even if he is far removed from his beloved Stanley persona. As "Simp," Laurel does indeed play a simple (and simpering) figure opposite Semon's usual crafty daredevil character. Semon is definitely the dominant half of this pair, but Laurel is sharp enough to know when he's been had and scrappy enough to retaliate. For two comedians with no real history of performing together, Semon and Laurel mesh surprisingly well, though their characters aren't defined beyond dumb-and-dumber caricatures. Laurel is basically just required to keep up with Semon's frantic pace, and he does so admirably.

In the final moments, Laurel is apprehended and Semon has the climactic chase all to himself. While this may strike some as selfishness on Semon's part, he does deserve credit for devoting as much footage to Laurel, a supporting player, as he did. At some point, *Frauds and Frenzies* was bound to be solely a Larry Semon comedy, and the chase, which is relatively brief, is funny and energetic enough to compensate for Stan's absence.

Frauds and Frenzies was another well-received Semon effort and the critics enjoyed Stan's participation, though they strangely failed to mention his name in the reviews, even when they were praising him. *Kinematograph Weekly* said, "Larry is doing time with his friend, who is every bit as ingenious and athletic as himself, and very nearly as comic.... It owes its mirth [to] the amusing antics of the two chief actors as to the swiftly moving adventures in which they are central figures."

Larry Semon became a popular comedian by speeding up the action and piling on the gags. Larry's "friend" would become a great comedian by slowing down the tempo and establishing how the gags were interconnected with his character.

After *Frauds and Frenzies*, Laurel returned to vaudeville, leaving any idea of a motion picture career behind. It is ironic that after Laurel's departure from Vitagraph, Oliver Hardy would become a prominent member of Larry Semon's stock company.

5

STAN AND BRONCHO BILLY

G.M. "Broncho Billy" Anderson was one of the true pioneers of cinema, having appeared in Edwin S. Porter's *The Great Train Robbery* (1903), and starring in some of the first Western films. The Broncho Billy series was the blueprint for nearly every Western series that would follow.

Anderson's series of cowboy films were produced for his own studio, Essanay, which he formed with George K. Spoor. The studio name was the first initial of each last name (S and A, Essanay). By 1915, Anderson's westerns were quite popular, as were several productions by the studio featuring such stars as Francis X. Bushman and True Boardman. It was late in 1914 when Essanay acquired the services of Charlie Chaplin, who, after his first year in films, had become the most popular star in American movies. Hiring Chaplin away from the Keystone studio was a major coup and required a lot of money, making the comedian the highest-paid star in motion pictures at that time. The 16 short films Chaplin made for Essanay in 1915 benefited from his full creative control, his artistic vision adding depth and substance to the otherwise slapstick two-reelers. This set a standard for all comedy movies to come afterward.

After Chaplin left Essanay the following year, the company sputtered to a halt, and Anderson sold his portion of the company to investigate independent production. One of his ventures was Macdon Pictures, which he formed in 1920. After re-establishing himself as a producer of popular Western films, Anderson looked into starting a comedy unit. He hired Essanay friends like Ben Turpin and Billy Armstrong to appear in what he called Jolly Comedies. When these films failed to take off, Anderson formed Amalgamated Producing. In January of 1921, a film entitled *The Lucky Dog* was produced, featuring Stan Laurel in the lead and, in a small role as a holdup man, Oliver Hardy.

The Lucky Dog

Cast

Stan Laurel	Stanley*
Florence Gillet	The girl
Oliver "Babe" Hardy	A bandit/Count De Chease

Credits

Jess Robbins	Director
Irving Reis	Cinematographer

Produced by Shiller Productions through the Amalgamated Producing Company.
No copyright registered.
Production dates: late January–early February 1921.
Released October 1921† by Sun-Lite series/Reelcraft via states'-rights.
Two Reels.

"Put 'em both up, insect, before I comb your hair with lead."
— Oliver Hardy meets Stan Laurel in *The Lucky Dog*

The Lucky Dog is the first time Stan Laurel and Oliver Hardy appeared in the same film. As such, it is a valuable and fascinating document of what would some day be the greatest comedy team in motion picture history. *The Lucky Dog* is routinely categorized as a Laurel and Hardy film, which it is by virtue of the fact that Stan and Ollie are in it. Aesthetically, however, it is a solo Laurel comedy, and Hardy's supporting role has taken on significance only in retrospect.

Unable to pay his rent, Stanley is literally tossed out into the street by his exasperated landlady. ("Pay your bill it's beginning to look like the war debt.") Gathering up his belongings, he inadvertently stuffs a stray dog in his satchel, and the canine becomes his new companion. Stanley is smitten with a young woman who also takes a liking to him, to the consternation of her suitor. A bandit commits an armed robbery and unwittingly stuffs the loot into Stanley's pocket. When the bandit holds Stanley at gunpoint, Stanley is bewildered by the wad of cash now in his possession and runs off with it.

Stanley tries to get rid of the dog but changes his plans when he encounters the young woman again. After wreaking havoc at a thoroughbred dog show, Stanley and his pooch ride home with the girl as the jealous suitor (who just happens to know the bandit with whom Stanley had a run-in) plans his revenge. The suitor and the bandit, the later posing as Count De Chease from

---

*Technically, the character is not referred to by name, though an intertitle identifies Stan as "Stanley Laurel."

†This release date is based on records that the film passed the New York censorship board at that time.

Stan Laurel (left) and Oliver Hardy (center) appeared together for the first time in *The Lucky Dog* (1921).

Switzerland, show up at the home intending to kidnap the girl and kill her father and Stanley. Their scheme unravels when Stanley recognizes the bandit and takes matters into his own hands. But it is the "lucky" dog that really saves the day by blowing up the two assailants with a stick of dynamite.

Produced by former movie-cowboy star G. M. "Broncho Billy" Anderson (one of the founders of the Essanay Film Manufacturing Company), *The Lucky Dog* served as a "pilot" for a projected series of Stan Laurel comedies. Anderson hired his old friend and associate Jess Robbins to direct. Robbins was currently directing comedies at Vitagraph and he, in turn, recruited Oliver Hardy, who was also working at the studio. For years, the exact production and release dates were undetermined due to the film's severely limited distribution, plus the fact that it was never registered for copyright. It was generally assumed to be from 1917, but thanks to the efforts of such dedicated scholars as Rob Stone, Bo Berglund and Randy Skretvedt, it was finally discovered that it was filmed in late January and early February 1921.* (Possibly due to

---

**For detailed accounts of this impressive detective work, see Randy Skretvedt's* Laurel and Hardy: The Magic Behind the Movies, Revised Edition *(Past Times Publishing Co., 1994) and Rob Stone's* Laurel or Hardy: The Solo Films of Stan Laurel and Oliver "Babe" Hardy *(Split Reel, 1996).*

the financial trouble of the studio, it does not appear that *The Lucky Dog* was ever reviewed in the trade papers.)

While *The Lucky Dog* may not be the best or funniest of Laurel's solo vehicles, its significance goes beyond merely being the first time Laurel and Hardy appear together in the same movie. The dynamic between the two actors is already evident, with Hardy exhibiting his seasoned screen persona and Laurel suddenly going from his snappy comic rhythm to a recognizable genesis of the Stanley character that would be borne out upon his eventual teaming with Hardy some six years later.

Laurel's stage training was often cited — and blamed — for his sometime broad gestures, even after he had evolved into the Laurel and Hardy team and began making talkies. In his book *Cavett*, Dick Cavett refers to Oliver Hardy's mannerisms as being "precise to the fingertips" while acknowledging the broader gestures of Stan Laurel. In *The Lucky Dog*, it is the broader gestures that prevail in the opening sequence. Stan is thrown out of his apartment for having so little money, according to one intertitle, he "couldn't buy metal polish for a thumb tack." Stan is booted, and his suitcase follows. This rudimentary sequence is actually quite amusing, with the irate landlady swinging at Stan with a broom, but missing and circling past him as he ducks to work with his luggage. Finally his timing is off, as he gets whacked with the broom, and flies into the street.

Laurel makes each movement "big." The woman's constant attempts to whack him with a broom are swirling gestures that nicely offset Stan's continually ducking into his bag and checking out the contents. He isn't aware of the woman's attempted assaults. He is inspecting his bag, oblivious to the landlady, ducking at just the right time. The perfect timing and the way in which the action is framed are major reasons as to why this sequence works so perfectly. The rhythm is consistent, right up to the time where Stan is knocked into the street.

Upon his landing, Stan dazedly envisions dancing nymphs playfully circling his body. It is a nice example of Laurel using the film medium (in this case, superimposed images) to enhance his comedy, the actor segueing far past his stage-trained limitations to offer a gag that is purely cinematic.

The dynamic between dog and comedian is a reasonably significant one, owing much to Charlie Chaplin's Essanay short *The Champion* (1915) or his First National release *A Dog's Life* (1918). How much Laurel might have been inspired by either of these films is open to conjecture, but it is certain his comic mind had the astute awareness of Chaplin, and the ability to understand how such a dynamic might be artistically successful.

Unlike Chaplin, who opens both of the aforementioned films as the dog's companion, Laurel instead presents his character as stumbling into a relationship with the dog. He tries to shoo it away, but the animal burrows into Stan's satchel when he isn't looking. This allows for another cinematic effect when the satchel starts scurrying away on its own, causing Stan to chase it and stumble into a robbery scene. It is Oliver Hardy portraying the holdup man, and Stan is his next victim.

This key scene offers a blueprint of the future Laurel and Hardy relationship. Neither Stan nor Oliver expected to become a team, and were not even aware that they would work together again. In later interviews, Stan indicates an awareness of Hardy at this time, and a respect for his talent as a comic heavy, but there was none of the insight that would inspire later Hal Roach studio directors (namely Leo McCarey, as legend has it) to notice the cohesion in their performances together.

Today, however, we can see this scene's portents due to our clear understanding of what the future would hold for Laurel and Hardy. The basic ingredients of either man's character already had the noticeable qualities that would define them later. Hardy, especially, already had many expressions and reactions in his comic arsenal.

There is a little bit of future Stanley in Stan's reaction to Hardy the bandit. Holding the dog, Stan is told to put up his hands. He puts up one, holding the dog in the other, switching hands when he is further instructed by Hardy to "put 'em both up." To comply, Stan hands the dog to Hardy, who then orders Stan to turn around. So Stan complies by making a complete turn and is facing Hardy once again. Laurel's inability to grasp simple commands and Hardy's exasperated reactions to his partner's illogical logic would become hallmarks of their style of comedy. Here, their rapport is strictly in its embryonic stages, but it is evident nevertheless.

Later, posing as Swiss royalty at the girl's home, Hardy attempts to shoot Stan in the head. When the gun jams, Hardy grabs another firearm but this one also jams. Stan, who has been cowering with his eyes shut and his fingers in his ears, becomes curious and offers to fix the gun. As he inspects the weapon, Stan unconsciously points it at Hardy, who angrily instructs him to point it in the opposite direction. Hardy is so concerned about getting his gun in working order that he doesn't realize his mistake in handing it over to Stan — and neither does Stan. As their eventual Stanley and Ollie personas would do, they get caught up in the smaller details of the moment without fully comprehending the magnitude of the situation until the last minute (in this case, when the gun discharges suddenly).

Aside from these noteworthy scenes, the rest of *The Lucky Dog* is an undistinguished farce comedy. Although Hardy figures prominently in the film's conclusion as well, there are no discernible opportunities for he and Laurel to play off each other as they had in the aforementioned sequences.

The Lucky Dog remained unseen for years,* so it was a revelation when footage turned up in Robert Youngson's *30 Years of Fun* (1963), the fourth of Youngson's feature-length compilations to utilize excerpts from classic silent-era comedies (following *The Golden Age of Comedy*, *When Comedy Was King* and *Days of Thrills and Laughter*). What audiences saw was a Laurel and Hardy that bore little resemblance to their familiar characters. Because the film stock of that era could not properly photograph his light blue eyes, Laurel wears dark make-up around his eyes that makes him look more like somnambulist Conrad Veidt in *The Cabinet of Dr. Caligari* than his loveable Stanley image. Hardy's appearance reflects the typical comic-villain roles he was playing at the time, although the make-up is not as extreme as the kind he was forced to wear in the Larry Semon comedies. (As the later Laurel and Hardy films revealed, Ollie's cherubic face radiated a natural warmth that would have been inappropriate for portrayals of heavies, comic or otherwise.)

Ironically, due to its uncopyrighted status, this once-obscure film has become one of the three most widely circulated Laurel and Hardy movies (the other two being *The Flying Deuces* and *Utopia*, a.k.a. *Atoll K*, which are also in public domain) and is passed off as a legitimate L and H comedy in numerous DVD collections. While *The Lucky Dog* is hardly a bona fide team effort, the greater availability of the film has allowed us access to one of the most important milestones in the careers of either Laurel or Hardy.

The Egg

Cast

Stan Laurel	Humpty Dumpty
Drin Moro	Stillwell's daughter
Colin Kenny	Gerald Stone
Tom Kennedy	Boss
Alfred Hollingsworth	Mr. Stillwell

Credits

Gilbert Pratt	Director

Working title: "The Carpenter"
A G. M. Anderson production. Copyrighted October 1, 1922.
Production date: April 1922.
Released September 4, 1922, by Amalgamated Producing Corporation/Metro Pictures Corp.
Two reels.

---

*In Laurel and Hardy: From the Forties Forward, Second Edition, Revised and Expanded *(iUniverse, 2009), Scott MacGillivray notes that 16mm prints of* The Lucky Dog *were available for rent from Kodascope, a division of Eastman Kodak, in 1928. The edition of* The Lucky Dog *currently in circulation derives from one of these prints.*

Made prior to *The Weak End Party* and *The Handy Man* but released before either film, *The Egg* shows Laurel continuing to mine humor from his character's working-class status within the parameters of an industrial job, while offering a comparison/contrast to the wealthy and privileged. These opening sequences make more of a cinematic statement than a comedic one, as the film cross-cuts between Gerald Stone, living in luxury on Fifth Avenue, and Humpty Dumpty (known to his fellow workers as "An Egg"), living in squalor on *Filth* Avenue.

The differences in their lifestyles and social conduct are further highlighted when the Egg catches a ride on the back of a fruit truck, sharing traffic with Stone, who is riding comfortably in a chauffeured car. The Egg samples some of the fruit, and blindly tosses aside any rotten ones he comes across. The disposed fruit flies into the faces of other drivers and passengers on the road, including Stone, who is outraged at the unmannerly working-class lout's behavior. In true comic fashion, the Egg remains oblivious to having done any of this.

Stone is on his way to the Rex Lumber Company (where the Egg is employed) with the intention of blackmailing Mr. Stillwell, the president of the firm. A note indicating his plans flies away with the wind, and ends up in the Egg's possession. He gives it little attention, but places the note in his pocket. Arriving late on his construction work site, Stan engages in a series of slapstick conflicts with his harried boss. There are many clever visual gags and some can be found in later films, including a de-facto remake, *The Noon Whistle* (1923), which would improve upon this foundation. The gag in which Stan looks around for his missing thumb (it is curled inside his fist) would turn up again in the Laurel and Hardy feature *Way Out West* (1937), and a lively bit where he runs in and out of adjoining lockers would be reused in *The Noon Whistle* and *Mandarin Mix-Up* (1924), and as late as *Swiss Miss* (1938).

Most of the slapstick sequences are comprised of harmlessly sadistic stuff involving lumberyard tools and supplies (Stan places a handful of nails in his mouth and winds up swallowing them, as Oliver Hardy would do repeatedly in *The Finishing Touch* [1928]). One gag upends viewer expectations by having Stan fall from a scaffold and landing *behind* a barrel of glue, rather than into it, which, in a Larry Semon picture, would have been the usual payoff.

A comic highlight occurs during a labor meeting, when Stan is recruited as the "fearless" leader of the company anarchists. He launches into a rousing but meandering speech, via title cards, citing how "in 1492, George Washington and the Smith Bros. gave us our Independence," and quoting Abraham Lincoln's immortal words: "A bird in the hand gathers no moss." As his delivery grows more impassioned, Stan waves a handsaw for emphasis and eventually slices through a wooden support beam, releasing a 500-pound weight inexplicably placed above his head. (This is the sort of illogical payoff you *would* find in a Larry Semon picture.)

Thanks to Stone's blackmail scheme, Mr. Stillwell is arrested for taking a bribe (Stone placed marked money in the company safe). The Egg overhears the charges against his employer and remembers the note he'd pocketed on the way to work. By providing the crucial piece of evidence, he saves Stillwell and ends up with Stillwell's daughter. The scene wherein Stan eavesdrops is reminiscent of the telephone gag in *The Weak End Party*, in which superimposed words are shown sliding along telephone wires. In *The Egg*, Stan is listening at the door as superimposed words slide directly into his ear! It is an inventive touch, and was probably Stan's idea rather than the director's.

Much of the humor springs from Laurel's interaction with his blustery boss, played by Tom Kennedy (1885–1965), an all-purpose comic foil who comes across as a generic heavy in *The Egg*. It wasn't until the advent of talkies that Tom's punch-drunk verbal delivery defined him as an oafish and sometimes sweet-natured lug.

Period reviews for *The Egg* were mixed, with *Film Daily* calling it "a cross between a Chaplin and a Larry Semon.... Most of the gags have been done before in several variations." *Kinematograph Weekly* offered the opposing opinion that "the fooling is often quite original." For *Bioscope*, the problem was not the material but Laurel himself: "Although he acts with a great deal of energy, Stan Laurel, who is featured in this picture, displays little sense of genuine comedy.... Although the star's performance lacks individuality, the action is fairly well worked up, thanks largely to skillful direction and the efforts of a hard working supporting cast."

While it is true that Laurel's screen persona, at this point in his career, was interchangeable with other nondescript comedians, *The Egg* still provides a good amount of slapstick fun and maintains enough plot conflict to fill its two-reel running time with something more than isolated gags. Laurel also continues to explore and comment on the class differences between the rich and the poor. Beneath the obvious comedy, the idea that Gerald Stone amassed great wealth through nefarious schemes only serves to underscore the nobility and heroism of a working-class lout like the Egg.

The Pest

Cast

Stan Laurel	Jimmy Smith
Glen Cavender	Landlord
Vera Reynolds	Tenant
Joy Winthrop	The pest

Hero .... Bulldog
Mae Laurel .... Woman in court (cut from final release print)

Credits

Jess Robbins .... Director
Irving Reis .... Cinematographer
Renaud .... Titles illustrations

Working title: "The Booklegger."
A G. M. Anderson production. Copyrighted May 10, 1923.
Released December 4, 1922, by Amalgamated Producing
Company/Metro Pictures Corporation.
Two reels.

Laurel's two-reelers for Anderson's production company continued to investigate gag situations with *The Pest*, which shows Stan attempting to define his style and establish himself as a film comedian rather than a comedian who merely appeared in films. There are set pieces and routines that Laurel would use again only a year or two later, refining and sometimes improving upon the original gags.

This time he is Jimmy Smith, a door-to-door book salesman who, in the opening sequence, is smiling with the gusto of an ultra-confident salesman

Stan Laurel in *The Pest* (1922).

and rattling off his pitch to a man standing in front of an iron gate. After Jimmy concludes his breathless spiel, a third man approaches the intended customer and begins speaking to him in sign language. As they wander off, a "Deaf and Dumb Institute" sign is exposed. (In these days of political correctness, such an outrageous gag might come under fire from hearing- and speech-impaired groups. In the silent era, however, every subject was fair game and no racial stereotype, physical handicap or emotional/behavioral issue was off limits.)

This gag sequence concludes as a woman (Joy Winthrop) comes out from behind the gate and Jimmy attempts to communicate with her via sign language. Of course, he is unfamiliar with sign language and merely flaps his hands about in an exaggerated manner. The woman, who is obviously not hearing- or speech-impaired, gives him an angry tongue-lashing, following him as he tries to walk away. Their walking evolves into a trot, and then a full-out run, before Jimmy finally eludes her. Winthrop is playing the title character, and she will turn up again.

This entire sequence would be repeated, tighter and more quickly paced, in the later one-reel Hal Roach production *Kill or Cure* (1923) in which Stan is peddling a bottled tonic rather than a book. (See entry for *Kill or Cure*.)

After the chase between Winthrop and Laurel, we come to a long set of outdoor stairs similar to those Laurel and Hardy would confront in their lost 1927 silent *Hats Off* and, more noteworthy, their Oscar-winning short comedy from 1932, *The Music Box*. This has caused some discussion, especially since the rediscovery and greater accessibility of *The Pest* (it was included in *Saved from the Flames*, a Flicker Alley DVD collection showcasing various films that were rescued from decomposition by such institutions as Lobster Films of France and Blackhawk Films in America). In his own study, Rob Stone indicates the steps are similar to those found in the later Laurel and Hardy films, but does not believe it is exactly the same location:

> The steps in *The Pest* are so new (concrete forms are still visible) that it is hard to compare them to those from *The Music Box* or even *Hats Off* since there are virtually no buildings near the stairs to use as reference points.

In *The Pest*, the steps are not utilized or emphasized in the same manner as the later films. Stan does not attempt to carry any bulky item up the long steps. He just goes up to avoid the pesty lady, only to find that she actually lives at the top of the stairway. Reacting in horror, he slides down the curb of the stairs, propelling him across the street and into a tree.

At least one other gag sequence in *The Pest* turns up in *Kill or Cure*. Jimmy approaches a building with five identical front doors. He rings each bell, steps back, and makes his passionate pitch to the five women who answer all at once.

He gets five doors slammed in his face in unison. Undaunted, he tries to be persistent, but is beaten up by a little man who lives behind one of the doors.

As this is a two-reeler, *The Pest* does have a subplot involving pretty Vera Reynolds at the mercy of evil landlord Glen Cavender. Since she hasn't the money to pay her mortgage, the landlord tries to force her into marriage. Jimmy comes to the rescue, of course, and upon this perfunctory plot point Laurel is able to hang a rather elaborate gag sequence. In an effort to avoid her overly protective bulldog, Jimmy dons a tiger-skin rug, and runs away. This causes scared reactions from onlookers, curiosity from the local dog catchers, and attention from the police. A pickpocket, running from the law, hides the wallet he's stolen in the pocket of a store mannequin. Jimmy steals the clothes to escape the tiger skin, and, upon returning to the woman's house, reaches in his own pocket and finds the money. He uses it to settle the mortgage and emerges as the hero.

As the Laurel comedies from this period go, *The Pest* is one of the funnier efforts. Its visual gags are impressive, and the comedian continues to convey much with his body and his face. Chaplin still casts a heavy shadow over Laurel's work, as the *Kinematograph Weekly* noted: "Stan Laurel gives promise of becoming a popular comedian and has great ability, although his footwork is strongly influenced by Chaplin."

Mixed Nuts

Cast
Stan Laurel . . . . Book salesman
Max Asher . . . . Doctor
Dave Morris . . . . Drunk

Credits
Mel Brown (and Robin Williamson, uncredited) . . . . Director
Jean M. F. Dubois . . . . Writer and editor
A G. M. Anderson production. No copyright registered.
Released circa 1925, by Samuel Bischoff, Inc.
Two reels.

Stan Laurel and G. M. Anderson had been shooting films for five months with no real success, so they decided to make a two-reeler as economically as possible. They took unused footage from *The Pest* (1922), combined it with sequences from *Nuts in May* (1917), Laurel's film debut, and bridged it all together with newly shot scenes to create *Mixed Nuts*, an interesting and surprisingly effective pastiche.

In *Mixed Nuts*, Stan is a salesman peddling a book about Napoleon. After getting hit on the head by a brick, he believes he actually *is* Napoleon, recruit-

Stan Laurel (seated) thinks he's Napoleon in *Mixed Nuts* (1925).

ing neighborhood children as soldiers to recreate famous battles. The kids dutifully obey his orders and throw rocks through windows. Stan is committed to an insane asylum where he continues to behave like the famed commander.

Laurel appears to be having a great time mimicking Napoleon's hand-in-coat gestures and militaristic mannerisms. His transformation recalls a similar one in the Laurel and Hardy feature *A Chump at Oxford* (1940), where a blow to the head causes sweet, simple-minded Stanley to become the aloof Lord Paddington, a master scholar and athlete.

The asylum sequences furnish several amusing moments, presenting three bearded doctors whose idiosyncrasies are every bit as ridiculous as Stan's Napoleonic posturing. Stan wanders out of the asylum and attempts to crack some hard-to-open nuts. (Real nuts, not his fellow inmates.) He puts one of the nuts on a trolley track, but the trolley car comes to a stop. He puts another one in front of a steam roller, but the vehicle also stops and the driver goes on his lunch break. Stan tries to drive the steam roller himself, only to lose control, crashing the vehicle. By the end of the picture, Stan regains his memory and is reunited with his girl.

Mixed Nuts incorporates unused footage from *The Pest*, which included some of Laurel's Napoleon transformation scenes. These sequences may have been deleted from *The Pest* because they would have taken the film off on a completely different tangent. The scenes wherein Stan uses a steam roller to crack nuts were lifted from *Nuts in May*, and this may be the only existing footage from this long-lost film. The insertion of this older material is obvious, as actors change in mid-scene (even to the point of wearing different costumes) and the edits are jumpy. Some of the newer scenes in *Mixed Nuts* repeat and rework gags from *Just Rambling Along* (1918), as Stan wanders into a café and winds up with pancakes in his hat.

Metro Pictures Corporation was displeased with the patchwork nature of *Mixed Nuts* and refused to release the film. To recoup his investment, G. M. Anderson sold it to independent producer Samuel Bischoff, who marketed *Mixed Nuts* on a "states'-rights" basis (meaning it was sold on a territorial basis to regional film exchanges). As a result, the film was never registered for copyright and an exact release date remains unconfirmed, although sources indicate it received limited distribution in 1925. By that time, Laurel's polished comedies of the period must have made *Mixed Nuts* seem all the more ramshackle by comparison.

The Weak End Party

Cast

Stan Laurel .... The gardner
Marion Aye .... Lily Smith
Henry Rattenburg .... Mr. Smith
Otto Fries .... Overseer
Colin Kenny .... Good Samaritan
William Gillespie .... Monocle Charley
Scott MacGregor .... Pinkerton Burns
Babe London .... Party guest

Credits

G. M. Anderson .... Director

Working title: "The Gardener"
A G. M. Anderson production. Copyrighted October 1, 1922.
Production date: January 1922.
Released October 2, 1922, by Quality Producing
Company/Metro Pictures Corporation.
Two reels.

With his next film, Stan Laurel investigates social mores, perhaps more prevalent in England, but still understood in the States. Society's reaction to the common working man is the underlying basis of the characters, contrasted with Stan's happiness at having the opportunity to enter high society, even if only through a fluke.

The plot deals with a society party where the number of dinner guests totals an odd and unlucky 13. Gardener Stanley is hastily tossed into the mix to make an even 14. Stan responds happily to this brief societal promotion and does his best to fit in. Meanwhile, Stanley's caretaker supervisor and one of the party guests are in cahoots to steal some rare jewels from the proprietors. Unwittingly, this is thwarted by Stan.

While *The Weak End Party* is nicely paced and very funny, most of its gags seem to be Stanley poking and prodding various people, first with garden implements, then with a pool cue. The variety of ways he devises to prod others is undeniably amusing, but there is little creative diversity. Several pool-table gags would be used to better effect in the Laurel and Hardy comedy *Brats* (1930), including one bit in which a marshmallow is mistaken for pool chalk.

Perhaps the most interesting scenes are the earliest, wherein Stan is shown working the grounds as a gardener, allowing Laurel to explore different ways to humorously use objects needed for his tasks. One interesting idea from a cinematic perspective involves the presentation of a phone call between two parties. Rather than use title cards, the dialog between the two parties on the phone is presented via superimposed words shown gliding across a shot of a telephone wire. When gardener Stan accidentally breaks the wire, the line of communication is lost, and the words are shown plummeting to the ground. Another example of Laurel's (or perhaps director Anderson's) imaginative grasp of visual humor is when a detective blows smoke into Stan's face. Stan catches the offending smoke in his mouth, then blows it out after the detective leaves.

Once Stan is allowed entry into society as an even-number party guest add-on, the aforementioned pool-table set piece is a highlight. Along with the gags that would later find their way into the Laurel and Hardy talkie *Brats*, there is also a fun bit in which Stan sees that his shot is about to hit the eight-ball, so he runs over and quickly stops it with his hand.

There is the usual deftness to Stan's accidentally poking and prodding those around him with something as unwieldy as a pool stick, but the gags are only funny in the most superficial manner. One gag is interesting in that it deals with sound in a silent film. A dog, under the pool table, is ripping apart an old rag, and Stan fears the sound he hears is his own pants ripping. When he realizes it is just the dog, he continues to play pool without worrying — but his own pants then do start to rip and he ignores it, still believing it to be the dog.

A deeper assessment of *The Weak End Party* is difficult since only the first reel was available for screening at the time of this writing. Yet based on this material, as well as accounts from the initial release, it can be safely concluded that *The Weak End Party*, despite some interesting ideas, is just a small step in Stan Laurel's development as a comedian and filmmaker. Nevertheless, while there may be a lack of comic diversity, the laughs are real and consistent.

The Handy Man

Cast

Stan Laurel . . . . Handy man
Merta Sterling . . . . Cook
Otto Fries . . . . Overseer
Harry Mann . . . . Mysterious stranger (the cook's husband)
Babe London . . . . Houseguest
Mathilde Comont . . . . Bride

Credits

Bob (Robert P.) Kerr . . . . Director
Bob Munson . . . . Writer
Irving Ries . . . . Cinematographer
A G. M. Anderson production. Copyrighted June 29, 1923.
Released March 12, 1923, by Quality Producing
Company/Metro Pictures Corporation.
Two reels.

Not to be confused with the same-titled 1918 comedy short starring Billy West and Oliver Hardy, *The Handy Man* was not distributed until March of 1923, although it had been filmed shortly after *The Weak End Party*, which had been released the previous October. The delay may have helped to avoid the obvious similarities between both films, which share the same basic framework and the same sets (for budgetary considerations), along with Stan Laurel and Otto Fries playing pretty much the same roles. Laurel is called a handy man here, but he's a gardener, as he was in *The Weak End Party*; Fries is once again his impatient overseer. However, the comparisons end there. *The Handy Man* is nowhere near as enjoyable as its predecessor.

As in *The Weak End Party*, the opening sequences of *The Handy Man* reveal Stan's ineptitude as he gamely goes about his assigned tasks. In the previous film, he accidentally trimmed a phone line during a conversation. This time, he inadvertently trims a rope supporting a swing upon which the hefty cook (Merta Sterling) is blissfully perched, causing her to plummet to the ground.

The plot centers around the cook, a heavyset woman who flirts with Stan and Otto, as well as every nearby male. Stan is smitten with the cook and wants to marry her. Otto reads in the newspaper that she is about to receive a sizeable inheritance, so he tries to steal her away from Stan.

There is a frenetic race to the altar with Stan and the cook in a horse-drawn carriage, rushing to the justice of the peace. In a bit that would be deemed objectionable by today's standards, she gets a face full of dirt just as they reach their destination, causing the justice to recoil in horror at the sight of her blackened face. "No, I'm white!" she protests, wiping off the grime as the justice sighs in relief. The union is interrupted by a mysterious stranger (seen lurking throughout the picture) who identifies himself as the cook's husband.

Stock characters, familiar slapstick gags, and racial humor can't possibly add up to a film of any real substance, and *The Handy Man* is one of Laurel's weakest efforts. Since he was working with movie directors who had no discernible style, Laurel seems to have been more concerned with the creation and execution of gags rather than devising ways to enhance them cinematically. Even after starring in several films, Laurel's screen persona remained ill-defined and did not show the sort of growth or maturity being demonstrated by Charlie Chaplin or (after several daunting experiments) Harold Lloyd. Nor did he immediately grasp the techniques of filmmaking, as did Buster Keaton.

The only consistent aspect of Stan's approach during this period was that he had settled into a niche as a working-class comedian. In *The Handy Man*, he is not at odds with high society, but for a change, operates within the parameters of other working-class people.

All of this is secondary to the ultimate question: Is the film funny? The answer is no, even if one makes allowances for the meager budgets and rapid shooting schedules involved. We can understand budgetary restrictions that force moviemakers to use the same sets over again. Offensive racial gags can be examined as artifacts from a time when poking fun at ethnicity was a long-standing tradition and political correctness was decades away from becoming a cultural checkpoint. And Stan's choice to concentrate more on gags than cinematic technique or even character development can be accepted. But none of this changes the fact that *The Handy Man* is trite, superficially amusing, and hardly representative of Stan Laurel's considerable gifts as a performer and creator of comedy.

Mud and Sand

Cast

Stan Laurel ...... Rhubarb Vaseline (often misquoted as "Vaselino")
Julie Leonard .... Caramel
Leona Anderson .... Filet de Sole
Mae Laurel .... Pavaloosky

Wheeler Dryden	Sapo
Sam Kaufman	Humidor

Credits

Gil Pratt	Director
Percy Pembroke	Assistant director
Irving Ries	Cinematographer
Thomas N. Miranda	Titles

Produced by G.M. Anderson. Copyrighted June 18, 1923.
Production dates: September 18–October 1922 (at Fine Arts Studio).
Released November 13, 1922, by Amalgamated
Producing Company/Metro Pictures Corporation.
Three reels.

With *Mud and Sand*, Stan Laurel established himself as a bona fide movie comedian by parodying *Blood and Sand*, which had been released only a few months earlier. The immensely popular feature film starred legendary romantic idol Rudolph Valentino as a matador whose triumph in the bullring leads to heartbreak and tragedy, and Laurel mercilessly satirized every aspect of the

Amateur matador Rhubarb Vaseline (Stan, center) tips his hat before facing the bull in *Mud and Sand* (1922).

original. It was not the first time a comedian lampooned film clichés; Roscoe "Fatty" Arbuckle parodied Westerns on more than one occasion during this tenure making short comedies at Paramount (1917–1919), and Charlie Chaplin spoofed not one but two 1915 film adaptations of Carmen in his *Burlesque on Carmen* (Essanay, 1916). But *Mud and Sand* represents a major step in the development of Laurel's film career and its success prompted him to embark upon a series of burlesques (or "travesties," as they were referred to in the trade papers) of then-current movies. The format provided Laurel with an ideal framework for his comic gifts, as he now had sturdy (and familiar) storylines upon which to hang imaginative and often outrageous visual gags. Additionally, it furnished him with a new outlet for his humor, by playing exaggerated versions of the original lead roles. Yet he also managed to imbue his performances with subtle touches that had been lacking in his previous starring vehicles. In the process of satirizing other actors, Laurel became a better actor himself.

Rhubarb Vaseline is a minor-league bullfighter who gets the opportunity to display his prowess at a big-time arena in Madrid. After "throwing the bull" for two years, he becomes the idol of Spain. But fame corrupts him, as he forsakes his faithful wife, Caramel, to pursue seductive vixen Filet de Sole and tango dancer Pavaloosky. After learning of his fling with Filet, Caramel deserts him and the broken-hearted Vaseline prepares for his final bullfight of the season. He is triumphant, but dies after being struck by a brick thrown by Pavaloosky.

Blood and Sand was a box-office smash for Rudolph Valentino, following closely on the heels of another hit, *The Sheik* (1921). Valentino's introductory scenes in *Blood and Sand* show him and his cohort playfully cavorting down a dirt road, toward the camera, giving the viewer the impression of a warm, respectful friendship. Little time is allotted to this build-up, but Valentino, a master at conveying intense emotion, is able to make their close relationship convincing.

Laurel offers a savage lampoon of this sequence as he is shown skipping down the road with his friend Sapo, both holding onto to the same lariat and behaving in an overtly effeminate manner. (For decades, there has been much discussion of the gay subtext alleged to exist in Valentino's films. Apparently, the subject was raised during those more innocent times as well, since contemporary accounts would often dismiss Valentino [to his chagrin] as a pansy or pretty boy whose appeal was limited to impressionable female moviegoers. Such claims did nothing to erode Valentino's enormous popularity [his onscreen charisma was undeniable], yet the subtext was still evident enough to make it ripe for parody.)

In *Blood and Sand*, Valentino and his friend approach a gated arena surrounded by a handful of spectators. His friend gamely goes into the ring to fight the bull, but gets gored and is carried out, seriously injured. The two friends bid each other goodbye, as the man dies in Valentino's arms. In vengeance, Valentino enters the arena and slays the bull.

In *Mud and Sand*, Vaseline and Sapo are lined up with other matadors outside a gated arena, awaiting their turn to display their bullfighting skills. One brave matador after another enters through the gate, only to be carried out a few seconds afterwards. Sapo gets his chance but he, too, is mangled by a bull and is removed on a stretcher. After Sapo bids him farewell, Vaseline enters the arena (and steps on his "dead" friend's face, as Sapo rises in pain) to avenge his death. While the remaining matadors wait outside the arena, a (prop) bull comes sailing over the gate. Vaseline steps out, makes a chalk mark on a scoreboard, re-enters the arena and tosses another dead bull over the gate. Vaseline is so confident he'll defeat the third and final bull that he makes a preemptive chalk mark. But this time, the bull throws *him* over the gate, and Vaseline hastily erases the score. Undaunted, he goes back inside and moments later the bull is carried out on a stretcher, as the arena attendant hangs his head and weeps.

While this sequence is very funny on its own terms, the satire is even more pointed if one is familiar with the corresponding scenes in *Blood and Sand*. Viewing this burlesque from a perspective nearly a century after the fact, it's easy to forget that the original film had been seen by virtually every member of the audience in 1922, making Laurel's satiric jabs seem all the more humorous.

Blood and Sand afforded Laurel so many scenes to parody that *Mud and Sand* runs three reels, longer than any of his other solo efforts. (He wouldn't star in another three-reeler until after he teamed with Oliver Hardy.) But the film never seems protracted and moves along at a brisk pace. The climactic bullfight affords Laurel an opportunity for some splendid physical comedy, as he tries to attract the attention of the apathetic beast by waving his cape and launching into a series of nonsensical dance movements.

What is most interesting about *Mud and Sand* is the uncanny accuracy of its satiric elements. Scenes recreate specific moments from the original picture, with a keen eye toward performance, scene composition and costume design. (As Pavaloosky, Mae Laurel is hardly the alluring temptress she's supposed to be, although she does perform a lively and amusing tango with Stan.) The lampooning extends to externals, with Stan's moniker Rhubarb Vaseline an obvious reference to Rudolph Valentino. The names of the supporting characters spoof the names in the original, such as Caramel (Carmen) and Filet de Sole (Doña Sole).

The significance of *Mud and Sand* lies in its burlesque of "serious" entertainment, removing the heaviness from melodrama by mocking it. In 1922, this approach seemed daring, subversive, and wickedly funny, and it garnered Laurel some of his best reviews to date. *Moving Picture World* called it "a crackerjack comedy that should please almost every audience." *Motion Picture News* found Stan's performance "exquisite," noting:

> Every now and then there comes to the screen a young man who "carries on" idiotically, who appears — casually observed — a mere clowning fool, but who, more thoughtfully considered, shows himself to be the rarest of all artists, a true buffoon, gifted with the power of bringing laughter which is strangely close to tears. Such a man is Charlie Chaplin; and such a man Stan Laurel is by way of becoming fast.

This comparison to Chaplin is a perceptive acknowledgment of Laurel's burgeoning talent as a screen comedian. Within a few short years, he would become the absolute definition of comic artistry.

When Knights Were Cold

Cast

Stan Laurel	Lord Helpus, a Slippery Knight
Mae Laurel	Countess Out, a Classy Eve
Catherine Bennett	Princess Elizabeth New Jersey, a Swell Eve
Scotty MacGregor	Sir Chief Raspberry, a Rough Knight
Billy (William) Armstrong	Earl of Tabasco, a Hot Knight
Will Bovis	Duke of Sirloin, a Tough Knight
Stanhope Wheatcroft	Prince of Pluto, a Bad Knight
Harry De More	King Epsom, a Good Knight

With
Dot Farley

Credits

Frank Fouce	Director
Irving G. Ries	Cinematographer
Thomas N. Miranda	Titles

Working titles: "Rob 'Em Good" and "When Knighthood Was in Flour."
A G. M. Anderson production. Copyrighted May 10, 1923.
Production date: December 1922.
Released February 12, 1923, by Quality Producing Company/Metro Pictures Corporation.
Two reels.

A parody of Douglas Fairbanks's *Robin Hood* (1922), *When Knights Were Cold* was originally titled "Rob 'Em Good," but while the film was in pro-

Stan Laurel is sentenced to death in the Robin Hood parody *When Knights Were Cold* (1923).

duction, a Bull Montana comedy short bearing the same name was submitted to Metro Pictures Corporation for release. Even though publicity material on Laurel's burlesque had already been issued, the title was changed to "When Knighthood Was in Flour," referencing another current feature, *When Knighthood Was in Flower* (1922) starring Marion Davies, before finally settling on *When Knights Were Cold.*

After the death of King Henry the 4711, the Prince of Pluto assumes the throne. Princess Elizabeth New Jersey is being held hostage, and when Lord Helpus tries to free her, the prince sentences him to death. But Helpus's band of merry men, led by a mysterious stranger, ride to his rescue. The stranger turns out to be King Henry the 4711, still very much alive, and all ends happily.

For years, *When Knights Were Cold* was unavailable for viewing, but Laurel retained fond memories of the long-lost film when discussing his solo work. In *Mr. Laurel and Mr. Hardy* (Doubleday, 1961), Laurel told his biographer, John McCabe:

I wish they'd re-release *When Knights Were Cold*. I guess maybe I'd like to see it again because it had one beautifully funny sequence that I've never seen in movies — either before or since. We had an army of knights in a chase sequence. There were over three hundred of them working with basket horses — you know, the circus clown-type horses, with the men's legs extending beneath the little papier-mâché horse built around them. It was hilarious, like some of those circus routines.

A running gag in *Monty Python and the Holy Grail* (1975) has King Arthur and his knights galloping along, on foot, as though they were on horseback. This may be a mere coincidence, but as the Pythons are acknowledged fans of Laurel and Hardy, they may have been familiar with Laurel's remarks. Also, the Python troupe's humor, like Laurel's, has roots in the British music hall tradition.

Reviewers had reservations about *When Knights Were Cold*. *Moving Picture World* noted, "Considerable cleverness has been shown in handling some of the stunts. It provides good entertainment.... However, it is hardly up to the standard of some of the other Stan Laurels and not as good as his *Mud and Sand*." *Motion Picture News* concurred, "The piece is not so funny as unique ... the humor [is] too labored."

Historian Rob Stone discovered the second reel of *When Knights Were Cold* at the Library of Congress and screened it at a comedy festival in the summer of 2010, to delighted audiences. Reports indicate that Laurel's memory of the gag sequence with the faux horses was accurate, and this presentation was a hilarious success.

Even though G.M. Anderson had an eight-film deal with Metro Pictures Corporation, *When Knights Were Cold*, the sixth entry, was the last production made under the arrangement. Explanations vary as to why the contract was not fulfilled. A few months before his death in 1971, Anderson told John McCabe, "[Stan and I] made some awfully good pictures, and I think we could have made even better pictures — but we just didn't have enough money in return bookings to make the ones we wanted to make."

By the time *When Knights Were Cold* was released (February 23, 1923), Laurel was already back at the Hal Roach Studio, working on *Under Two Jags*. (The Anderson-produced *The Handy Man*, made before *When Knights Were Cold*, was released a month later.) Just as Laurel had fond memories of the film, G. M. Anderson had fond memories of Laurel:

"Stan was a wonderful fellow — so cheerful around the lot. He just made you feel good the minute he walked in. Not only that, he was always very much concerned with making the picture a success if it meant working extra long hours and doing things that weren't easy. Not a complaint from Stan, ever."

6

Stan Returns to Hal Roach

While G.M. Anderson continued to release his Laurel comedies throughout the early 1920s, Laurel re-signed with Hal Roach in 1923. Unlike the previous time Laurel worked for Roach, when Stan was a fledgling comic substituting for a contracted series that had ended abruptly, the comedian was now established in films.

When Laurel had formerly been under his employ, Roach was a partner in the Rolin Film Company. Now Roach was the head of the Hal E. Roach Studios and was challenging Mack Sennett's supremacy in the marketplace. By the end of the twenties, Roach managed to eclipse Sennett as the leading producer of short comedies in America. So in January of 1923, Stan re-signed with Roach. The original contract is as follows:

> This letter is to reduce to written form the substance of our conversations covering your engagement by this studio as follows:
> 1st- The engagement is to begin on Monday, January 29th, 1923, and to continue for twelve (12) weeks.
> 2nd- You are to render services as an actor, playing the leading part in comedies of not less than one reel in length, to be starred and featured, and agree herein to use your best efforts at all times during the continuation of this engagement to produce the highest grade of work, and further agree to give us fullest co-operation possible to accomplish this result in an efficient manner.
> 3rd- It is mutually agreed that this engagement may be terminated by either party upon two (2) weeks notice to the other party, provided however that should an unfinished picture be in progress, either at the termination of this agreement or at the termination of the two weeks notice period herein provided, that you will continue the engagement until such time as the picture then in progress is completed in a satisfactory manner.
> 4th- It is mutually agreed that the Hal E. Roach Studios have the sole right to your services during the continuance of this agreement, and you will not render services to any other individual or firm for any purpose whatsoever unless the consent of the Hal E. Roach Studios is first obtained.
> 5th- It is agreed that you will abide by such reasonable rules and restrictions

6. Stan Returns to Hal Roach

Stan (right) poses with current boss Hal Roach (left) and former boss Fred Karno, circa 1923.

as are laid down by the studio for the guidance of others in its employ in a similar capacity, and will report promptly for work when requested to do so.

6th- You hereby grant to the Hal E. Roach Studios full privileges of publicity and advertising, both for yourself personally and for the pictures in which you are to appear, with the provision that all advertising of pictures in which you appear shall mention your name in a prominent manner.

7th- It is mutually agreed that the salary for this engagement shall be $300.00 per week, payable on Saturday of each week.

8th- In case of shutdowns on account of strikes, fire, acts of God, or other causes over which we have no control, it is agreed that this engagement will be suspended during the continuance of such shutdown and that it shall be extended for the length of suspension.

9th- It is hereby agreed that the Hal E. Roach Studios shall have the right to renew this agreement for a further period of one year at the rate of $400.00 per

In 1923, Stan re-signed with Hal Roach and was given a big buildup as a star on the verge of greatness.

week and another additional year at the rate of $500.00 a week, at any time prior to the termination of this engagement, by written notice, it being understood that should this option be exercised a standard form of contract will be entered into.

10th- It is agreed that the signatures of the parties to this agreement appearing below shall indicate their respective acceptances of the provisions above set forth.

Yours very truly
HAL E. ROACH STUDIOS by
Warren Doane, Vice President

Roach's initial plans were to feature Laurel in one-reelers, alternating with an established series of Paul Parrott comedies. Midway through 1923, however, Stan's films were extended to two reels in length and the Parrott series was dropped altogether. Parrott would pursue a career behind the camera as a writer and director. (For more on Parrott, see the entry on *Do You Love Your Wife?* [Rolin; filmed 1918, released 1919].)

If the comedies produced by G.M. Anderson revealed the initial rumblings of Stan Laurel's comic potential, especially burlesques such as *Mud and Sand* (1922), it is his output at the Roach Studios that solidified his star status. Laurel investigates a lot of new possibilities, and expands upon ideas and concepts he established under Anderson. It is a most productive and significant period in the comedian's solo career.

Under Two Jags

Cast

Stan Laurel	A stranger
Katherine Grant	Princess
Mae Laurel	Cheroot
William Gillespie	Commandant
Charles Stevenson	Arab

With
Sammy Brooks (unconfirmed), Roy Brooks

Crew

George Jeske	Director
C. Brandenberg	Assistant director
Frank Young	Cinematographer
J. V. White	Props

A Hal Roach production. Copyrighted June 6, 1923.
Production dates: February 3–10, 1923 (at the
Hal Roach Studios and Universal City).
Released June 3, 1923, by Pathé Exchange.
One reel.

Under Two Jags, Laurel's first film after returning to the Hal Roach studio, is one of his lesser travesties. It purports to be a parody of *Under Two Flags*

(1922; based on the book by Ouida), and while there are some references to the original story, they will be lost on those who are unfamiliar with it. *Under Two Jags* is an underwhelming effort and today is seen at a disadvantage since surviving prints are missing nearly all of the intertitles. As a result, the identities of the characters and their motives are unclear, and the storyline is often puzzling.

At a desert outpost in Dhumbell, a stranger goes into a saloon filled with Foreign Legionnaires. Enlisting in the legion, he quickly establishes himself as the most incompetent soldier in the company. Just as the stranger is about to be executed, Cheroot, a saloon girl who has fallen in love with him, rushes to the rescue.

There are a few amusing if perfunctory gags, such as Stan blowing the suds off a glass of beer and having it fly into an officer's face, and opening a champagne bottle that sprays its contents on everyone within range. The marching and drill maneuvers provide some fun, as Stan is unable to keep in step with the rest of the troop. When he tries to scale a stone wall, it collapses under his weight — a gag that played better and more logically when Oliver Hardy did it in *Habeas Corpus* (1928). Stan is energetic and agile throughout, but overall *Under Two Jags* is quite underwhelming.

Once again, Mae Laurel is a member of Stan's supporting cast, and once again she proves to be bereft of talent and appeal. Mae Charlotte Dahlberg was Stan Jefferson's vaudeville partner, and after she came up with a new surname for him ("Laurel") she began using the name professionally as well. (Although they never married, she later claimed to be Stan's common-law wife and sued him.) Her lack of talent was matched by her overbearing demeanor. Producers always balked at her inclusion (and intrusion), but Stan had the power to insist she be cast in his pictures.

Playing a princess with whom Stan becomes smitten, pretty Katherine Grant, a Roach contract player who worked with Charley Chase, makes her first appearance with Laurel in *Under Two Jags*. A former beauty-contest winner, Grant was a fine comic actress who reportedly contributed a lot of creative ideas to the films in which she appeared, but just as she was on the brink of stardom, she became another Hollywood tragedy. On December 8, 1925, Grant was struck by a hit-and-run driver and never fully recovered. Hal Roach paid for her medical expenses; in May 1926, he told a reporter, "She screened perfectly, and in my opinion developed into the most proficient actress in the profession. We expected great things of her and for her until this happened. We wanted her back as quickly as possible." But Grant suffered a physical and mental breakdown and in 1929 she was placed in a sanitarium, where she died on April 2, 1937, one month shy of her 33rd birthday.

There is no real connection to *Under Two Jags* and the later Laurel and Hardy legion-themed comedies *Beau Hunks* (1931) and *The Flying Deuces* (1939), aside from the similar setting. *Under Two Jags* was well received in its day, but it falls in the "For Fans Only" category now.

The Noon Whistle

Cast

Stan Laurel .... Tanglefoot
James Finlayson .... T. O'Hallahan, the foreman
Katherine Grant .... Secretary
William Gillespie ...... President of the Bankrupt Lumber Company
Sammy Brooks .... Short millworker
Noah Young .... Millworker
Jack (John B.) O'Brien .... Millworker

Credits

George Jeske (and Jay Howe, uncredited) .... Director
W.P. Hackney .... Assistant director
Frank Young (and Ernie Crockett, uncredited) .... Cinematographer
Lloyd French, Harry Bayfield .... Props

A Hal Roach production. Copyrighted April 27, 1923.
Production dates: February 13–22, 1923.
Released April 29, 1923 by Pathé Exchange.
One reel.

Though he garnered the most critical success with his travesties, Laurel never abandoned the comedies in which he played a working-class lout trying to accomplish various tasks in an industrial situation. This setup would later serve him and Hardy well in numerous films, including the two-reelers *The Finishing Touch* (1928) and *Busy Bodies* (1933), both of which have similarities to *The Noon Whistle*.

The Noon Whistle is similar to Laurel's earlier film *The Egg* in that a construction site is the backdrop for a series of clever comic set pieces. But while *The Egg* has an accompanying plot to fill out its running time, this one-reeler is unencumbered by such excess and simply presents Stan's inept exploits at a lumberyard. *The Noon Whistle* further benefits from the presence of James Finlayson as the harried foreman. While veteran comedian Tom Kennedy was an effective comic foil in *The Egg*, the combative relationship between Finlayson and Laurel is significant as being established here and would be developed further over the following years. Fin, as he has been affectionately called, would later become the most noted supporting player in Laurel and Hardy's stock company. His initial encounters with Stan in *The Noon Whistle* are a portent to Fin's unforgettable presence in such later Laurel and Hardy films as *Big Business* (1929), *Chickens Come Home* (1931), *The Devil's Brother* (1933), *Our Relations* (1936) and *Way Out West* (1937).

In assessing a film like *The Noon Whistle*, one must center upon how the gags are staged and executed. They are often clever, usually funny, and sometimes familiar. A few were used before by Laurel in other films. But the beauty of the one-reel films Laurel starred in during this period is their compact, fast-paced approach to simple situations. The Laurel and Hardy films were especially noteworthy for getting a great deal of humor from the simplest of premises. Hence, *The Noon Whistle* is an effective training ground for Laurel's later, and most noted, output at the Hal Roach Studios.

Because Laurel is always cited as the creative force behind his films, even at this stage of his career, it is difficult to discern the input of George Jeske, the credited director. Certainly anything stylistic is more akin to Laurel's vision rather than Jeske's, a man who never developed any recognizable directorial style.

The opening scene in the lumber yard is a nice burst of well-timed and constant movement within the frame. Derided by the company president for their laziness ("They lean against each other when they loaf!," he rants), the workers are shown standing around singing in harmony rather than attending to tasks. Foreman Fin approaches and the men scurry frantically, each grabbing a large board and heading toward some level of activity. This sequence is a perfectly timed piece of slapstick choreography. The workers, all with boards placed on their respective shoulders, scurry within the frame, frantically trying to find a place to "look busy" and avoid the foreman's wrath. They weave in and out of each other, carefully tilting their boards so as not to cause any sort of collision. Only seconds long, the scene nicely establishes the fast-paced slapstick that follows, and offers some wonderful visuals that really use the concept of constant movement within the frame. It is as stimulating a physical scene as any in Laurel's solo canon.

Stan's entrance has him sliding into the scene and knocking down Fin, who gets up and starts after the errant worker. Stan runs away, and ensuing attempts to elude the foreman result in a fast-moving, carefully timed and well-choreographed chase sequence. It isn't simply a foot chase between the two; Stan picks things up, turns, walks, runs, bends, steps to one side, and performs a veritable dance in his avoidance of Fin, who follows him in kind. Their adversarial relationship is established immediately.

The Noon Whistle is a series of slapstick set pieces, with Stan trying to accomplish tasks and Fin getting the brunt of whatever backfires. Stan is constantly dropping objects on Fin, from heavy boxes to slipper boards. (At one point, the groggy foreman tries to revive himself by splashing a few drops on his face from a nearby water bucket.) At least two gags were to be used again by Laurel. One, which had already been used in *The Egg*, has Fin trapping Stan in one of a row of lockers, shutting all the doors in rapid succession so that the bumbling worker has been trapped. Stan comes from behind the lockers and helps Fin complete his task. This bit would be repeated, with variations, in *Mandarin Mix-Up* (1924), and the later Laurel and Hardy feature *Swiss Miss* (1938).

Another great gag has Stan on one end of a long board. The board passes through the frame, extending further and further as if it is several yards long. When the other end shows up on screen, Stan is carrying it from that position as well. This is definitely a Laurel idea, nodding to his interest in surreal slapstick, and would turn up again in *The Finishing Touch* (1928) and *Great Guns* (1941).

The ending is abrupt and inconclusive, but the gag situations are fast and funny. Sometimes they are rather elaborate, such as when Stan shimmies up a ladder, with Fin on the other end. Stan carrying a heavy sack causes the ladder to tip in his favor, and Fin, trapped within the rungs at the other end, rises up in a see-saw effect. As he lowers, his feet get stuck in a bucket of hot glue.

The Noon Whistle was well received at the time of its release. *Motion Picture News* noted, "Stan Laurel proves himself a considerable comedian in this snappy comedy.... There is not a dull moment ... there are probably few screen comedians who could get as much real humor out of the action as Laurel does."

White Wings

Cast

Stan Laurel	"Our Hero"
Katherine Grant	Nursemaid
Jimmy (James) Finlayson	First dental patient
Marvin Lobach	Policeman
George Rowe	Good Samaritan
William Gillespie	Onlooker
Mark Jones	Third dental patient

Credits

George Jeske	Director
W. P. Hackney	Assistant director
Frank Young	Cinematographer
Lloyd French	Prop man

A Hal Roach production. Copyrighted April 27, 1923.
Production dates: February 2–23, 1923; retakes February 27.
Released May 23, 1923, by Pathé Exchange.
One reel.

Plotless and entirely gag-driven, *White Wings* is an undistinguished but pleasant throwback to the early Mack Sennett/Keystone comedies, and conveys a similar freewheeling, off-the-cuff spirit. To compensate for the paucity of material, Stan puts his energy and charm into overdrive, and for the most part he manages to make us forget that no real fuel powers his comic engine.

As the picture opens, Stan, introduced as "Our Hero," is an aspiring street sweeper who gets into a territorial scuffle with a rival sweeper. The hassle ends when an oncoming automobile whisks Stan and the rival's cart to another section of town, where he inadvertently switches the cart with a baby carriage. Mistaken for a kidnapper, Stan panics and flees with the baby, pursued by a nursemaid and a policeman. The nurse safely recovers her charge, but the cop, determined to make an arrest, doggedly chases Stan. Because of the white coat he's wearing, Stan is mistaken for a dentist giving curbside demonstrations of "painless" tooth extractions. After three hapless patients endure Stan's unorthodox (and hardly pain-free) procedure, the policeman decides to have a troublesome tooth yanked, which results in poor Stan literally winding up in the arms of the law.

White Wings isn't the funniest or most inventive of Stan Laurel's solo comedies, but it speeds along at a breezy pace to offer a variety of amusing gags along the way. Laurel's creativity with visual humor is at work, even if his gift for cinematic structure is placed on the back burner.

The start of the chase offers perhaps the most striking visual comedy in the film, with the wild image of Stan hidden under the baby's outlandishly elongated gown; the baby sits atop his head, making them look as though a six-foot infant is running amuck through the streets. We are offered no footage of Stan planning this disguise or even donning it. He just suddenly appears in the next shot as the giant baby, shocking passersby and two men on a park bench who react by toppling backward, bench and all, into a river.

Later, Stan, sans child, strikes stationary poses among monument statues in an effort to elude the cop. Of course, the deception is completely transparent—the derbied, white-coated Stan stands out like a lighthouse in the middle of all those stone figures—but such ingratiating lapses of logic (and verisimilitude) are a key factor of visual humor, especially during the silent era. Film historian Rob Stone has cited this sequence as an embryonic forerunner of the climactic set piece in Laurel and Hardy's *Early to Bed* (1928), in which Hardy hides in a fountain to elude an uncharacteristically retaliatory Laurel. (Variations of this statue gag also appear in Bing Crosby and Bob Hope's *Road to Morocco* and Abbott and Costello's *Pardon My Sarong*, both 1942 releases, and Hope's own *Let's Face It* from 1943.) For his part, Laurel pushes the sequence one better when "Our Hero" reaches down and tickles the cop's ear. When the cop abruptly turns around, Stan has struck a different pose. The cop scratches his head, confused as to whether that "statue" was in a different pose only a few seconds earlier.

The concluding dentistry sequence is the weakest passage in *White Wings*, partly because no real buildup is given to it, but primarily because it isn't nearly as amusing as what preceded it. (Behind drawn curtains, Stan uses a mallet to anesthetize patients, a gag that quickly grows tiresome.) Nevertheless, the routine does provide Stan with the opportunity to use James Finlayson as a comic foil, even though Fin's footage (as Stan's first patient) is regrettably brief. The wild, fast-paced chase opens the film with such a bang, and the gags are so over-the-top (at one point the cop, strapped to a chair, falls into a mud puddle with another man and struggles to get out in order to keep chasing Stan), that the more sedate, and less creative, dentist sequence ends the film on a disappointing note.

As in many of his pre–Hardy films, Stan's screen character is still largely undefined, beyond an energetic, enterprising scrapper who isn't above taunting his pursuers. Throughout *White Wings* he repeatedly looks into the camera, as when he offers a sweet smile to the audience after he lifts the baby from the carriage or giddily prepares to kick the cop in the posterior. (Stan shares his unabashed delight with the audience —*twice*— before delivering the final blow.)

Rotund Marvin Lobach, playing the indefatigable officer, would turn up in supporting roles in other Laurel solo comedies. Lobach also appeared in assorted comedies for Hal Roach and Mack Sennett, but his most notable (make that *dubious*) appearances, in relation to Stan Laurel, were in a series of cheaply made two-reel comedies produced by Artclass/Weiss Brothers, in which Lobach and former Hal Roach star Harry "Snub" Pollard were teamed to capitalize on the popularity of Laurel and Hardy during the late 1920s. (Though fascinating to view as a point of comparison, the contrived Pollard-Lobach efforts are bereft of the qualities that make the L and H films so special.)

White Wings is yet another Hal Roach production that makes good use of outdoor locations, and appreciative movie buffs will delight once again in seeing Culver City and the neighboring areas that have become familiar terrain to silent-comedy aficionados. But as far as Laurel's career is concerned, *White Wings* is most significant for seeing him explore more possibilities for visual gags, investigating some of the medium's more surreal aspects. The baby head on the adult body is the sort of bizarre image that might be something of a harbinger to later gags, including Stan and Ollie with their heads twisted backward (in *The Live Ghost*, 1934) or their legs wrapped around their necks (in *Going Bye-Bye!*, 1934). Even as late as 1945, Stan and Ollie become walking skeletons after meeting up with a nefarious character who, throughout the entire film (*The Bullfighters*), had been threatening to "skin them alive."

After a few years in films, Stan Laurel's development as a comedian and filmmaker was progressing slowly, but even in a standard-yet-funny effort like *White Wings*, we already notice discernible advancement in both areas. He effectively frames the statue sequence with the cop in the foreground and himself elevated in the background. His sudden entrance as the baby-man is one of constant and rapid movement that dictates the pace of the next few sequences. Laurel was learning to understand the language of cinema as he continued to tap into his ideas for visual comedy.

Pick and Shovel

Cast

Stan Laurel	Miner
Katherine Grant	Foreman's daughter
James Finlayson	Foreman
George Rowe	Cross-eyed miner
William Gillespie	A. Worthless (mine owner)
Sammy Brooks	Little miner
Mah Jong	Mule

Credits

George Jeske	Director
W. P. Hackney	Assistant director
Frank Young	Cinematographer
Lloyd French	Props

Also known as *The Pick of the Miners*.
A Hal Roach production. Copyrighted May 12, 1923.
Production dates: February 26–March 5, 1923.
Retakes: March 9, 1923.
Released June 17, 1923, by Pathé Exchange.
One Reel.

Pick and Shovel is another single-reel comedy that presents Laurel as a low-level laborer who runs afoul of co-workers and management. As he did in *The Egg* and *The Noon Whistle*— as well as the subsequent *Collars and Cuffs, Gas and Air, Oranges and Lemons* and *Short Orders*—Stan attempts to mine gags (literally, in *Pick and Shovel*) from a specific workplace. This time, the results are far less effective than in similar efforts.

Stan, a bumbling miner, is smitten with the foreman's daughter, to the chagrin of her father. However, when the mine floods, Stan rises to the occasion and rescues his sweetheart.

The mineshaft is the centerpiece of the film, much like the assembly line

The likenesses of Katherine Grant, Stan Laurel and a mule named Mah Jong are featured on this poster for the *miner* comedy *Pick and Shovel* (1923).

was the centerpiece of the opening scenes of Charlie Chaplin's *Modern Times* (1936). Whereas the factory setting allowed Chaplin to depict the dehumanization of employees (in addition to using the location for a series of brilliant sight gags), Laurel uses work-related implements and props for a reel's worth of pain-and-pratfall humor. While it may seem ludicrous to compare Chaplin's major feature-length production to Laurel's disposable short, it does serve to illustrate Laurel's ideas about comedy. Discussing *Modern Times* years later, Stan claimed that Chaplin had no intention of delivering social commentary; he simply felt that putting his tramp character in a factory setting would be good for a lot of laughs. Laurel's remarks overlook aspects of Chaplin's style (as Chaplin matured, his humor definitely had a point of view), but his words clearly revealed his own comedic style. It is obvious in a film like *Pick and Shovel* that Laurel thought this particular setting would be good for some laughs, pure and simple, without any thought of exploring social subtexts.

Pick and Shovel benefits from a cast of reliable Roach Studio perennials, especially the wonderful James Finlayson, who would prove to be a valuable comic foil for Stan throughout most of the Laurel and Hardy years. And perky, dimpled Katherine Grant is once again a charming leading lady, continuing to show the promise that Hal Roach saw in her. Grant and Laurel have a cute flirtation scene in which they stand on either side of a mule, playing with its ears and speaking through them like an intercom.

Unfortunately, the humor is devoid of any real punch. The opening sequence is perhaps the funniest, as Stan, in an iris shot, is seen attired in fur coat, tuxedo and top hat, standing in front of a booth marked "Check Room." Then the iris opens and he is revealed to be a humble mine worker preparing to start the day. Reaching for his pick and lunchbox, he dutifully prepares to enter the mineshaft with his co-workers but stands too far off and remains at the surface after the platform descends. As the foreman starts to berate him, the distracted Stan plummets down the shaft, falling past the platform and reaching the bottom before the others do.

Laurel's pantomimic skills are evident in a set piece in which he takes a smoke break. Unaware that oil from his miner's cap has dripped into his pipe, Stan is taken aback by the small explosion caused when he lights it. Undaunted, he tries to light oil-stained cigarettes, with the same results. Finally, he settles for chewing tobacco, but the oil has tainted its flavor. This sequence would be a throwaway in most other Laurel comedies, but in a lesser entry like *Pick and Shovel*, it's a highlight.

In a scene that predates similar bits in the Laurel and Hardy comedies *The Second Hundred Years* (1927) and *The Hoose-Gow* (1929), albeit closer in spirit to The Three Stooges, Stan repeatedly pokes his co-workers with his pick while trying to work within a tight space. Yet this passage fails to register and not even a wild climax involving explosives and a flood can inject much life into the proceedings.

Pick and Shovel is a well-produced but disappointingly pedestrian effort made during an otherwise interesting period of Laurel's film career.

Kill or Cure

Cast

Stan Laurel	"Live wire" agent
Katherine Grant	The maid
Mark Jones	"Speedy" Sam
Noah Young	Car owner
Eddie Baker	Sheriff
Helen Gilmore	Aggressive woman
George Rowe	Man standing in front of Deaf and Dumb Institute
William Gillespie	Institute doctor
Sammy Brooks	Little non-customer
Charles Stevenson	Door-slamming non-customer

Credits

"Perc" (Percy) Pembroke	Director
W. P. Hackney	Assistant director
Frank Young	Cinematographer
Lloyd French	Props

A Hal Roach production. Copyrighted June 17, 1923.
Production dates: March 6–13, 1923.
Additional scenes filmed April 7 and 9, 1923.
Released July 15, 1923, by Pathé Exchange.
One reel.

A remake of *The Pest* (1922), *Kill or Cure* is a funnier film and, running only one reel in length, is much faster paced.

Stan plays a door-to-door salesman (or merchandising "agent," as they were known) peddling Prof. I.O. Dine's Knox-All, a multi-purpose tonic that can be used as (among other things) medicine, cleanser, hair restorer, or insecticide. Despite his spirited technique, Stan never gets anywhere: After delivering a breathless sales pitch, he discovers his potential customer is a deaf mute; a maid pays him with a counterfeit coin; an ornery motorist refuses to buy a bottle, despite getting his car polished for free; and doors repeatedly slam in his face. His only successful sale is to "Speedy" Sam, a drunk who uses the tonic for an alcohol substitute.

Some film historians contend that the one-reel format did not allow comedians enough time to create a characterization of any real depth, and thus limited them to a series of superficial gags. And, in many instances, this is true. But in *Kill or Cure*, the lack of character development doesn't prevent Laurel from being a likable comic figure. He's so persistent in trying to make a sale and so eager to achieve a measure of success that the viewer gains a rooting interest in his exploits. In spite of continual setbacks, he never loses his inherent playfulness, which makes him even more appealing. And without being saddled with a plot, Laurel fires off one gag after another, coming up with numerous variations on a single theme. *Kill or Cure* isn't a bona fide comedy classic, but it does deliver several solid laughs.

Kill or Cure begins with the same routine that opened *The Pest*: Stan is enthusiastically explaining the merits of his wares to an oblivious man standing in front of an iron gate. When the man is summoned away via sign language, a "Deaf and Dumb Institute" sign is revealed. Undaunted, Stan then tries to communicate with a woman walking out of the establishment by using nonsensical hand gestures. But she turns out to be an institute worker who is neither hearing- nor speech impaired and she launches into an angry (and apparently loud) tirade, chasing poor Stan down the street. *Kill or Cure* repeats another set piece from *The Pest*, as Stan approaches a building with four identical doors, encountering rejection at every one.

In *The Pest*, Stan sold books; in *Kill or Cure*, he's peddling an all-purpose elixir, which allows greater opportunity for humor. Its usages are endless — not only does it cure physical ailments, it can polish metal — as Stan sets out to prove to curious motorist, played by perennial foil Noah Young. Stan diligently cleans Young's filthy automobile, even using his shirt sleeve as a rag, until it is shiny and spotless. But Young ungraciously complains that his car has "shrunk" like a wool sweater in the wash, refuses to buy a bottle, and tosses Stan off to the side. In his sole display of anger in the film, Stan retaliates by grabbing a sack of flour from a nearby grocery store and empties its contents all over the car and the motorist. This sort of justified outburst anticipates Laurel and Hardy's "reciprocal destruction" routines.

The Pest was an entertaining comedy, but, as with many of Stan's earlier two-reelers, it had a protracted subplot. *Kill or Cure* simply presents Stan's adventures as a salesman, and does so with a smoother flow and a more decisive rhythm to the comedy. There is an interesting Chaplinesque moment after Stan realizes the maid has paid him with counterfeit currency. His cheery smile fades as he picks up his traveling bag and walks dejectedly down the sidewalk (away from the camera), with his hands behind his back. Within seconds, however, the bouncy stride returns to his step and he marches off in search of his next customer. It's an intriguing bit that probably would have played better if it had come at the end of the film rather than the middle.

The only real missteps are the repeated cutaways to "Speedy" Sam, a drunk who tries to elude the sheriff so he can enjoy a swig of the tonic. Otherwise, *Kill or Cure* is a very funny comedy that ranks as one of Stan Laurel's better solo efforts.

Collars and Cuffs

Cast

Stan Laurel	Laundry worker
Mark Jones	Foreman of Rough and Wet Laundry
Katherine Grant	Laundry worker
Eddie Baker	Pants presser
George Rowe	Pedestrian
Sammy Brooks	Card-playing laundry worker
Jack Ackroyd	Cop

Credits

George Jeske	Director
W. P. Hackney	Assistant director
Frank Young	Cinematographer
Lloyd French	Props

A Hal Roach production. Copyrighted May 12, 1923.
Production dates: March 14–20, 1923.
Released July 1, 1923, by Pathé Exchange.
One reel.

When silent comedy is recalled by those who have only had limited exposure to the genre, they tend to conjure up images of relentless slapstick and protracted chase sequences, presented within a loose structure. Of course, this sweeping generalization overlooks the subtle artistry inherent in the finest films of Chaplin, Keaton, Lloyd and Langdon. But the truth is that many silent-era comedy shorts are simply formless collections of fast-paced sight gags provoked by a single theme or locale, and this unpretentious approach can often be highly entertaining when the gags are clever and varied and the performers are in sync with each other. Such is the case with *Collars and Cuffs*, one of the liveliest and funniest of Stan Laurel's solo efforts and arguably the best of his "occupational" comedies. As he continued to explore the working man's world for comic opportunities, Laurel was honing his cinematic technique, learning how to present a gag on film for maximum effect.

Set at the aptly named Rough and Wet Laundry, *Collars and Cuffs* opens with an interesting gag in that it is, essentially, an audible one for a silent movie. Katherine Grant is stretching the fabric each time Stan, who is ironing, bends over, causing him to believe he has ripped his pants.

The uninitiated should be aware that "silent films" were never referred to as such until the advent of the "talkies." Until that time, movies were simply movies, without any adjective to note the lack of a soundtrack. So when gags involving the emission of specific sounds and noises were presented in films during this period, performers had to physically convey their responses to whatever they were supposed to have heard.

Laurel takes the fabric-ripping gag a step further. After realizing his error, he actually does rip the seat of his pants while ironing, causing the female workers to react in horror, and his foreman (Mark Jones) to respond with outrage. But Stan keeps working at his post, blissfully unaware of the situation.

Most of *Collars and Cuffs* is an extended chase, as the foreman pursues Stan throughout the laundry (the equipment serves as props for slapstick gags). While the foreman is angry, Stan remains playfully aloof. At one point, Stan evades the foreman and joins a card game. This interval initially seems to throw the rhythm of the comedy off-kilter, yet when Laurel returns to the card game at various intervals during the chase, the frequency of these disruptions give the sequence a welcome tone of unbridled wackiness.

The messiness of laundry work had been used previously as a source for humor, most notably in the Keystone comedy *Dirty Work in a Laundry* (1915). *Collars and Cuffs* contains gags that are bigger in scope than most farces of this type, yet without the excessiveness found in the Larry Semon comedies at Vitagraph and (later) Chadwick Studios. Semon's outsized, no-holds-barred gags were often so far over the top that they produced startled reactions rather than laughter. Laurel tempered his bigger gags with physical grace and a variety of movement within the structure.

At the conclusion of *Collars and Cuffs*, a large washing machine goes haywire, capturing the boss in its soapy confines, covering him completely with lather. Abbott and Costello performed a similar bit in *Rio Rita* (MGM, 1942), with Lou Costello trapped in an industrial-sized washing machine, and the humor is enhanced by the brisk editing of the sequence. The editing in *Collars and Cuffs* is also an asset and extends the gag beyond the machine itself, as the soapy water spills out of the laundry and onto the street, causing cars to spin out of control and pedestrians to slip and fall. Responding police officers hurry into the laundry and are so caught up in the messiness that they dive into a clothes hamper to avoid the tumult. Stan attempts to flee, but he's unable to produce any traction on the slippery soapsuds and winds up running in place.

Despite its lack of deeper substance, or perhaps because of it, *Collars and Cuffs* is one of Stan's most delightful one-reel comedies on a purely visceral level. Examining Laurel's output chronologically, it is at first difficult to discern his exact contributions as a writer and/or a director, since he did not receive screen credit in either capacity. Laurel's later stint at Roach, when he would limit himself to just writing and directing, allows us to better assess his comic vision, so when revisiting these earlier efforts, we have a clearer picture of his creative input. *Collars and Cuffs* certainly bears the Stan Laurel stamp in its consistent inventiveness. The film remains as entertaining today as it was at the time of its initial release when the *Moving Picture World* enthused, "The situations have been cleverly devised ... sure to please lovers of rough-and-tumble comedy." Indeed!

Gas and Air

Cast

Stan Laurel .... Phillup McCann
Katherine Grant .... Lunch counter operator
Charles Stevenson ...... Bolt, the foreman of Weak End Gas station
Eddie Baker .... Motorist in need of gasoline
With
Noah Young, Roy Brooks

Credits

Percy Pembroke .... Director
W. P. Hackney .... Assistant director
Frank Young .... Cinematographer
Lloyd French .... Props
A Hal Roach production. Copyrighted June 7, 1923.
Production dates: March 20–27, 1923.
Retakes: April 6–7, 1923.
Released July 29, 1923, by Pathé Exchange.
One reel

With *Gas and Air*, Laurel again eschewed his successful movie-parody format to find humor in working-class settings. This had served him well on most of his one-reel comedies, and had established his career as far back as his initial few films.

As Rob Stone has noted, Roach studio records reveal *Gas and Air* began filming the very day that *Collars and Cuffs* wrapped. Both are gag-driven comedies centering around a single workplace, yet the laundry setting in *Collars and Cuffs* offered ample opportunity for fast-paced, messy fun and an even messier climax. In *Gas and Air*, the comic potential of the gas station setting seems more limited.

Service station jokes were to be used countless times over the years, especially by The Three Stooges (*Violent is the Word for Curly, Slaphappy Sleuths, Pardon My Backfire*). Even a movie as (relatively) recent as Jerry Lewis's *Hardly Working* (1981; filmed in 1979) has a scene with the comedian bumbling through time-honored gags as a service attendant (the car hood hitting Lewis in the face as it opens; neglected gasoline causing an explosion, etc.). Laurel does similar things in *Gas and Air* but does save the most inspired comedy for a later portion of the film. In an outrageous sequence, a truck hits a fat man crossing the street, causing the vehicle to fall completely apart. Stan then must step within the truck, lift the remaining chassis, and walk it back to the service station for repairs. It is a clever visual, and easily the highlight of the picture.

Stan also revisits the opening of *Pick and Shovel* when he arrives in a top hat and long coat, only to remove both and reveal he is merely a worker at the site, and not the wealthy customer as his manner of dress would lead us to believe. Later, Stan employs another gag involving perceived appearances as he dons a disguise in order to "trick" a car into functioning properly.

What prevents *Gas and Air* from being as enjoyable as *Collars and Cuffs* is that it does not have the same sense of rhythm or structure. The many gags, often quite funny, do not flow as well, resulting in a film that is merely a series of comic sequences rather than a unified whole. There's plenty of activity during the opening moments — at breakfast, Stan can't break open a hard-boiled egg; Stan pushes a vehicle up a ramp and it winds up crashing into a line of barrels; Stan tries to control a vehicle as it drags his boss down the street — but these bits do not have a cumulative effect, so even some of the funnier gags become rather tiresome.

Existing prints of *Gas and Air* are incomplete, ending abruptly with an out-of-control water hose, so it may be difficult to fully assess the merits (and faults) of the film at this time. However, a review in *Motion Picture News* seems to have been on the right track: "The gags are for the most part of a stereotyped order, but they are good for a laugh where the audience is not too exacting about the originality of the humor supplied them." Stan Laurel's fertile comic mind would be put to much better advantage in other subjects.

Oranges and Lemons

Cast

Stan Laurel	Sunkist sap
Katherine Grant	Little Valencia (the girl)
Eddie Baker	Orange Blossom (the foreman)
George Rowe	Worker
Sammy Brooks	Worker
Mark Jones	Worker
Martin Wolfkeil	Worker

Credits

George Jeske	Director
Clarence Hennecke, W. P. Hackney	Assistant directors
Frank Young	Cinematographer
Ham (Hamilton) Kinsey, Lloyd French	Props

6. Stan Returns to Hal Roach

A Hal Roach production. Copyrighted June 7, 1923. Production dates: March 28–April 6, 1923. Released August 12, 1923, by Pathé Exchange. One reel.

For years, *Oranges and Lemons* was the most accessible of Stan Laurel's solo efforts, thanks to numerous 8mm and 16mm prints available on the collectors market and from film-rental outlets. (Even today, transfers of these old prints frequently turn up on DVD as part of various "Comedy Classics" collections.) Many Laurel and Hardy fans introduced to Stan's pre–Ollie work via this film were surprised to discover the aggressive fellow on display bore no resemblance to the beloved comic figure to whom they were accustomed.

Stan picks and packs the title fruits in *Oranges and Lemons* (1923).

The frenetic pacing and mechanical gags are closer in style to a standard Larry Semon comedy, minus Semon's penchant for racial jokes and animal abuse.

There is no plot to speak of in *Oranges and Lemons*. Stan is a fruit picker and packer at a citrus grove, where he proves to be a menace in the orchard and the packing plant. His incompetence enrages the foreman and his combativeness antagonizes his co-workers. Before long, an angry mob is chasing Stan all over the workplace.

Oranges and Lemons is a lightning-paced one-reeler, brimming with visual gags. Yet few of these gags elicit genuine laughter because Stan isn't playing any sort of character here, just an unsympathetic catalyst for mayhem. He's clearly intended to be the underdog, but it's difficult to root for a nonentity, especially one with such a temperamental streak. (His co-workers want to wring his neck and, after a while, you can't blame them.)

Even his romance with Katherine Grant is underdeveloped, although *romance* is too descriptive a term to employ here since their relationship is merely implied. The only scene featuring the couple (done in cutaways — they're never in the same frame!) consists of Katherine playfully tossing oranges to Stan faster than he can catch them. Then she disappears completely, which is a shame because their brief byplay contains the only sliver of humanity in the film.

Stan's comic timing is the greatest asset of *Oranges and Lemons*. The gags, as perfunctory as they are, benefit from his physical prowess, as when he attempts to climb a rubbery ladder or jumps upon a makeshift seesaw to propel packing crates to a co-worker on an upper level. There's a beautifully executed routine in which Stan repeatedly eludes an irate Eddie Baker by nimbly weaving back and forth through a pair of swinging doors. However, as good as the individual set pieces are, the film is too disjointed for these moments to have any cumulative effect. Plus, the humor is often too mean-spirited to qualify Stan as a nominal hero, and this miscalculation is off-putting. In other films, Stan could be a mischievous, self-serving scamp and still win over the audience. But here he's a borderline sadist who provokes most of the fights and is quick to perform a triumphant little dance after tormenting a victim.

Oranges and Lemons was just another stock item to roll off the comedy-short assembly line, yet reviewers felt it was on par with Laurel's past efforts. *Moving Picture World* said, "About up to the average of previous numbers in which this comedian has been featured as it contains quite a few laughs." *Motion Picture News* encouraged exhibitors to book it: "If you want a reel of action with a generous measure of rough and tumble incident and slapstick fun, here's the film to supply your demand."

At one point, Stan is seen running on a conveyor belt moving in the opposite direction. That image serves as a metaphor for *Oranges and Lemons* and other characterless, gag-driven comedies he was turning out during this period: a lot of energy is expended, but he doesn't get anywhere. The greatness in Stan Laurel would not fully emerge until he developed a distinctive comic personality that would separate him from the third-rate, interchangeable silent-screen clowns who routinely made comedies as uninspired as this one.

Short Orders

Cast

Stan Laurel	Short-order cook/waiter
Marie Mosquini	Cashier
Eddie Baker	Café owner

Jack Ackroyd .... Customer
George Rowe .... Chef
Mark Jones .... Customer with tough steak
Charles Stevenson .... Customer

Credits

Percy Pembroke .... Director
Ralph Ceder .... Director (retakes, uncredited)
Clarence Hennecke .... Assistant director
Robert Doran, Frank Young .... Cinematographers
Ham (Hamilton) Kinsey, Lloyd French .... Props

Alternate title: *Super Service.*
A Hal Roach production. Copyrighted August 11, 1923.
Production dates: April 13–23, 1923.
Released September 2, 1923, by Pathé Exchange.
One reel.

Short Orders dishes up a potpourri of gags dealing with food preparation (it's a health inspector's nightmare), yet most are too derivative of better material seen in other, similarly themed comedy shorts. And without defined characters or a storyline, the gags have no resonance or momentum. The unremarkable *Oranges and Lemons*, Stan's previous effort, seems like Chaplin's *Modern Times* by comparison.

The film is simply a series of incidents based on a single situation: Stan doubles as a short-order cook and waiter (the only waiter, in fact) at a cheap café. Chaplin, Keaton, and Arbuckle had repeatedly (and hilariously) mined this setting as a source of rich humor; a host of minor comics liberally borrowed their ideas and, in some instances, the same gags. To Stan's credit, he tries to put his own spin on the material, but far too often he relies on the belief that outrageousness is naturally funny. That certainly isn't always the case, and that's certainly not the case here. When Chaplin, Keaton, and Arbuckle prepare meals in the kitchen, the tasks are executed with illogical logic (i.e., using the blades of a fan to slice carrots). But when Stan and the chef imitate lumberjacks and use a crosscut saw to slice cheese, it's too impractical and silly to be amusing. (It also raises the question why such a small establishment with so few customers would require the services of a cook *and* a chef.)

Stan does come up with nice variations on standard gags. In many other comedies, a pair of swinging doors leading to and from the kitchen would signal disaster: people getting hit in the face, dishes and trays being knocked to the floor, and so forth. None of that happens here as Stan effortlessly glides through these potential weapons. At one point, one door thoughtfully holds itself open and doesn't close until Stan gives it approval to do so. Stan gives the time-honored "stinky Limburger cheese" routine a moderate twist by having the chunk of cheese secured on a leash, jumping around like a wild animal as he attempts to slice it. The odor is so potent that a patron's derby keeps popping off his head every time he raises the cheese sandwich to his mouth.

One clever running gag has Stan the short-order cook transforming himself into Stan the waiter by simply raising the bottom of his apron and tying it around his neck, revealing a vest, collar and tie attached underneath.

But Stan also overplays his hand by trying to be too clever. In various films, Arbuckle and Keaton performed (separately) a window-cleaning bit in which they were seen using a rag to meticulously clean a window (in a kitchen door, automobile door, or telephone booth), making sure every inch of it was spotless, only to reach *through* the window when they were finished, revealing that there was no glass pane at all. In the hands of Arbuckle or Keaton, it's a beautifully sustained bit of pantomime. Stan's variation, however, flattens the whimsical nature of the gag: Stan cleans a soaped-up window — it's clearly a *real* window — and when he's finished, he steps through it. (Which raises another question: Why does the *backroom* kitchen have *storefront* windows?) The original routine played fair with the audience because it was performed in a single, continuous take. Stan's version is undermined by a cutaway shot that bridges two (obvious) separate takes. This sort of cinematic "cheating" ruins the magical quality of the bit.

As in *Oranges and Lemons*, the so-called leading lady (Marie Mosquini in this film) gets the short shrift. There's no romantic angle, and the only scene Stan shares with her is when he sees her crying and tries to comfort her, only to discover she's peeling onions. (Why is the cashier peeling onions? Shouldn't the chef or the short-order cook be doing that?)

This inexplicable display of compassion distracts Stan long enough for him to put too much salt on a steak, making it impossible to be cut with a knife. The customer's complaining proves to be the last straw for the boss, who fires Stan on the spot. Stan grabs his hat, the tough steak, and his umbrella (embarrassingly, concealed silverware spills out of it) and exits.

Walking past a shoe-repair shop, Stan notices his feet have practically worn through the soles of his shoes. Not wanting to let food go to waste, he uses the tough steak for replacement leather, only to have a pack of hungry dogs follow him down the street. This final gag may be the most notable one in the film, if only because it predates a similar bit in the Laurel and Hardy feature *Way Out West* (1937) in which Stan utilizes a piece of inedible lunchmeat for the same purpose.

The *Exhibitors Trade Review* didn't rave about *Short Orders*, although they could have been harsher: "Stan Laurel's effort is a fairly amusing picture of what happens to restaurant orders as well as those who try to eat the sometimes strange results. At times the action is a bit obvious and lacking spontaneity. But it is good for a number of laughs."

Save the Ship

Cast

Stan Laurel . . . . Husband
Marie Mosquini . . . . Wife
Mark Jones . . . . Father-in-law

Credits

George Jeske . . . . Director
Clarence Hennecke . . . . Assistant director
Robert Doran . . . . Cinematographer
Ham (Hamilton) Kinsey, Harry Bayfie . . . . Props
A Hal Roach production. Copyrighted November 19, 1923.
Production dates: April 30–May 5, 1923; retakes July 7–11
Released November 18, 1923, by Pathé Exchange.
One reel.

For *Save the Ship*, the cast and crew spent six days filming off the coast of Santa Catalina Island. Ten days after shooting wrapped, Stan began work on another one-reeler, *A Man About Town*. Two months later, five days of retakes were required to put the finishing touches on *Save the Ship*, which turned out to be Laurel's final single-reel starring short. Despite all of the time and effort expended upon the production, this is one of Laurel's least interesting comedies.

Without an actual plot, *Save the Ship* consists of a series of gags strung together by a simple premise: Stan, his wife and in-laws live in a tent on a floating platform out in the ocean. (Published synopses state that the family is on a holiday, but that isn't made clear in existing prints of the film.) The lack of genuine terra firma doesn't faze Stan, as he raises chickens and meticulously tends to his garden, situated right behind the tent. When his attempts to catch fish in the traditional manner prove futile, he uses a rifle to shoot flying fish out of the sky. But the firearm has been accidentally overloaded with gun powder, and the resulting blast sinks the unorthodox vessel. A motorboat rescues Stan's wife and mother-in-law, while Stan and his father-in-law scramble aboard an attached rowboat. To keep warm, the father-in-law starts a fire that destroys their craft, but Stan is too preoccupied with a game of solitaire to notice.

Placing the action on the platform and in the surrounding ocean limits the scope of the film, as too much time is devoted to repetitious fishing gags

(Stan catches the hook on the seat of his pants and keeps pulling his trousers down). Laurel does manage to utilize the restrictive setting for a few inventive visuals. The seagoing garden is an inspired bit of lunacy, as are the flying fish Stan catches but can't hang onto.

As Laurel set his sights on a forthcoming series of longer, two-reel comedies, his final one-reel efforts seem hurried and slapdash, and *Save the Ship* is a good example of this. The film is full of high spirits (there's plenty of motion in this motion picture) and races along at a fast clip, so while it may not be consistently funny, it isn't dull either. Period reviews were charitably favorable, although *Motion Picture News* offered this rather non-committal assessment: "All in all, the comedy is a fairly good one, if you like that sort of stuff."

Save the Ship is the cinematic equivalent of fast food: indistinguishable from a lot of other mass-produced fare, yet not impossible to tolerate. If you like that sort of stuff.

A Man About Town

Cast

Stan Laurel	A man about town
Jimmy (James) Finlayson	Hunko, the store detective
Katherine Grant	The wrong woman
George Rowe	Cross-eyed barber
Mark Jones	Another cross-eyed barber
Charles Stevenson	Shop assistant
Eddie Baker	Cop
Sammy Brooks	Little man with hat
Sunshine Har	Bit
Sam Lufkin	Bit

Credits

George Jeske	Director
Clarence Hennecke	Assistant director
Frank Young	Cinematographer
Ham (Hamilton) Kinsey	Props

A Hal Roach production. Copyrighted August 11, 1923. Production dates: May 15–22, 1923; retakes May 25. Released September 16, 1923, by Pathé Exchange. One reel.

A Man About Town keeps things moving fast enough to sustain its simple (if ludicrous) premise for an entire reel, although without any distinctive gags or set pieces it's never anything more than a mildly enjoyable time-filler.

Riding on a street car, Stan asks for directions and the conductor instructs him to follow another passenger, a young woman who will be transferring to the same car Stan will need to take to reach his destination. When she gets off, Stan dutifully follows her but accidentally winds up shadowing a different, similarly dressed woman, then finally another. The "wrong" woman wanders into a department store where Stan's seemingly suspicious behavior catches the eye of Hunko, the store detective. After Stan runs out of the store to keep up with the woman, the detective continues to tail the "suspect." The woman becomes aware of Stan's presence and tells a policeman, "That hungry looking man has been following me." With the cop and Hunko in hot pursuit, Stan prepares to board a streetcar when he pauses to taunt his pursuers. While doing so, the streetcar departs and a police patrol wagon pulls up, as Stan distractedly hops aboard that vehicle instead.

The final gag is the only moment when Stan behaves like the cocky go-getter he played in some of his other solo efforts. The rest of the time, he's a childlike innocent, although more of a blank slate than an actual character. But the idea of Stan being given a simple directive and taking it to the literal extreme is indicative of the Stanley we would come to know in the Laurel and Hardy era.

For most of *A Man About Town*, Stan is blissfully unaware he's being pursued by the detective, which creates a markedly different relationship between Stan and co-star James Finlayson. Finlayson is still his adversary, but since Stan isn't conscious of it, he has no reason to foster a rivalry. Instead, it becomes a comedy of frustration: Finlayson's frustration in trying to get the goods on Stan, as well as Stan's frustration in trying not to lose track of the woman he's supposed to follow. It's an intriguing exercise, with the comic skills of the two comedians compensating somewhat for the skimpiness of the material.

Some of the humor typifies the casual tastelessness found in many vintage comedies, with gags that would be considered the height of insensitivity in these (allegedly) enlightened times. In the department store sequence, for example, Stan inadvertently exposes a female shoplifter who was stuffing garments in the back of her coat. Later, the detective spies a customer with a prominent bulge in the back of his jacket. The detective angrily confronts the man and lifts his jacket, only to discover he's a hunchback. In a barbershop sequence, Stan (biding his time while the woman he's been following stops at a beauty parlor) and the detective are both unnerved by a pair of cross-eyed barbers. As William K. Everson noted in *The Films of Laurel and Hardy* (Citadel Press, 1967): "If such gags seem tasteless or 'sick,' it should be remembered that comedy in the silent era was a wide-open field. Race, religion, minority groups, sex, all of these were kidded mercilessly, and because they were kidded equally, there was never any feeling of discrimination or resentment, as long as the individual gags were funny."

The *Moving Picture World* noted that the basic premise led to "amusing but no unusual complications." That pretty much sums up *A Man About Town*.

Roughest Africa

Cast
Stan Laurel .... Prof. Stanilaus Laurello*
Katherine Grant .... Min Laurello (professor's wife)
James Finlayson .... Lieut. Hans Downe
George Rowe .... Cross-eyed Simpo-Sap

Credits
Ralph Ceder .... Director
Clarence Hennecke, Robert A. Golden .... Assistant directors
Frank Young .... Cinematographer
George Stevens .... Assistant cinematographer (unconfirmed)
Carl Himm .... Editor
H. M. Walker .... Titles
Ham (Hamilton) Kinsey, Harry Bayfield .... Props
Byron Vreeland .... Grip
Tony Campanaro .... Monkey trainer

"Expedition sponsored by the
Artichoke University of Bellpepper Rapids."
A Hal Roach production. Copyrighted November 9, 1923.
Production dates: May 31–June 16, 1923.
Retakes: June 28–July 6, 1923.
Released September 30, 1923, by Pathé Exchange.
Two reels.

During the 1920s, African-safari documentaries such as Mr. and Mrs. Martin E. Johnson's *Jungle Adventures* (1921) and H. A. Snow's *Hunting Big Game in Africa with Gun and Camera* (1922) chronicled the death-defying exploits of wildlife experts who risked their lives to capture footage of various savage beasts. Stan realized that the self-important solemnity of these films was ripe for satire, and his burlesque of the genre, *Roughest Africa*, is one of his best parodies.

Professor Stanilaus Laurello, a big-game hunter known as "Bhanana Pheel" ("Big Boss"), and his trusty cameraman, Lieut. Hans Downe ("Twoo Sphot" or "Little Boss"), leave the civilization of Hollywood and embark upon an expedition to the jungles of Los Angeles to film Laurello's latest documentary. With native burden bearers ("Simpo-Saps") transporting the barest essentials (including golf clubs, bass fiddle, piano, bathtub, icebox and barrels of

---

*Most sources cite the character's name as "Stanislaus," but it is "Stanilaus" in the actual film.

Glass slide advertisement for *Roughest Africa* (1923).

liquor), Laurello hops into a taxicab as the journey begins. Making a "slight detour" through assorted territories and landscapes — the Lumbago Mountains, the Kitchen Range, Asia Miner (Local 325) — they reach the Hypo-Dermo Islands, where Laurello's (literal) brush with a wild porcupine leaves him with a backside full of quills.

While Laurello baits ostrich traps with frankfurters, a bear wanders onto the campgrounds and pandemonium erupts. Laurello repeatedly tries to shoot the bear but each time Hans Downe is on the receiving end of the gunfire. Laurello manages to capture the bear in an ostrich trap, only to plunge into the same pit when a mischievous monkey pulls the release lever. Laurello's encounter with an elephant results in the pachyderm being shot from the inside after it swallows his gun.

In Bulla-Bulla, Laurello plays his bass fiddle to attract a lion, but the tactic backfires when a dozen of them start chasing him through the jungle.

After swimming across a crocodile-infested river (with one croc nipping at the seat of his pants), Laurello retreats to the safety of the taxicab, unaware that a skunk has joined him for the ride.

Roughest Africa successfully skewers the artifice of jungle documentaries by continually exposing Laurello as a bumbler who takes every opportunity to preen for the camera. Even after he's been mauled by a bear, the professor tips his pith helmet and flashes a triumphant (if forced) smile. None of Laurello's ineptitude is lost on his cameraman Hans Downe, who scoffs at the professor's failed attempts at staging "natural" events.

The film is loaded with funny visual gags, beginning with our introduction to Laurello, who is sitting amongst a row of Capuchin monkeys. (A title card helpfully informs us that "the Professor is fifth from the left.") In a beautifully executed sequence we see, in a long shot, an ostrich chasing Laurello across the horizon, from left to right. Their paths cross with Downe, who's being chased by a bear and running in the opposite direction. Laurello and the ostrich quickly turn on their heels, as the bear chases the two men and the oversized bird across the horizon, from right to left.

The most memorable set piece involves "the thrill of my first elephant chase," as Laurello peers through binoculars, unaware that one of the beasts has snuck up behind him. Laurello fires a few ineffectual shots until a cross-eyed Simpo-Sap advises the clueless hunter to shoot it between the eyes. Laurello nervously approaches the elephant, shakes hands with its trunk and, with a piece of chalk, draws a target on its forehead. He pulls out his pistol but spends so much time striking poses of the camera that he doesn't notice the elephant has retreated, so the gun is now pointed at the animal's rear end.

After a failed attempt to capture the elephant, Laurello produces his pistol again, but the animal swallows it. Undaunted, Laurello grabs another pistol and ties a rope around the trigger. Sprinkling the gun with salt, he places it into the elephant's mouth, and once he's sure it has reached the stomach, he pulls the rope. The gun goes off and the elephant disappears in a cloud of smoke — only to have the carcass (rather, a prop elephant) crash-land seconds later.

A surprising element that gives *Roughest Africa* a real satiric punch is the authenticity of the interaction between Laurel, Finlayson and the animals. As Finlayson rests on a cot, a real bear comes along and licks the top of his head. There are no cutaways to a stuntman in a bear costume, as Fin shares a close-up with the genuine article. Likewise, Stan's eye-to-eye encounter with an elephant is done, for the most part, with a real elephant. (As in nearly all films requiring the services of an elephant, a domesticated Indian elephant is used because they're tamer and easier to train than the larger-eared African variety.) When Stan plays a bass fiddle to attract lions, one of them gets close enough to breathe down his neck, making his scared reaction all the more amusing. Ironically, this sort of convincing interaction is often lacking in legitimate travelogues.

The comedic chores are divided between Laurel and Finlayson, who by now have established an effortless rapport. The self-assuredness of Laurello's first-person narrative (via title cards) is sharply contrasted by the incompetence of his actions and by Downe's frequent ridiculing of his boss. Both men are deathly afraid of the wild beasts, only Downe doesn't pretend otherwise. Stan's skills as a pantomimist and physical comedian are given wide range here as he spends the bulk of the picture reacting to the animals or fleeing from them.

The only real glimpse of the Hardy-era Stanley we get is in the final scene, where the professor winds up sharing the backseat of the taxicab with a skunk. At first, he's unaware of the presence of his aromatic traveling companion and assumes the foul odor is emanating from his cigar. The slow realization of his predicament foreshadows those wonderful moments in Laurel

James Finlayson (left center) and Stan discover the natives are restless in *Roughest Africa* (1923).

and Hardy comedies when Stanley gradually begins to grasp the severity of whatever "nice mess" he's gotten himself into.

Katherine Grant's limited footage as Min Laurello, the professor's wife, hardly justifies her second-billing status. The rest of the cast — aside from the animals — are mostly anonymous supporting actors playing native "Simpo-Saps." Their blackface make-up may seem politically incorrect in these supposedly enlightened times, but their exaggerated, minstrel-like appearance was meant to be satiric and should be taken in that context.

The longer-than-usual shooting schedule yielded so much footage that Hal Roach decided to release *Roughest Africa* as a two-reeler, Stan's first Roach production in that format. The film was well received, as indicated by the *Motion Picture News*: "This one is a humdinger, just the thing to make any program sparkle with a hilarity that will be refreshingly relished.... To those who have viewed the African pictures this burlesque should prove a riot; to those who have not seen them, *Roughest Africa* will treat them to hilarious revelations."

During the 1960s, an abridged version of *Roughest Africa* (retitled *The Hunter*) received considerable exposure on television as part of the syndicated *Comedy Capers* series. Young viewers, who were discovering silent comedy in general and Stan Laurel in particular, found this film irresistible, despite having no knowledge of the subject being spoofed. What they responded to was a very funny man doing very funny things, and that assessment still applies today. (For more on *Comedy Capers*, see Appendix.)

Scorching Sands

Cast

Stan Laurel	Stan
James Finlayson	James
Katherine Grant	A beautiful captive
George Rowe	Cross-eyed chieftain
Mark Jones	Ali Bamboo
Merta Sterling	Princess Hormona
Billy Engle	Arab
Sammy Brooks	Diminutive Arab

Credits

Robin E. (Bobby) Williamson	Director
Clarence Hennecke	Assistant director
Frank Young	Cinematographer
Ham (Hamilton) Kinsey, Harry Bayfield	Props

A Hal Roach production. Copyrighted November 9, 1923.
Production dates: June 18–25, 1923.

Retakes (directed by Ward Hayes): July 24–26, 1923.
Released December 9, 1923, by Pathé Exchange.
One reel.

Although the title references the Paramount Pictures feature *Burning Sands* (1922), *Scorching Sands* is not a direct parody. Both films are set in the desert, and the similarity ends there.

A beautiful American tourist is kidnapped by Ali Bamboo and his gang of thieves. Meanwhile, Stan and James, two intrepid explorers stranded in the desert, discover Bamboo's hideout, which they mistake for a pharaoh's temple. Just as the chieftain sentences the intruders to death, the hideous Princess Hormona declares that she wants one of them for herself. Stan and James want nothing to do with her, but the captive tourist convinces them that the only way to escape is to charm the princess, whether they like it or not. When they accidentally push the princess into a swimming pool, the explorers grab the tourist and beat a hasty retreat. Stranded in the desert once again, Stan and James's camel reappears to help them make a convenient getaway.

A run-of-the-mill entry, *Scorching Sands* breezes along at a fast clip but is not as successful as other Laurel gag-laden one-reelers (such as *Collars and Cuffs* and *The Noon Whistle*) because it attempts to cover too much ground in too little time. The subplot dealing with the kidnapped tourist and Ali Bamboo's gang is largely ignored after the first few minutes, rendering these scenes pointless. (It appears this portion of the narrative was severely diminished by subsequent retakes that expanded other sequences.) The film is notable for casting James Finlayson as Laurel's accomplice rather than nemesis, but the introduction of extraneous players only dilutes the potential of their teamwork. Additionally, there's not enough of a contrast between Laurel and Finlayson's barely defined characters to make it an effective partnership.

There are a few amusing touches, as when Laurel and Finlayson enter the temple and sign what they believe is a guest book, unaware that it is actually an order of execution. When Laurel is about to be decapitated, he fluffs up a large pillow and places it in the oversized basket beneath the executioner's chopping block.

Scorching Sands is a handsome, elaborate production. The ornate temple (complete with a swimming pool), décor and costumes seem as though they were designed for a feature film rather than a humble one-reel short. Apparently, Hal Roach either increased the budget or, more likely, utilized standing sets.

The primary interest of *Scorching Sands*, from a historical perspective, is that it reunited Stan with Robin E. Williamson, who directed Laurel's very first film, the long-lost *Nuts in May* (1917). Williamson's contributions to

Scorching Sands are not immediately discernible, at least not more so than Laurel's other directors from this period. It has been acknowledged that, by this time, Laurel was really supervising the productions while the credited director just kept things moving.

Scorching Sands received surprisingly favorable reviews, with the *Motion Picture News* commenting, "Stan is just getting the knack of what is wanted in the way of comedies and it is only a question of time before producer Hal Roach will have given exhibitors a money maker of the Harold Lloyd caliber, for Stan is original and tries to put over something that is thoroughly new — and he succeeds admirably in *Scorching Sands* which is a rapid series of hot laughs."

In 2000, *Under Two Jags*, another Laurel solo comedy, was released on DVD under the title *Scorching Sands* as part of *The Lost Films of Laurel and Hardy: The Complete Collection, Volume Eight.* The confusion apparently stemmed from the fact that the first intertitle in *Under Two Jags* reads, "Scorching Sands — Far out on the great Desert of Dhumbell." The back of the DVD case misidentified the short as *Scorching Sands*, although the liner notes cited that "it appears to be the different film *Under Two Jags*."

The Whole Truth

Cast
Stan Laurel .... Husband
James Finlayson .... Defense lawyer
Earl Mohan .... Lawyer/florist
Helen Gilmore .... Wife
Jack Ackroyd .... Clerk
Wallace Howe .... Pharmacist
Charles Stevenson .... Jewish tailor

Credits
Ralph Ceder .... Director
Frank Young .... Cinematographer (*Roughest Africa* footage)
A Hal Roach production. Copyrighted November 9, 1923.
Released November 4, 1923, by Pathé Exchange.
One reel.

Just prior to embarking on his new series of two-reel comedies, Stan Laurel had another one-reeler left to make in order to fulfill his contractual obligation. With the assistance of producer Hal Roach and director Ralph Ceder, Laurel crafted a one-reel comedy out of unused footage from his previous films, primarily *Roughest Africa*, shooting new scenes as a framing device. The resulting pastiche, *The Whole Truth*, is one of Laurel's funniest one-reelers. That it is so well-assembled and cohesive is a testament to his skills as a filmmaker. (For more on Ralph Ceder, see the entry for *Zeb vs. Paprika*.)

The Whole Truth opens with Stan's wife pleading her case in a courtroom, complaining on the stand that her husband "went out for a cigar" and "must have gone to Havana" because he did not return home for months. Rather than use a pretty ingénue like Katherine Grant, Laurel instead cast homely, shrewish Helen Gilmore in the role of his spouse. This choice of actress heightens the comic value of the situation, as a dapper Stan enters the courtroom and is greeted enthusiastically by all the female spectators. (In fact, the audience is comprised of nothing but women.) Stan is so popular with the ladies that he even poses for a picture.

Stan takes the stand and, after his defense attorney approaches him and says, "Remember our story and try not to laugh," he recounts his reason why he never made it home. This sets us up for an excuse that will undoubtedly be preposterous.

Stan's excuse is related in flashback and involves discarded footage from *Roughest Africa*, which had just completed retakes (June 28 to July 6) and would make it to theaters in September, two months before *The Whole Truth* was released. The unused footage could have been the catalyst for this one-reeler. Some of the flashback scenes involve a very funny battle that Laurel and Finlayson have with a rhinoceros. The rhino costume is quite elaborate and realistic, and, as Rob Stone has noted, it is curious that this amusing (and expensive) footage was deleted from the original. (Laurel, or even Roach, might have wondered how they could salvage these scenes.)

In *Roughest Africa*, the safari scenes were supposed to be set in the Dark Continent, but in *The Whole Truth*, Laurel and Finlayson (who was Stan's cameraman in the original story) are squirrel hunting in New Jersey, which makes their encounter with a rhino too far-fetched for the judge to accept — although the all-female audience bursts into applause after Stan finishes his tall tale.

The judge orders Stan to take a truth-serum pill, and Stan launches into another flashback (unused footage from another Laurel comedy, title unknown) that shows him buying a bouquet for his wife. Unbeknownst to Stan, the flowers get dipped in chloroform and there is a nice running gag where everyone who sniffs the bouquet falls into a deep sleep. Variations on this gag continue until Stan happens by a storefront mannequin holding a bouquet. Stan smells the dummy's flowers and then takes a whiff of his own to compare. He is knocked out by his own bouquet, just as the store owner comes outside. Seeing that Stan is a much more lifelike dummy, he replaces the original mannequin. So much time elapses that Stan has grown a full, thick beard before he wakes up.

Upon returning home, Stan is thrown out by his wife. He sits dejectedly outside his house, crying. The flashback ends and the scene cuts back to the courtroom where, in wrapping up the story, Stan continues to weep. (This is, of course, years before Laurel's trademark "cry," so this early display of tears is an interesting portent of things to come.)

Stan's second explanation is accepted as the truth. His wife forgives him and the now-happy couple leaves the courtroom. But as he exits, Stan turns to the camera and, with a wink and a smile, reveals that he never swallowed the pill. This triumphant ending is gratifying, and Stan's character comes off as a loveable rascal rather than an untrustworthy womanizer.

Assembling a film out of unrelated scraps of footage is usually a dubious achievement at best, and for fans of silent comedy, *Triple Trouble* (1918), a Charlie Chaplin two-reeler cobbled together from unused Chaplin footage, will immediately spring to mind. The difference, however, is that *Triple Trouble* was assembled by Essanay two years after Chaplin left the studio and was beyond the comedian's creative control, while Laurel was able to supervise *The Whole Truth*. Given its patchwork nature, *The Whole Truth* is remarkably effective, tightly structured, and very funny.Reviews for Laurel's final one-reeler were enthusiastic. *Moving Picture World* called it "lively and entertaining," and *Motion Picture News* remarked, "Hal Roach gets right down to business.... He doesn't waste a foot.... This is a splendid reel and entertainingly funny throughout."

Though *The Whole Truth* was made for purely economic reasons, it serves to illustrate the strides Laurel was making as a filmmaker. Compiling unrelated scenes and making them work within the context of newly shot footage would be a budget saving device used in short comedies well into the 1950s (a handful of Three Stooges films were made this way after Shemp Howard's death, with actor Joe Palma doubling for the deceased Stooge in the new footage).

While he still didn't enjoy the same degree of creative control that Chaplin and Keaton had at the time, Stan Laurel was gradually working his way to *auteur* status.

Frozen Hearts

Cast

Stan Laurel	Olaf
Katherine Grant	Sonia
May (Mae) Laurel	Madame XX
James Finlayson	General Sappovitch
Pierre Couderc	Count Alexis Pifflevitch
George Rowe	Cross-eyed soldier
Sammy Brooks	The General's second
William Gillespie	Spectator at duel

Stan Laurel is "Funfully Yours" in this autographed publicity shot for *Frozen Hearts* (1923) (courtesy Paul Gierucki).

Jack Gavin .... Bit
Earl Mohan .... Bit

Credits

Jay A. Howe .... Director
Clarence Hennecke .... Assistant director
Frank Young (and Jack Roach, uncredited) .... Cinematographer
T. J. Crizer .... Editor

H. M. Walker .... Titles
Ham (Hamilton) Kinsey .... Props
"From the celebrated novel by Pistachio Filbertsky."
(A burlesque on *Enemies of Women* by Vincent Blasco-Ibañez.)
A Hal Roach production. Copyrighted November 23, 1923.
Production dates: July 27–August 11, 1923.
Released October 28, 1923, by Pathé Exchange.
Two reels.

The freewheeling comedic style of Stan Laurel's parodies of then-current movies was completely different from the disciplined, character-driven approach he would strive for during his partnership with Oliver Hardy. In his "burlesques," Stan played caricatures rather than characters, and the travesty angle allowed him to indulge in every off-the-wall, exaggerated gag he could devise. Although these films offer little to no indication of the beloved comedian Stan would eventually become, they represent some of his best pre-Hardy work. *Frozen Hearts* is one of the better Laurel lampoons, filled with outrageous visuals and amusing title cards by the great H.M. "Beanie" Walker. ("Sonia's father had sworn to let his whiskers grow until a St. Louis team won the pennant.")

The film opens in the little Russian village of Popoffski during the fall of 1888. Olaf, the son of a humble pool shark, is in love with a peasant girl named Sonia. Just as Olaf and Sonia are making marriage plans, Count Alexis Pifflevitch enters the picture and sends Sonia off to Petrograd, where she is to become a court dancer. A defiant Olaf is arrested but manages to subdue the Count, steal his uniform and follow Sonia to Petrograd.

At the Royal Court, the mysterious Madame XX uses her feminine appeal to entice all the officers, much to the consternation of her lover, General Sappovitch ("Sap" for short). When Sonia appears on the scene, however, the general ignores Madame XX, who then makes a play for the newly arrived Olaf, the faux count. Sonia catches Olaf cuddling with Madame and begins flirting with the general to make Olaf jealous. Olaf intercedes and the general challenges him to a duel, with swords as the weapon of choice. They duel in the courtyard during a raging snowstorm. After a lengthy stretch ("sixteen innings"), it's a draw so the exhausted participants bring the fight indoors to settle it with guns. As Olaf and the general are about to fire, Madame XX hits the light switch; when the lights go back on, the duellers are still standing, but all of the spectators have been shot. The real Count Pifflevitch shows up and argues with the general over who gets to kill Olaf. While this new battle erupts, Olaf and Sonia make their getaway.

Even though *Frozen Hearts* runs out of steam before its conclusion, there are enough funny moments to make it worthwhile. After Sonia is ordered to

Petrograd, Olaf sneaks into her room to bid her farewell. She hands him a picture of herself as a mournful Olaf tells her, "I'll always wear it next to my heart"—as he proceeds to stuff it into his back pocket. Opening the door to leave, Olaf turns back to kiss Sonia goodbye. Olaf opens a second door, located a few feet behind the first door, then goes back to embrace Sonia once more. He opens a third door, embraces Sonia yet again, and backs away while blowing kisses, only to topple out of an open window, landing squarely on Count Pifflevitch and two of his guards.

The count sends for a firing squad to execute Olaf. But the first marksman's vision is so impaired he sees six images of Olaf. ("Shall I fire into the crowd?" he asks.) Next up is a cross-eyed soldier, who winds up killing the guards standing on either side of Olaf, as well as shooting the count in the posterior.

After subduing the count (this occurs behind closed doors so we're left to assume that brains, such as they are, conquered brawn), Olaf dons the officer's uniform and makes plans to head for Petrograd. One of the film's best sight gags has Olaf opening a desk drawer and pulling out a carpet-sized map of Russia marked "Vest Pocket Edition."

In Petrograd, as Olaf prepares to enter the Royal Court, a mound of snow falls off the roof and covers him completely. He resourcefully uses a horse's wagging tail to brush himself off. Once inside, Olaf greets two of the guests; opening his cigarette case, Olaf offers one gentleman a cigarette, the other a piece of chewing tobacco, then reaches in and produces an already-lit pipe!

For his courtyard duel with General Sappovitch, Olaf strips down to reveal a delicate corset with bows. He even stops the fight at one point to adjust his shoulder strap. As they engage in furious (and unorthodox) swordplay, their seconds argue over dueling regulations and get into violent brawl as a hot dog vendor plies his trade.

Frozen Hearts satirizes the conventions of Russian literature—separated lovers, military oppression, unsavory nobility, palace intrigue—and the handsome production values and costume design give it an air of authenticity. (We're not claiming it's in the same league as an Erich von Stroheim production, but for a modestly budgeted comedy short it's still impressive.) Stan and the supporting cast seem to be enjoying themselves immensely, with Katherine Grant making an appealing leading lady and James Finlayson proving once again to be a peerless comic foil. The weak link, as usual, is Mae Laurel (billed as "May Laurel"), who is hardly the irresistible siren she's supposed to be portraying. This wouldn't be an issue, perhaps, if she had the comedic gifts to compensate for it, but the other performances only serve to magnify her shortcomings. At least she doesn't ruin the picture.

Motion Picture News evidently preferred Stan's burlesques to his regular line of comedies: "[Laurel] seems to have his heart in his work and goes about it in a way that impresses you ... there is every indication that straight plays furnish the most food for fun-provoking by Stan."

Stan's parodies may not have had a great impact on his artistic growth, but the format did stimulate his natural creativity and further encouraged him to find humor in any given situation.

The Soilers

Cast

Stan Laurel	Canister*
James Finlayson	Smacknamara
Ena Gregory	Helen Chesty
Mae Laurel	Cherry LaFlip
George Rowe	Brewery
Jack Ackroyd	Justice of the peace
Billy Engle	Prospector/henchman
Eddie Baker	Canister's assistant
Jack Gavin	Prospector
Marvin Lobach	Henchman
Martin Wolfkeil	Henchman

With
Katherine Grant, Sammy Brooks, Jack O'Brien,
Al Forbes, Joe Bordeaux.

Credits

Ralph Ceder	Director
Clarence Hennecke, Harry LaMar	Assistant directors
Frank Young	Cinematographer
T. J. Crizer	Editor
Hal Conklin	Writer
H. M. Walker	Titles
Ham (Hamilton) Kinsey	Props

A Hal Roach production. Copyrighted November 23, 1923.
Production dates: August 20–September 1, 1923.
Released November 25, 1923, by Pathé Exchange.
Two reels.

For most of its length, *The Soilers* is a fitfully amusing burlesque of *The Spoilers* (the version released August 5, 1923) and the best-selling Rex Beach novel (1906) upon which that film was based. During its final third, however,

---

*In some prints, Stan's character is identified as "Bob Canister." For this film and many other titles covered in this volume, we have referenced the Lobster Films edition released on DVD by Kino On Video.

6. Stan Returns to Hal Roach

Stan Laurel is a literal two-gun hero in *The Soilers* (1923).

The Soilers kicks into high gear with a hilariously protracted brawl between Stan and James Finlayson, elevating this entry to the front ranks of Laurel's solo efforts.*

The time is the late 1890s; the setting is the Alaskan territory where a two-fisted daredevil named Canister ("Glennister" in the original) owns a string of gold mines. Smacknamara ("McNamara" in the original), a crooked

---

*A one-reel condensation of The Soilers *circulated on the 8mm and 16mm home-movie market for years, and this is how many Stan Laurel fans were introduced to the film. In its edited form, the emphasis was on the climactic brawl; most of this footage was retained.*

lawyer, conspires to seize control of Cannister's holdings. As tempers escalate, Canister and his assistant dynamite the camp grounds of Smacknamara's Double Cross Mining Company. Vowing to break his enemy with his bare hands, Canister confronts Smacknamara at the Silver Dollar Dance Hall and Saloon, a gambling establishment owned by Brewery, a reformed soda clerk. A violent brawl ensues and Canister emerges victorious, but no one aside from an effeminate cowboy really notices or cares.

Even if one is familiar with the source material, *The Soilers* plays like a series of thinly connected set pieces because the original storyline has been stripped down to its barest essentials. The actors' exaggerated gestures lampooning rugged heroics and unbridled skullduggery are passably amusing but without a sturdy narrative to support these antics, they quickly become repetitious.

Most of the supporting characters lack definition and purpose, especially Helen Chesty ("Helen Chester" in the original) and Cherry LaFlip ("Cherry Malotte" in the original), the hero's girl and the saloon gal, respectively. Aside from providing thumbnail representations of the opposite ends of womanhood, their presence is ultimately pointless since they contribute so little to the film. Of course, in-depth characterizations should not be expected to turn up in a freewheeling parody that deals strictly in superficial stereotypes, but even superficial stereotypes need to be properly integrated into the basic framework.

As the hero, Stan is square-shouldered and steely eyed in the face of adversity. As the heavy, James Finlayson snarls and rants his way through every situation. While watching Laurel and Finlayson interact is always of interest, there's only so much they can accomplish within the restricted parameters of the caricatures they're playing. The one-note characters paint these two talented comedians into an artistic corner, and the only way to salvage the proceedings would be to break loose with an outrageous, no-holds-barred climactic sequence. Fortunately, that's exactly what happens.

Every movie version of *The Spoilers* (1914, 1923, 1930, 1942 and 1955) culminates in a barroom brawl between hero and protagonist. Events have been building up to this moment and when it finally arrives, the resulting knock-down, drag-out fight is distinguished by its length and sheer brutality, as Good literally battles Evil. Stan takes this intense set piece and satirizes it for all it's worth.

The showdown begins in Smacknamara's office, located above the saloon. Canister enters and nails the doors shut so he can have a final confrontation with Smacknamara, only to have seven of Smacknamara's henchmen pop out from behind the bookcase, closet, and the supposedly secured doors. But the grizzled gang members flee in terror at the sight of a mouse, leaving the hero to settle the score, one-on-one, with his rival. Canister tosses his gun aside ("I'm gonna break you with my bare hand") and then wrestles the gun from Smacknamara. (He doesn't exactly wrestle it away — he bites Smacknamara on the wrist.) As Smacknamara grabs a letter opener and tries to stab Canister, an effeminate cowboy wanders into the office. Blissfully unaware that Smacknamara has Canister pinned to his desk, he rifles through some papers until he finds the specific page he's looking for (he has to raise Canister's head off the desk to get it) and nonchalantly sashays out the door, while Canister and Smacknamara stop and stare in bewilderment.

Resuming their battle, fists and furniture fly as the increasing savagery of the fight produces bruises and blood — all of which go unnoticed by the cowboy who merrily skips in and out of the room, completely unfazed by the mêlée.

Reduced to hitting each other with pillows, Canister and Smacknamara fall through a second-floor window in a flurry of feathers and broken glass, onto the wooden walkway below. Still enmeshed in their struggle, they continue to furiously duke it out inside the saloon. In the original story, the townsfolk gather to watch the battle but here the customers dance and gamble without paying the slightest attention to the ruckus.

When Canister finally subdues Smacknamara, our hero desperately seeks the approval of the apathetic saloon patrons ("I broke him with my two bare hands," he says repeatedly). There are no cheers or expressions of gratitude — even his girl walks off with another man. Broken in body and spirit, Canister staggers outside, where he encounters his lone supporter: the swishy cowpoke, who appreciatively tosses him a flower, still in the flower pot.

The ferocity of the climactic brawl gives the sequence a satiric punch that's missing from the rest of the picture. The relentless brutality of the original fight is both lampooned and replicated, and as in all successful parodies, the humor retains some of the dramatic weight of its source material. The inclusion of a stereotypical "pansy" character may strike some viewers as insensitive, but those scenes, performed without malice, are undeniably funny and provide a sly contrast to the testosterone-fueled "he-man" action.

The Soilers is an example of how a rousing finale can make an audience overlook a lackluster start, though the *Motion Picture News* was generally unimpressed with the results: "Stan Laurel is not seen to as good advantage as in many of his past comedies. The comedy is too far fetched, and the fight scene, while uproariously funny in spots is entirely too dragged out.... While the whole thing is of course a travesty and travesties are made to be ridiculous even this sort of thing can be overdone.... There are spots of humor in the action, but this one is hardly up to the standard of the general run of Hal Roach comedies."

Mother's Joy

Cast

Stan Laurel	Basil Dippytack/Magnus Dippytack
James Finlayson	Baron Basil Buttontop
Ena Gregory	Maid
Mae Laurel	Miss Flavia de Lorgnette
Helen Gilmore	Dottie Buttontop Dippytack
Jack Ackroyd	Attorney McFumble
George Rowe	Waiter
William Gillespie	Party guest
Charlie Hall	Party guest

With
Joe Bordeaux, Earl Mohan, Laura Roessing,
Glenn Tryon, Charles Lloyd.

Credits

Ralph Ceder	Director
Harry LaMar	Assistant director
Frank Young	Cinematographer
T. J. Crizer	Editor
H. M. Walker	Titles
Ham (Hamilton) Kinsey	Props

A Hal Roach production. Copyrighted December 24, 1923.
Production dates: September 10–21, 1923.
Released December 23, 1923, by Pathé Exchange.
Two reels.

Mother's Joy has so many things going for it that it's regrettable the results aren't better. The premise is a good one, there are some imaginative visual gags, and the performances possess an engaging comic energy, yet the film never quite reaches its full potential.

Dottie Buttontop, the only daughter of aristocrat Baron Buttontop, elopes with "that handsome scoundrel" Magnus Dippytack. Magnus deserts Dottie and she begs her father for forgiveness ("I've come home to eat") as she introduces him to his infant grandson Basil, named after the baron. But when the child begins making rude gestures, the temperamental baron banishes mother and child from his house. Years later, a remorseful baron tracks them down and invites them to return.

At a belated coming-out party, the baron introduces his grandson to a prospective bride, wealthy heiress Miss Flavia de Lorgnette. Despite Flavia's general disinterest in young Basil—and young Basil's blatant interest in the baron's pretty new maid—their engagement is announced. At the altar, however, Flavia refuses to exchange wedding vows, claiming she's taken a dislike to the groom. Basil admits he's taken a dislike to her as well. With that, the minister storms out, declaring, "I've taken a dislike to the whole outfit!"

Mother's Joy, as the title indicates, lampoons the old-fashioned, heavy-handed melodramas that dealt with familial secrets, regrets and redemption. During the later phase of his career, Stan would no longer rely on silly character names and other accoutrements, but these elements work well enough within the context of this film's lightheartedly satiric tone. During a flashback, we're introduced to Magnus Dippytack — Stan wearing a handlebar mustache and outlandish muttonchop sideburns. The get-up ensures an easy laugh but Stan wisely underplays his gestures, letting his ridiculous appearance speak for itself.

Later, when the disgraced Dottie (dressed in a cape and covered in snow) returns home and introduces her father to his grandchild, we see Stan clad in an infant's gown and bonnet, lying in an oversized basket. The effect is genuinely funny and bizarrely convincing, foreshadowing the brilliant Laurel and Hardy short *Brats* (1930), in which oversized sets allowed Stan and Ollie to portray young children. (This technique was also used for their gag appearance as babies in *Wild Poses*, an Our Gang short released in 1933.) Conversely, when the baron shows his attorney a photo of mother and child taken a few years afterwards, the image is funny because it's so patently unconvincing: an obvious composite shot featuring a miniature image of Stan standing next to a full-sized image of Helen Gilmore.* The verisimilitude of the baby-basket gag is what makes it work but the photo gag depends upon its inherent phoniness, revealing that Stan was astutely aware of the key differences between both comedic concepts.

When we're finally introduced to the grown-up heir ("a drinking image of his father"), he's a cabman with a horse-drawn coach. Basil picks up a fare but before arriving at his destination, a noon whistle blows and he stops to have lunch in the middle of a busy intersection. With traffic whizzing past, he sets up a table and serves a plate of hay to his grateful horse. This charming interlude was filmed at an actual intersection of downtown Culver City, a location seen frequently in Hal Roach comedies of the era. As was so often the case, pedestrians gathered to see what was going on. (Although by 1923, a movie crew in the neighborhood must have been a fairly common sight.)

**Helen Gilmore had previously worked with Stan in* Kill or Cure. *She would appear in the subsequent Laurel comedies* Postage Due, Zeb vs. Paprika, Near Dublin *and the Laurel-directed* Chasing the Chaser, *as well as the Laurel and Hardy films* Their Purple Moment *and* Two Tars.

Basil and Dottie feel awkward rubbing shoulders with the baron's upper-crust associates. The accident-prone Basil can't even bow without falling head over heels down the stairs (an impressive stunt Laurel performs without the use of a double). Refreshingly, Stan isn't the pugnacious character seen in some of his other solo films. While Basil isn't exactly the childlike Stanley of the Laurel and Hardy movies, Stan allows himself to be bullied and doesn't entertain the idea of retaliating, which is completely unlike his earlier comic persona. Yet he's still adult enough to flirt openly (albeit innocently) with the maid every time she enters the scene.

Once it is established that Basil and Dottie are fish out of water, *Mother's Joy* becomes a series of increasingly unsubtle sight gags. Dottie forces Basil to sing, in hopes that his vocalizing will impress the party guests. As Basil emotionally warbles "Mother Hold My Aching Head," his off-key screeching causes a picture to fall off the wall, while his tears land on a potted flower, accelerating its growth. (This early example of the "Laurel cry" is interesting from a historical perspective, although here it's just a comic device and not part of an actual characterization.) The guests endure the assault on their eardrums as long as they can, until Basil starts reaching for higher notes, at which point they all flee the house in disgust.

During his initial foray into society, Basil Dippytack is a shy, bumbling innocent. As he grows comfortable with the lavish trappings, his behavior becomes more rambunctious. At the (later) engagement party, he steals a seat at the crowded dinner table, drenches the baron in grapefruit juice, and has guests scrambling for the exits once again when he offers to sing in lieu of giving a speech.

The plot thread involving Basil's engagement to Flavia seems to have been added primarily to give Mae Laurel something to do, although her participation could hardly be called a bona fide performance. Perhaps to accommodate her limitations an actress, the minor role simply requires her to be haughty and unresponsive. (In contrast, Ena Gregory projects more personality in a single close-up than Mae does in all her footage combined.) Mae is basically a walking clothes rack, and on that level, she fills the requirement adequately enough.

Film historians Richard W. Bann and Rob Stone have noted the parallels between Basil and Flavia's aborted wedding ceremony and Stan's real-life relationship with common-law wife Mae. Like their onscreen counterparts, Stan and Mae never did tie the knot (for various reasons, chiefly because Mae's husband refused to grant her a divorce), and mutual "dislike" severed their private and professional relationship. It's intriguing to surmise what, if anything, was going through their minds as they were performing this scene, though Stan would have utilized a good comedic idea regardless of how it may have reflected upon his personal affairs.*

Audiences and critics, unaware of what was going on in Stan's private life, judged *Mother's Joy* on its own merits. The *Exhibitors Trade Review* felt it had "a more consistent and effective line of fun than some of his other recent efforts. There are some highly amusing incidents and altogether it should please the average audience."

If *Mother's Joy* had sustained a more consistent level of inventiveness, it might have emerged as one of the better Stan Laurel comedies. As it stands, it's an uneven, amusing effort that runs out of gas before reaching its conclusion.

Near Dublin

Cast

Stan Laurel	Con Corrigan
Ena Gregory	Colleen Dugan
James Finlayson	Sir Patrick
George Rowe	Officer O'Toole
Dick Gilbert	Old man Dugan
Fred Karno, Jr.	Villager
Helen Gilmore	Villager
Jack Gavin	Villager
Mae Laurel	Villager
Leo Willis	Villager
William Gillespie	Man with fiddle
Sam (Sammy) Brooks	Barn dance musician

With
Jimmy Kelly (James T. Kelly), Jack Ackroyd, Earl Mohan, Glenn Tryon, L. Loback, Charles Hall, Pat Kelly, Billy Engle, Ed Baker, Charlie Lloyd.

Credits

Ralph Ceder	Director
Harry La Mar	Assistant director
Frank Young	Cinematographer
H. M. Walker	Titles
T. J. Crizer	Editor
Ham (Hamilton) Kinsey and Sherbourne Shields	Props

During his partnership with Oliver Hardy, Stan utilized the aborted-wedding idea in Our Wife *(1931) and* Me and My Pal *(1933), and, to a lesser extent,* Pack Up Your Troubles *(1932). The idea was also used for the pilot of a projected Laurel and Hardy radio series in 1941. Edgar Kennedy and Patsy Moran co-starred in the pilot and returned to perform the same duties when the sketch was revived for a 1943 installment of Armed Forces Radio's* Mail Call *series. Historian Scott MacGillivray has noted that this sketch is known variously as "The Wedding Party," "The Wedding Night," and "The Marriage of Stan Laurel."*

A Hal Roach production. Copyrighted February 20, 1924.
Production dates: September 26–October 9, 1923.
Retakes (directed by George Jeske): December 16–17, 1923.
Released May 11, 1924, by Pathé Exchange.
Two reels.

A takeoff on romantic musical plays set in Ireland, such as the works of Chauncey Olcott (*Mavourneen, Sweet Inniscarra, Old Limerick Town*), *Near Dublin* has a solid supporting cast, nice production values, and a sturdier-than-usual plotline. It just isn't terribly funny. To be fair, the film does attempt to be something a little more than a flat-out parody. Still, this creative ambition doesn't compensate for the lack of strong gag sequences.

In the little village of Shillalah, Con Corrigan is the mailman who knows everyone's personal affairs because he reads all their correspondence. Con's sweetheart is the lovely Colleen Dugan, whose father owes back rent to Sir Patrick, a brick merchant and landlord. Sir Patrick informs old man Dugan that he'll forget about the money if he can marry Colleen. Incensed by this offer, Con pays the debt, launching a rivalry between the two men.

At a barn dance, a blindfolded Con tries to take a bite out of an apple on a string. A practical joker replaces the apple with a brick that smacks Con in the face. Con retaliates by clobbering the prankster with the brick, setting off a brick-hurling melee between all the partygoers (who came prepared with concealed bricks just in case a fight broke out). Sir Patrick storms in with Officer O'Toole in tow and has Con arrested for "defrauding the mails."

From his jail cell, Con looks on as Colleen struggles to fend off Sir Patrick's amorous advances. Escaping from jail, Con comes to Colleen's rescue, only to have Sir Patrick break a chair over his head. Con pretends to be dead and Colleen has Sir Patrick arrested for murder.

During Sir Patrick's trial — held at the all-purpose barn — Con hides in the hayloft and delights in tossing bricks at his foe. When Con's presence is discovered, the superstitious villagers think he's a vengeful ghost and flee in terror. Con and Colleen join hands and skip down the street, with Sir Patrick and Officer O'Toole in hot pursuit.

The humor in *Near Dublin* relies heavily on knockabout physical antics and crude Irish stereotypes (the villagers love their bricks and their booze), so it's rather surprising to find passages that are fairly subdued. Stan is first seen riding horseback, reading a letter he is about to deliver and laughing uproariously at its contents. As he hands the opened letter to the indignant recipient, he grins knowingly and brushes one index finger against the other to indicate the naughty nature of the correspondence. Yet another delivery is handled in an entirely different manner. After he overhears a woman brag about how well her

(Front row, left to right) Stan Laurel, Ena Gregory, Mae Laurel and James Finlayson at a village barn dance in *Near Dublin* (1924). Mae is more prominent in this photograph than she is in the actual film.

son is doing in America ("He's Vice-Janitor in a bank"), Stan doesn't have the heart to give her a letter from her son, stating he's been sent to prison. Stan rips up the letter rather than be the bearer of the bad news. (James Finlayson observes Stan destroying the letter and later charges him with defrauding the mail.) Stan plays the scene with utter sincerity, using minimal facial expressions to convey his compassion. There's no comedic payoff to this scene, nor does Stan's character display this trait at any other time. Aside from setting up the reason for his later arrest, it's a poignant set piece that has little connection to the rest of the film.

Stan's character wavers from being a spirited funster to a fairly straightforward leading man (in a light-comedy vein), but he's never really a full-fledged bungler or buffoon. Although he has no trouble getting into predicaments, he's quite resourceful when need be. He manages to escape from his jail cell by crawling around on his hands and knees, pretending to look for something on the floor. Intrigued by Stan's actions, curious cop George Rowe joins in the search, even though he has no idea what he's looking for. As Rowe becomes increasingly distracted, Stan slips out the door. The sequence is typical of *Near Dublin*'s comic set pieces: it's cleverly conceived and executed, yet only comes across as mildly amusing at best.

Repetition also negates the effectiveness of the humor. During the trial sequence, Stan hides in the hayloft and throws a brick at Finlayson, hitting him in the head and knocking him unconscious. The gag is executed three times, each time in the same manner with the same results. The lack of a strong comic payoff (or *any* comic payoff) is curious and surprising.

Other scenes, like the aborted letter bit, are not played for laughs. The romance between Stan and Ena Gregory is sweetly rendered, not quite a parody of romances in straight plays but more like an imitation of one. Even when other characters and situations become broadly exaggerated, the Stan-Ena relationship seems to operate on a different level. James Finlayson's villainy is mostly a comic caricature but there are moments when his performance enters the realm of pure melodrama.

The disjointed nature of the film may have been further complicated by the changes insisted upon by the distributor. Historian Rob Stone has noted that the Pathé Exchange objected to a funeral sequence in the initial cut and deemed it unsuitable for release. To appease them (and bridge the missing footage), retakes were done by George Jeske, who was not the original director. It's doubtful the removal of the funeral scene did irreparable damage, but it probably didn't help matters either.

Upon its initial release, *Near Dublin* was well-received by reviewers. *Motion Picture News* enthused, "Here is a travesty on the well-known Irish plays that will undoubtedly register big and it is well produced, affording Stan Laurel one of the best and most novel comedies he has had for quite a while. James Finlayson, Ena Gregory, and George Rowe have the prominent roles and a large cast help put this comedy over in most excellent style.... Yes, this one is very funny." *Moving Picture World* enjoyed it too, although they didn't rate it as highly: "While it lacks some of the snap of the previous Laurel comedies, it is nevertheless amusing and the plot and atmosphere are quite out of the ordinary."

For years, *Near Dublin* only circulated in a truncated edition made available to the home-movie market. This eight-minute abridgement did an injustice to the original, as mediocre as it may be, with haphazard re-editing and substandard print quality laying waste to whatever virtues the complete version possesses. It wasn't until 2004, when Kino on Video released the Lobster Films restoration on DVD, that the two-reel version of *Near Dublin* was accessible to the general public.

Near Dublin is one of Laurel's weaker solo efforts, yet it's not without some intriguing, if misfired, ideas.

Smithy

Cast

Stan Laurel	Smithy
Ena Gregory	Secretary
James Finlayson	Sergeant
Jack Gavin	Foreman
William Gillespie	President of Woodhead Bros. Contractors
Glenn Tryon	The general manager (the other Smith)
Eddie Baker	Captain
George Rowe	Cross-eyed worker
Marvin Lobach	Fat worker
Fred Karno, Jr.	Worker
Sammy Brooks	Short man waiting in line

Credits

George Jeske	Director
L. E. Dill	Assistant director
Frank Young	Cinematographer
T. J. Crizer	Editor
H. M. Walker	Titles
Ham (Hamilton) Kinsey, Sherbourne Shields	Props

Also known as *The Home Wrecker*.
A Hal Roach production. Copyrighted January 20, 1924.
Production dates: October 11–20, 1923.
Released January 20, 1924, by Pathé Exchange.
Two reels.

One of the strongest Stan Laurel solo efforts from this period, *Smithy* is a nicely constructed comedy that allows Laurel to display the full range of his gifts for physical clowning. His execution of potentially hazardous stunts gives him an affinity with Buster Keaton, although no one would ever mistake Stan's overt mugging for Buster's stoicism.

Smithy, the laziest dough boy in the 372nd infantry, gets discharged from the Army. He secures a job at a construction site, where his ineptitude endangers his co-workers, particularly his former sergeant, who has also found employment there. While Mr. Smith, the general manager, is away, the new office boy mistakenly delivers a letter meant for Smith to Smithy, putting him in charge of all construction work. Smithy promptly fires his old sergeant and makes the foreman do some of the actual labor. The president of the company rushes to the site after discovering the error, but the structure has already been completed by Smithy and the crew. As the boss admires a job well done, one of the workers removes the final support beam and the entire building collapses like a house of cards. Smithy re-enlists in the Army, only to find the vengeful sergeant waiting for him.

For those unfamiliar with Laurel's solo comedies, *Smithy* is a good place to start. While Stan's brash character bears little resemblance to his sweet-natured persona in the Laurel and Hardy films, there are enough funny gags and inventive stunt work to satisfy the viewer. Though it runs less than five minutes in length, the opening Army sequence establishes Smithy as a slacker who fouls up a simple marching exercise when he becomes tangled up in his own belt — a portent to his ineptitude in other areas. ("Awkward squad" drills were a staple of military comedies and variations of this routine turned up in the Laurel and Hardy comedies *With Love and Hisses* [1927], *Pack Up Your Troubles* [1932], *The Flying Deuces* [1939] and *Great Guns* [1941].)

The construction-site setting provides ample opportunity for physical humor. Smithy's attempts to carry an awkward roll of tar paper to the site's roof, via a ladder, causes him to drop the object, become entangled in the ladder, and continually fail at his task, while the foreman fumes. Laurel, for perhaps the first time in his film career, milks this situation for its full potential. Laurel and Hardy were (and are) acclaimed for their ability to deftly milk a single comic situation and in *Smithy* we see Stan beginning to do this, rather than fire off a series of stand-alone gags. His repeated climbing up and down the ladder never seems protracted because he comes up with a variety of gags based on this single idea.

As he did in other films, Stan performs his own stunts, but here they seem even more impressive because they're frequently done at considerable heights. Scampering across a slanted rooftop, he drops debris on his co-workers and gets tar-soaked wooden shingles stuck to his hands, feet and backside. Vigorous attempts to remove this sticky material nearly cause him to slide off the roof. These breathtaking moments anticipate scenes of Stan and Ollie perched on skyscraper girders in *Liberty* (1929) and the boys trying to put up a radio aerial in *Hog Wild* (1930).

Laurel had used the construction premise in *The Noon Whistle* (1923), in which he and James Finlayson had the same combative relationship they do in *Smithy*. When Smithy discovers that one of the workers is his old sergeant, he greets him merrily but gets an angry response. Of course, Smithy had just sawed a wooden plank without realizing the sarge was standing on the other end, causing him to plummet to the ground. Stan would inflict just as much injury to Oliver Hardy in their construction-themed comedies *The Finishing Touch* (1928) and *Busy Bodies* (1933).

Smithy recalls Buster Keaton's brilliant *One Week* (1920), which chronicles Buster's attempts to build a house from scratch. Laurel's hyperactive, happy-go-lucky character is nothing like Keaton's Great Stoneface persona (in *Smithy*, Stan still can't resist playing directly to the camera), but there are similarities in each comedian's concentration on gag situations and pacing the humor in a more deliberate manner, without the hurried, helter-skelter quality of much '20s-era slapstick. As a filmmaker, Laurel had not matured as quickly as Keaton had, but his growth was discernible and he was continuing to learn creative lessons that would prove invaluable to his later career.

Smithy garnered enthusiastic reviews. The *Motion Picture News* stated that the construction scenes "should arouse the most lethargic to hearty laughter." The *Exhibitors Trade Review* called it "one of [Laurel's] funniest performances.... The military camp scenes are novel [and] the building process in which everything falls off the roof is hilarious entertainment."

In the 1960s, Blackhawk Films released an abridged version of *Smithy* to the home-movie market. Running a little over one full reel and missing the opening and closing Army sequences, this edition subsequently turned up on various "Comedy Classics"-type video collections before Kino International and Lobster Films made the complete two-reeler available on DVD. Yet even in its truncated form, *Smithy* is a fine example of Stan Laurel's comedic talent and blossoming cinematic skills.

Zeb vs. Paprika

Cast

Stan Laurel . . . . "Dippy" Donawho (Paprika's jockey)
James Finlayson . . . . Major Glanders Botts
George Rowe . . . . "Cockeye" Hawkins (Zeb's jockey)
William Gillespie . . . . Archibald Sinclair
Ena Gregory . . . . Mrs. Sinclair
Sammy Brooks . . . . Trainer
Eddie Baker . . . . Stable hand/trainer
Dick Gilbert . . . . Stable hand/trainer
Jack Ackroyd . . . . Jockey club member
Billy Engle . . . . Jockey club member
Helen Gilmore . . . . Racetrack spectator
Mildred Booth . . . . Racetrack spectator

With

Charles Hall (unconfirmed), Fred Karno, Jr., L. Loback, Jack O'Brien, Earl Mohan, Al Forbes, Charlie Lloyd, Al Ochs, Noah Young (unconfirmed), Harry Rattenberry.

Credits

Ralph Ceder . . . . Director
Harry La Mar . . . . Assistant director
Frank Young . . . . Cinematographer
T. J. Crizer . . . . Editor
A. H. (Al) Giebler . . . . Titles
Ham (Hamilton) Kinsey, Sherbourne Shields . . . . Props

A Hal Roach production. Copyrighted January 26, 1924.
Production dates: October 23–November 6, 1923.
Released March 16, 1924, by Pathé Exchange.
Two reels.

The first world championship of horse racing was held at Belmont Park (Long Island, New York) on October 20, 1923. "The International," as it was called, showcased a match race between Kentucky Derby winner Zev and Epsom Derby (England's most prestigious race) winner Papyrus. A record crowd of 50,000-plus spectators turned out for the highly publicized event, looking on as Zev easily defeated Papyrus to win the $100,000 purse.

British Pathé Exchange Inc. purchased the exclusive film rights to the International for a reported $50,000. Pathé utilized 30 cameras to document the race and the track events leading up to it. Although observers felt that the race didn't live up to all the hype, those who were unable to attend still had an interest in seeing it. Pathé was able to deliver an edited version of their two-reel film on the evening of October 21 (a little over 24 hours after the event) for a premiere screening at the Lumberg Theater in Niagara Falls, New York. With the Zev-Papyrus contest still in the headlines, *Zeb vs. Paprika* began production on October 23.

Watching *Zeb vs. Paprika* today, viewers are unlikely to be familiar with the historic race, which begs the question whether one's enjoyment of this parody is dependent upon knowledge of the actual event. The answer is no. References to specific participants are made (as evidenced by the film's title), yet *Zeb vs. Paprika* remains a spirited, consistently amusing racetrack-themed comedy, even for those who might not catch the in-jokes.

Major Glanders Botts, owner of the European (read: British) thoroughbred Paprika, challenges Archibald Sinclair,* owner of the American race horse Zeb, to a match for the international championship at the Uphilldown Track in the United States. Paprika's jockey is "Dippy" Donawho† ("one of the best jockeys that ever slipped headache powder to a rival horse"), and Botts puts him through a strict exercise regimen to ensure victory. At the start of the race, the horses break free from their harnesses, forcing Dippy and rival jockey "Cockeye" Hawkins to pursue them on foot. Catching up with the horses, both jockeys ride furiously to the finish line and Dippy crosses first. But the jubilation is short-lived, as Mrs. Sinclair points out that Dippy has mounted Zeb, not Paprika. Dippy, Botts, and Paprika head back to Europe in defeat.

Harry F. Sinclair, the founder of Sinclair Oil, was the owner of Zev. Sinclair was a central figure in the Teapot Dome scandal.
 †*In the Zev-Papyrus race, Steve Donoghue was the jockey for Papyrus.*

In *Zeb vs. Paprika*, Stan foregoes the manic, exaggerated expressions and the smug giddiness often found in his other solo comedies. He instead uses wide-eyed wonder, blank-faced puzzlement, and deadpan cunning as effective counterpoints to the mayhem swirling around him. This comparative subtlety is indicated by his introduction: Dippy enters the Maison Pierre ("in plain English, Pete's Place") Jockey Club attired in a oversized, brightly striped tweed cap, riding breeches and boots, and puffing on a pipe-shaped cigarette holder. Stan does not overplay his hand in calling attention to these comic affectations, as he carries himself with the aplomb of an aristocrat, giving his character the "half-assed dignity" (as Laurel described it) he and Oliver Hardy projected in their later films. His entrance is all the more humorous because, right off the bat, Stan's height (five feet nine inches) makes him an unconvincing jockey.

To whip Dippy into fighting shape, Botts orders a group of trainers and stable hands to "rub him down to ninety-five pounds." The gang pounces on poor Dippy, creating a human dog pile. Dippy crawls out from under the mass of flailing arms and legs (no one notices that he's gone so the pummeling continues without him) and gets on a scale. Because his weight is still 181 pounds, he throws himself back into the fray. Crawling out again, he gets back on the scale and discovers he's *gained* 18 pounds! He dives into the brawl once more, only this time Botts has been mistaken for Dippy, so Botts gets mauled instead. As a result, it's Botts, not Dippy, who gets *rubbed down* to the goal weight.

Not every gag hits the mark. When Botts instructs a burly trainer to take Dippy and "work off his surplus fat," the trainer grabs Dippy by the neck and hauls him into the dressing room, closing the door behind them. Within seconds, the door reopens and Dippy emerges, dressed in exercise togs, dragging the now-unconscious trainer by the neck. Exactly how Dippy speedily dispatched a larger opponent goes unexplained, and while Laurel was able to produce laughs by leaving certain details to the viewer's imagination, here the payoff is too abrupt to succeed.

Compare the execution of this gag to a better-crafted set piece in the Laurel and Hardy two-reeler *Unaccustomed As Were Are* (1929), in which a vengeful Edgar Kennedy beckons Stan to step into the apartment hallway. Kennedy has already beaten up Ollie, who expects his pal to receive a similar thrashing. But when Stan returns unharmed, Ollie is astonished. What Ollie doesn't know (but the viewer does) is that Mrs. Kennedy (played by Thelma Todd) clobbered Edgar before he had the opportunity to lay a finger on Stan. As Stan bids goodbye, an incredulous Ollie discovers an unconscious Kennedy lying in the hallway. This sequence is wonderfully funny because of the way it toys with the viewer's — and Ollie's — expectations. Because we know what actually transpired, Ollie's surprised reaction provides a perfect capper. On the other hand, the gag in *Zeb vs. Paprika* is based solely on the element of surprise and, by contrast, it doesn't have the same impact. As in virtually all the Laurel and Hardy comedies Stan personally supervised, the gags in *Unaccustomed As We Are* spring from character interaction and plot development. (The team's first "all-talking" film, *Unaccustomed* also benefits from the shrewd use of sound effects to evoke offscreen calamity.) The difference in how these two separate sequences are conceived and executed keenly illustrates Laurel's growth as a writer, comedian and filmmaker.

A lively workout routine gives Stan ample opportunity to display his physical agility. Dippy sprints around the gym (nimbly skipping like a kindergartener on a playground lot) then dashes out of the building, followed closely by Botts and his crew. No matter how hard Dippy tries to elude his tenacious pursuers — hiding around corners, running in reverse — he is unable to shake them. Finally, Botts ties a rope around Dippy's neck and forces Dippy to run in circles, as though he's a wild stallion that needs to be broken.

Hungry jockey "Dippy" Donawho dons a disguise so he can grab a bite to eat in *Zeb vs. Paprika* (1924).

In the mess hall, Dippy is denied his meal ("No eats till after the race!," Botts warns him), so the hungry jockey masquerades as the cook and winds up devouring an entire chicken dinner. When he sees Dippy's bloated stomach, Botts utters an easily lip-read "Oh shit!" that makes the immediate intertitle ("He's got a *swell* chance to win the race!") funnier than intended.

Just before the start of the race, Dippy attempts to enter the track grounds but a pair of ticket-takers won't let him past the front gate, despite his protests that he's a jockey. At the admission window, Dippy accidentally purchases four tickets. Unable to get a refund, he strides up to the gate and confronts the ticket-takers who refused him admittance. He hands one of them a single ticket, enters, snaps his fingers, then exits and shuffles over to the adjacent gate, where he pulls the same routine, then returns to the first gate to repeat the ritual. But Dippy pays for his petulance: in haste, he hands over his last ticket and then cockily exits, only to realize he's shut out once again. (An infuriated Botts comes along and drags him inside.)

The climactic horse race, filmed at a real racetrack, is fast-paced and exciting. The byplay between Dippy and rival jockey Hawkins is amusing. Dippy taunts Hawkins, who reaches over to strangle him in mid-race, as Botts nervously cheers from the stands. The authenticity of the setting enhances the humor, and in an impressive bit, Laurel's stunt double slides off the back of his horse, grabs its tail, and is dragged across the turf. Cinematographer Frank Young nicely shot the entire sequence, T. J. Crizer crisply edits, and director Ralph Ceder, who would later become one of the finest second-unit directors in Hollywood, stages the action well.*

Audiences of the era knew which horse won the actual race, and so here their expectations are upended when Paprika is triumphant, only to deliver a final twist when it's discovered that Dippy was on the wrong steed.

The film concludes with an absurd image that most likely sprang from the fertile mind of Stan Laurel. Out on the ocean, Dippy and Botts are in an undersized rowboat (Dippy is rowing, Botts holds him at gunpoint) heading back to Europe, towing Paprika behind them on a raft.

Zeb vs. Paprika went into release five months after the Zev-Papyrus race, though it didn't damper the enthusiasm of moviegoers and reviewers. *Moving Picture World* noted, "Stan Laurel has crowded a lot of good stuff, quite a bit of which is original, in this burlesque.... This comedy reaches the happy

---

*Comedy fans will fondly recall Ceder's expertise as a second-unit stunt director. His credits include the chariot chase in Eddie Cantor's Roman Scandals *(1933), the torpedo chase and flying sequences in Abbott and Costello's* Keep 'Em Flying *(1941), and the automobile chases that climax two W. C. Fields pictures,* The Bank Dick *(1940) and* Never Give a Sucker an Even Break *(1941).*

medium which qualifies it for any audience — either uptown or downtown, or in the town hall." *Motion Picture News* stated, "There is plenty of action in this one.... This one should be good for a great many hearty laughs."

Stan's performance in *Zeb vs. Paprika* has more in common with his persona in the initial Laurel and Hardy films than it does to the hyperactive gesturing associated with a number of his solo efforts. Though he's a bundle of energy throughout, his restrained facial expressions convey a childlike inability to grasp the situation. This strengthens his interaction with James Finlayson, who reacts with Hardyesque frustration at Stan's transgressions. While this Stan Laurel is far from the Stanley we will come to know and love, *Zeb vs. Paprika* reveals that facets of his later persona are already in place and just need to be refined.

Postage Due

Cast

Stan Laurel . . . . Willy Worst
James Finlayson . . . . Postal Inspector Hawke
George Rowe . . . . Photographer/Postal customer
Ena Gregory . . . . Woman at photographer's studio
Eddie Baker . . . . Crook
Dick Gilbert . . . . Crook
William Gillespie . . . . C. W. Lyons (Chief Postal Inspector)
Martin Wolfkeil . . . . Postal worker
Jack Ackroyd . . . . Sleeping man in post office

With
Fred Karno, Jr., Sammy Brooks, Jack O'Brien,
Billy Engle, Al Forbes, Charles Hall, C. Lloyd,
Al Ochs, Helen Gilmore, Mildred Booth.

Credits

George Jeske . . . . Director
L. E. Dill . . . . Assistant director
Frank Young . . . . Cinematographer
T. J. Crizer . . . . Editor
Hal Conklin . . . . Titles
Ham (Hamilton) Kinsey, Sherbourne Shields . . . . Props
A Hal Roach production. Copyrighted January 26, 1924.
Production dates: November 5–14, 1923.
Released February 17, 1924, by Pathé Exchange.
One reel.

When assessing movies from a perspective decades removed, there is a tendency, unconscious as it may be, to pass judgment on certain films based on their production history or factors other than the finished product. By doing so, the discussion becomes more about what the movie isn't rather than what it actually is. The perception that *Postage Due* was a rushed production (shooting began the same day *Zeb vs. Paprika* was completed) diminishes its worth in the eyes of some historians. While it may not be the most sterling example of Stan Laurel's solo work — there's nothing in it that's remotely character driven — it is superior to a number of his other efforts and contains enough Laurel touches to indicate Stan had more on his mind than simply meeting the production deadline.

Willy Worst wants to send a picture of himself to his sweetie; after an unproductive stop at an automatic photo booth, he drops by a photographer's studio to have a postal (photo postcard) taken. Willy strikes a pose as Venus — in a tutu (!) — just as Hawke, an overzealous postal inspector, passes by the studio and spies shots of scantily clad men and women on display. Hawke storms in and warns the photographer, "These risqué pictures can't go through

Glass slide advertisement for *Postage Due* (1924).

the mail. They slow up the postman." Despite Hawke's intense scrutiny, Willy manages to get his postal made and heads to the post office, where the eagle-eyed Hawke is now examining shipments to ensure against violations. As Hawke browbeats a customer — "There's no stamp on this letter.... You could get twenty years for that" — Willy realizes he dropped his postal into the mail slot without affixing a stamp. Panic-stricken, Willy jumps over the service counter to retrieve his postal, with the suspicious Hawke in hot pursuit. During the ensuing chase through the processing area, they slide down chutes and conveyor belts and leap into oversized sorting bins. While hiding in a mail sack, Willy encounters two crooks (who were also hiding in sacks) breaking into the post office safe. Although Willy tries to foil the robbery, he's apprehended as a member of the gang. As he's carted away, Willy exclaims, "If you find my postal, send it in care of the warden."

Stan's introductory sequence in *Postage Due* offers a nice contrast to the frantic antics that follow. Sitting in a photo booth, preparing to have his picture taken, Laurel meticulously grooms himself and tries to strike the most photogenic pose possible. But after he inserts a coin, the glare of the bright light startles him, ruining his composure as his eyes pop and his mouth falls open. (It's not difficult to imagine Laurel's later Stanley character performing this same routine, though more deliberately paced and minus the overplayed gestures Stan indulges in here.)

The session at the photographer's studio (note the portrait of Hal Roach on the wall) is more silly than funny, with a heavy reliance on Stan cavorting around in a ballerina costume — foreshadowing, somewhat, his later full-fledged female impersonations in later Laurel and Hardy films. But the sequence does serve to set up the adversarial relationship between Stan and postal detective James Finlayson.

In an amusing scene at the post office, Stan attempts to inscribe his postal but can't find a pen that works properly and keeps grabbing replacement pens from under the nose of an increasingly baffled customer (George Rowe, who also played the photographer; this is a separate character).

Once the chase commences, *Postage Due* really kicks into high gear, as Stan desperately searches for his postage-less postal while trying to elude Finlayson. Both comedians display considerable physical dexterity, with Stan's nimble agility being particularly impressive. (The hectic, off-the-cuff spirit is similar to the wild amusement-park chase in *Sugar Daddies* [1927], which also starred Laurel and Finlayson and tossed Oliver Hardy into the mix for good measure.) *Postage Due*'s finale could hardly be called inspired but it's undeniably lively and chuckle provoking. On that level, it achieves its modest artistic goal.

Reviews for *Postage Due* were favorable. *Moving Picture World* noted, "There is action in the film from start to finish, and it should prove a good comedy for the average audience." *Kinematograph Weekly* declared, "The fertile gagsters and first rate comedians in Stan Laurel, James Finlayson and George Rowe keep the pace brisk and the incidents bright."

It's easy to undervalue a film like *Postage Due*, especially within the context of Stan Laurel's screen career. Yet it remains an enjoyable (if unremarkable) diversion, and that's no small accomplishment considering how many other comedies fail to meet that requirement.

Brothers Under the Chin

Cast

Stan Laurel, Ena Gregory, James Finlayson, Noah Young, Wiliam Gillespie, Sammy Brooks, Jack Ackroyd, George Rowe, Fred Karno, Jr., Jack O'Brien, Al Ochs, Eddie Baker, Martin Wolfkeil.

Credits

Ralph Ceder .... Director
Harry La Mar .... Assistant director
Frank Young .... Cinematographer
A. H. Giebler, Hal Conklin .... Writers
T. J. Crizer .... Editor
H. M. Walker .... Titles
Ham (Hamilton) Kinsey, Sherbourne Shields .... Props
A Hal Roach production. Copyrighted April 18, 1924.
Production dates: November 15–December 3, 1923 (at Balboa, California).
Released April 13, 1924, by Pathé Exchange.
Two reels.

Another of the handful of Stan Laurel solo films for which no print is known to exist (at the time of this writing), *Brothers Under the Chin* featured Laurel and Finlayson as orphaned twins who are adopted by different families. Some 20 years later, Stan is shanghaied and ends up on a ship run by Fin, a ruthless captain. Stan is treated poorly until Fin notices a birthmark under Stan's chin that matches his own, and realizes he has found his long-lost brother.

While the plotline appears to be another excuse for a parade of working-class gags, Rob Stone observes that a scene in which the entire crew becomes seasick was a bit ahead of its time, although for the wrong reasons. *Motion Picture News* duly noted that "the prolonged and wholesale vomiting is not comedy but rather sickening to the average audience." Other reviews shared this opinion. This kind of outrageous passage has become commonplace in modern movies, but it is quite interesting that bodily-function humor at this level could find its portent in a comedy from the silent era. Laurel liked surrealism and sometimes enjoyed pushing the envelope, but more boorish behavior never appealed to him. While the scene does not sound particularly clever or funny, the fact that bodily-function gags are now a staple of family-oriented entertainment is an indication of how far we have — or haven't — come. (Progress is not always artistically beneficial.)

Reviewers did enjoy the opening scenes set at an orphanage, in which Laurel and Finlayson play infants. Oversized furniture and props (including the bassinet left over from *Mother's Joy*) made the comedians look diminutive, a comic idea that would be brought to hilarious fruition in the Laurel and Hardy two-reeler *Brats* (1930).

Wide Open Spaces

Cast

Stan Laurel . . . . Gabriel Goober
Ena Gregory . . . . Girl
James Finlayson . . . . Jack McQueen

With

George Rowe, Noah Young, Sammy Brooks, Jack Ackroyd, Martin Wolfkeil, Vera White, Patsy O'Byrne, William Gillespie, Fred Karno, Jr., Jack O'Brien, Al Ochs, Eddie Baker, Chet Brandenburg, Harry Bayfield, Dick Gilbert, Harry Rattenberry

Also in the original *Wild Bill Hiccough* version:

Billy Engle . . . . Phil Sheridan
Charles Dudley . . . . A. Lincoln
Al Forbes . . . . General Custer
Mae Laurel . . . . Calamity Jane

Credits

George Jeske . . . . Director
L. E. Dill . . . . Assistant director
Frank Young . . . . Cinematographer
A. H. Giebler, Hal Conklin . . . . Writers
T. J. Crizer . . . . Editor
H. M. Walker . . . . Titles
Ham (Hamilton) Kinsey, Sherbourne Shields . . . . Props

Filmed and previewed under the title *Wild Bill Hiccough*.
A Hal Roach production. Copyrighted June 30, 1924.
Production dates: December 5–15, 1923
Released July 16, 1924, by Pathé Exchange.
Two reels.

Western films are central to the development of cinema, the most famous early example being Edwin S. Porter's seminal *The Great Train Robbery* (1903). Within a decade, the genre had produced enough clichés to make them ripe for parody. Roscoe "Fatty" Arbuckle's *Moonshine* (1918) is a particularly good example of spoofing Western conventions, highlighted by visuals devised by Arbuckle's apprentice, Buster Keaton.

Stan Laurel targeted *Wild Bill Hickok* (1923; directed by Clifford Smith), a feature-length Western starring William S. Hart, and satirized it as *Wild Bill Hiccough*. Laurel's parody was completed and previewed under this title, but when the film was submitted for release, it was rejected by the Pathé Exchange for scenes the distributor found objectionable. (There is no documentation as to the exact content of these scenes, although there are indications that the original cut contained offbeat and edgy humor.) Revisions were required, but by this time Stan had left the Roach Studios and was already making comedies for producer Joe Rock. With Laurel unavailable to appear in retakes or supervise the restructuring of the film, title writer H. M. Walker was left with no other option than to remove the objectionable scenes and piece together the remaining footage the best he could, reinstating previously discarded shots in an attempt to fill in the gaps. This overhauling forced Walker to rewrite the intertitles and alter the plotline in order to preserve some sense of continuity. The resulting two-reeler no longer came off as a specific burlesque of *Wild Bill Hickok*, so the name of Stan's character was changed to Gabriel Goober and the film was rechristened *Wide Open Spaces*. In later interviews, H. M. Walker remarked that he was unhappy about having to completely re-edit *Wild Bill Hiccough* since he felt it was far superior to the mangled edition that was finally released.

In *Wide Open Spaces*, Easterner Gabriel Goober journeys to the wild and woolly West, and discovers squatters have seized his property. The sheriff makes Goober his deputy, and the tenderfoot goes about reclaiming his land from the band of robbers. There are no existing prints of *Wild Bill Hiccough*, and only half a reel of *Wide Open Spaces* survives, so no detailed comparisons or evaluations can be made. Based on the disconnected sequences that do exist, *Wide Open Spaces* appears to have been a very funny Western satire with imaginative visual gags. Goober serenades his beloved horse with a large bass violin and uses a chair instead of a saddle as a mount. He exhibits the stoicism of William S. Hart, carrying himself about in a majestic fashion, with his hand inside his jacket and resting on his heart. During a shootout with several bandits, Stan calmly fires his six-shooters while the victims react with comically overplayed death scenes.

Reviewers were divided on the merits of the film. *Motion Picture News* noted, "It is laughable and a rather broadly drawn satire that will surely entertain the majority of audiences.... Very Good." The *Moving Picture World* was less enthused: "The comedy has its high spots ... but, taken all in all, it seems to have somewhat less fun than most of those preceding it in which Stan Laurel has appeared ... the scenario writer did not give him many ideas to work with."

Without the opportunity to view *Wide Open Spaces* in its entirety, we are unable to support or challenge either opinion. However, the few minutes that do survive indicates that it was one of Laurel's better solo comedies.

Rupert of Hee Haw

Cast

Stan Laurel	The King/Rudolph Razz
James Finlayson	Rupert of Hee Haw
Mae Laurel	Princess Minnie
George Rowe	The Duke of Bromo
Pierre Couderc	The Duke of Aspirin
Billy Engle	Short officer
Martin Wolfkeil	Rotund officer
Ena Gregory	Rupert's maid
Mickey Daniels	Boy who kicks Rudolph
Mary Kornman	Girl cheering for Rudolph
Ernest "Sunshine Sammy" Morrison	Boy cheering for Rudolph
Joe Cobb	Boy cheering for Rudolph
Jackie Condon	Boy cheering for Rudolph
Sammy Brooks	Little palace guard
Eddie Baker	Uniformed officer
Charles Lloyd	Soldier
Jack Gavin	Servant
Irene Lentz	Lady T. Pott Dome
Pal	Mad dog

With
Jack Ackroyd, Al Forbes, Al Ochs, Gary Horton,
Alita Cruze, Dick Gilbert, Harry Bayfield.
(Contrary to previous filmographies, Johnny Downs
does not appear in this movie.)

Credits

Percy Pembroke	Director
Lloyd French	Assistant director
Freeman Rollins	Second assistant director
Clarence Hennecke, Leo McCarey	Assistant direction (uncredited)
Frank Young	Cinematographer
T. J. Crizer	Editor
H. M. Walker	Titles
Ham (Hamilton) Kinsey, Sherbourne Shields	Props
"Count Innerarityski"	Authority on court etiquette

Alternate titles: *Coleslaw* and *Rupert of Cole Slaw*.

A Hal Roach production. Copyrighted May 12, 1924.
Production dates: December 20–26, 1923 and January 2–12, 1924.
Released June 24, 1924, by Pathé Exchange.
Two reels.

A takeoff on the Ruritanian romance-adventure tale *Rupert of Hentzau*, *Rupert of Hee Haw* (facetiously referenced in the credits as "A Sequel to *The Prisoner of Zebra*") is the weakest of Laurel's movie burlesques. While a handful of clever gags are overwhelmed by far too many repetitious pratfalls, the main problem is that the original story has been rendered incomprehensible. Without the sturdy foundation of a coherent plot, the satire comes off as disjointed and pointless.

Princess Minnie is not happy about being engaged to the king, who spends his waking hours staggering around the palace in a drunken stupor. The princess sends for Rudolph Razz, a paramour who bears a striking resemblance to the king. An incriminating letter from the princess to Rudolph has been intercepted by the Duke of Aspirin, so Rudolph passes himself off as the king and

James Finlayson's ire is raised as Mae Laurel flirts with Stan Laurel (right) in *Rupert of Hee Haw* (1924).

tries to retrieve the stolen note. The search leads to Rupert of Hee Haw's mountain hideaway, where Rudolph and Rupert engage in a swordfight. With assistance from a mad dog, Rudolph subdues Rupert and retrieves the letter. To his shock, the message reads: "I never want to see you again!" A dejected Rudolph looks on as the princess runs off with the less-than-dashing Duke of Bromo.

Stan plays a dual role and neither part fully exploits his range, though as the drunken king, he executes some impressive physical stunts, such as falling backwards over a banister and landing on a staircase. Performed in a single take, it's funny and cringe-inducing at the same time. These early scenes contain a couple of imaginative visuals. When we're introduced to the king, he's already inebriated. As he gingerly attempts to make his way to the door, the entire wall closes in and smacks him in the face, knocking him to the floor. (This simple yet clever effect was accomplished by having the freestanding wall pushed from behind.) Later, the king is offended by the sound of a cuckoo clock and fires a rifle at the mechanical bird within, resulting in a flurry of feathers flying out of the clock.

Stan is lively as Rudolph Razz, performing a jaunty dance step when he gets excited, yet it doesn't obscure the fact that he's not playing a character — he's merely an energetic gag machine. This approach can have its merits, especially in a superficial parody such as this, but as the gags get increasingly lame, the antics grow tiresome.

What really sinks *Rupert of Hee Haw* is its needlessly confusing plotline. The king, whom we're led to believe will be one of the major characters in the story, just wanders off. Later we're informed he died but the exact cause or circumstances are never made clear. Supporting characters are not properly introduced or defined, so their identities and motives remain a mystery. (Who is the Duke of Aspirin and why is he blackmailing the princess, aside from requisite villainy?) Out of the blue, a fleeting reference to Rupert is made ("Rupert of Hee Haw knows all — He's a seventh son!"), yet when he finally turns up, we still don't have a clue as to who he is or why he should suddenly be in possession of the princess's letter.

Without defined characters or a coherent storyline, the gags are piled on without rhyme or reason. When four people slip on the same banana peel (and two more trip over one of the victims), it's a sly exaggeration of a joke that was as old as the hills even then. Regardless, it comes off as uninspired and a bit desperate, especially when a rotund officer's tumble results in an earthquake-like tremor.

For someone who is essaying the title role, James Finlayson is afforded little screen time, turning up only near the end of the film to engage in swordplay with Stan. (Ena Gregory also has a surprisingly minor role as Rupert's

(Left to right) Unidentified player, Mae Laurel, Billy Engle, Stan Laurel and George Rowe in the disjointed burlesque *Rupert of Hee Haw* (1924).

maid.) As usual, Laurel and Finlayson work well together and there are some nice comic touches during their duel — Rupert grabs the sword with the longer sheath, only to discover it has a much shorter blade; Rudolph stops mid-fight to sample a box of chocolates, politely sharing the contents with Rupert and his maid — but this all comes too late to salvage the film.

It may seem unreasonable to criticize *Rupert of Hee Haw* from a perspective several decades removed. After all, this was a satire of a then-current property and its target audience was no doubt familiar with the original plot and characters that are now being called into question. To make aesthetic demands on a humble little picture that was made primarily to fulfill a distributor's contract and was never intended to be viewed years (let alone *decades*) after its initial release may strike some as the height of absurdity.

Nevertheless, it should be noted that many older movies *do* withstand this sort of scrutiny. In the case of the Stan Laurel burlesques, efforts such as *Dr. Pyckle and Mr. Pryde*, *Roughest Africa*, and *The Soilers* remain hilariously inventive examples of the form, even if one is unfamiliar with the subjects being lampooned. Therefore, *Rupert of Hee Haw* can be held to the standards of the other Laurel satires and, accordingly, be considered a misfire.

Short Kilts

Cast

Stan Laurel	McPherson's son
James Finlayson	McGregor's son
Mickey Daniels	McPherson kid
Ena Gregory	McGregor's daughter
George Rowe	Blacksmith/Member of McHungry clan
Mary Kornman	McGregor kid
Leo Willis	McGregor
Jack Gavin	McPherson
Martin Wolfkeil	McHungry's son
Sammy Brooks	McHungry
Helen Gilmore	Mrs. McHungry

With
Patsy O'Byrne, Joy Winthrop, Ouida Wildman,
Charlie Lloyd, Al Ochs, Al Forbes

Credits

George Jeske	Director
Leo McCarey	Assistant director
Freeman Rollins	Second assistant director
Frank Young	Cinematographer
T. J. Crizer	Editor
H. M. Walker	Titles
Charley Oelze	Props

A Hal Roach production. Copyrighted August 2, 1924.
Production dates: January 16–24, 1924.
Released August 11, 1924, by Pathé Exchange.
Two reels.

With a premise centering around two feuding families, *Short Kilts* is simply a hillbilly tale transplanted to Scotland, and the change in setting allows for plenty of jokes about stereotypical Scottish frugality and combative temperament. There's no shortage of comic ideas, which underscores the fundamental problem: the film is content to trot out one idea after another, yet few are developed beyond the basic concept. So if the idea of a group of kilt-wearing men playing musical chairs is amusing to you, then you may derive a fair amount of enjoyment from these antics. However, for those who expect a little more from the talented folks involved, *Short Kilts* is a mild farce at best. It may be better than its poor reputation would indicate, but the thin material is unworthy of Stan and his enthusiastic co-stars.

The McPhersons host a party attended by the McGregors and the McHungrys. McPherson's son loves McGregor's daughter, and McGregor's son is smitten with McPherson's daughter. A dispute over a game of musical chairs devolves into a violent squabble, and the patriarchs declare there will never be marriages between the clans. Undaunted, McPherson's son whisks the McGregor girl off to the justice of the peace and ties the knot. The McGregor lad does the same with his betrothed, and both families reconcile their differences. At the double-wedding celebration, they resume the game of musical chairs and another brawl erupts.

Filmed at the Hal Roach Studios and the original Samuel Goldwyn lot (which had formerly been the Triangle Studios and would later become Metro-Goldwyn-Mayer), *Short Kilts* is always on the verge of being funnier than it actually is. In an early scene, young McGregor (James Finlayson) comes home and notices his family is about to have supper. "Stop!" he urges, "Don't eat — We're invited out!" So the McGregors head straight over to the McPhersons, where, to their dismay, they're asked to sit off to the side and wait until the McPhersons finish their meal. As the McPhersons stuff their stomachs, old man McGregor glowers at his mortified — and starving — son. Later, when invited to another gathering at the McPhersons, the McGregors decide to eat first, a strategy that backfires spectacularly since the McPhersons wind up serving a sumptuous feast. With their bellies already filled with porridge, the McGregors can't bring themselves to touch any of the food, though young McGregor makes a gallant attempt and places a single bean on his plate.

These ideas sound amusing, and they *are* amusing, yet just as the viewer starts to anticipate a bigger payoff, the scene shifts to another setup. This occurs repeatedly over the course of two reels and what we're left with is a tame comedy that doesn't know how to exploit its best ideas.

Nevertheless, a tame payoff is better than no payoff at all, which is one of the problems with the elopement sequence. Stan and Ena head to a blacksmith who doubles as the justice of the peace (who is also a member of the McHungry clan), with Jimmy and his betrothed (the actress playing this role is uncredited) serving as their witnesses. Yet when Jimmy asks Stan to return the favor, Stan adamantly refuses, leaving Jimmy in tears. This odd, humorless resolution reveals a cruel streak in Stan's character that is completely unnecessary. As it is, Stan hardly has a character to begin with (he's a garden-variety simpleton, without a tangible personality or point of view), and his ungrateful gesture, played straight, sways the audience sympathy to Finlayson. Later, Finlayson shows up with his new bride, with no explanation offered as to how the couple got hitched without the required witnesses. So there's no payoff *and* no logic to any of this.

One of the film's merits is that Laurel generously shares the spotlight with the supporting cast. Whether unintentional or not, James Finlayson comes across as more likable than Stan because he's less aggressive and more put-upon. Despite Laurel's above-the-title billing, both share the comic chores equally, though Finlayson seems to have a better grasp of the character — or caricature — he's playing. (Finlayson, a Scotsman, has a grand time lampooning Scottish stereotypes.) Leo Willis and Jack Gavin are fittingly robust as the heads of their respective households — even if Willis was actually three years younger than his "son." Nine-year-old Mickey Daniels and eight-year-old Mary Kornman enliven the proceedings as a pair of mischievous kids. Both were already comedy-short veterans, having starred in Hal Roach's Our Gang series since 1922.

Moving Picture World found the film passably amusing, with reservations: "The original idea, that of satirizing a Scotchman's reported frugality, was an excellent one, but it has not worked out, it seems, as vividly as possible. The subject, nevertheless, has much to commend it and will be liked by audiences indulgent toward routine slapstick stuff." *Motion Picture News* offered an audience-specific recommendation: "This one will please those who like their entertainment rough and of the home spun order."

After completing *Short Kilts*, Stan left Hal Roach — more precisely, Stan was let go. Only 12 of the 13 Stan Laurel comedies announced for the season were made and he still had four years left on his contract. Yet Roach dismissed him, allegedly due to Stan's personal problems — namely Mae Laurel. Her interference disrupted the productions (she continually demanded to be cast as his leading lady) and her volatile private conduct had an adverse affect on Stan's professional reliability. Concerned that this bad situation would become even worse, Roach dropped Stan from the roster.

Within a month, Stan found himself making comedies for independent producer Joe Rock.

7

STAN LAUREL AND JOE ROCK

Shortly after leaving the Hal Roach Studios for the second time, Laurel signed a deal with independent producer Joe Rock (1893–1984). Rock started in the movie business as a stuntman and bit player at the Vitagraph studio in New York. Vitagraph paired him with Earl Montgomery for a series of short comedies before the studio split them up for solo films. In the early 1920s, Rock formed his own independent production company and eventually gave up his career as a performer. Rock was producing short comedies starring Jimmy Aubrey when he and Laurel were introduced by a mutual friend, director Percy "Perc" Pembroke.

By now Laurel had a poor reputation in the industry due to his relationship with Mae Laurel. The havoc she was creating in his personal life bled into his professional career, and no producer or studio wanted to deal with an unreliable Stan or a volatile Mae. So Rock signed Stan with the stipulation that Mae not be involved with the films. Rock could not get the New York-based Selznick Distributing Corporation to agree to a Stan Laurel series, but Rock decided to go ahead and produce the Laurel films anyway. Laurel had just picked up $400 as a final payment from Roach, and was advanced another $1,000 from Rock to live on while the first few films in this new series were made. It was not until the third entry, *Monsieur Don't Care*, that the distributors were convinced that the series would be worthwhile.

In addition to not appearing in the films, Mae Laurel was also banned from the set during production. Mae's resentment festered and the situation came to a head when the crew went to Lake Arrowhead to shoot location scenes for *The Snow Hawk* (1925). Mae demanded to come along on the trip, and Rock relented as long as she steered clear of the actual filming. Sometime after their arrival, Mae lied to Stan, telling him that Rock had made sexual advances to her. In truth, Rock had spent that day with his visiting wife,

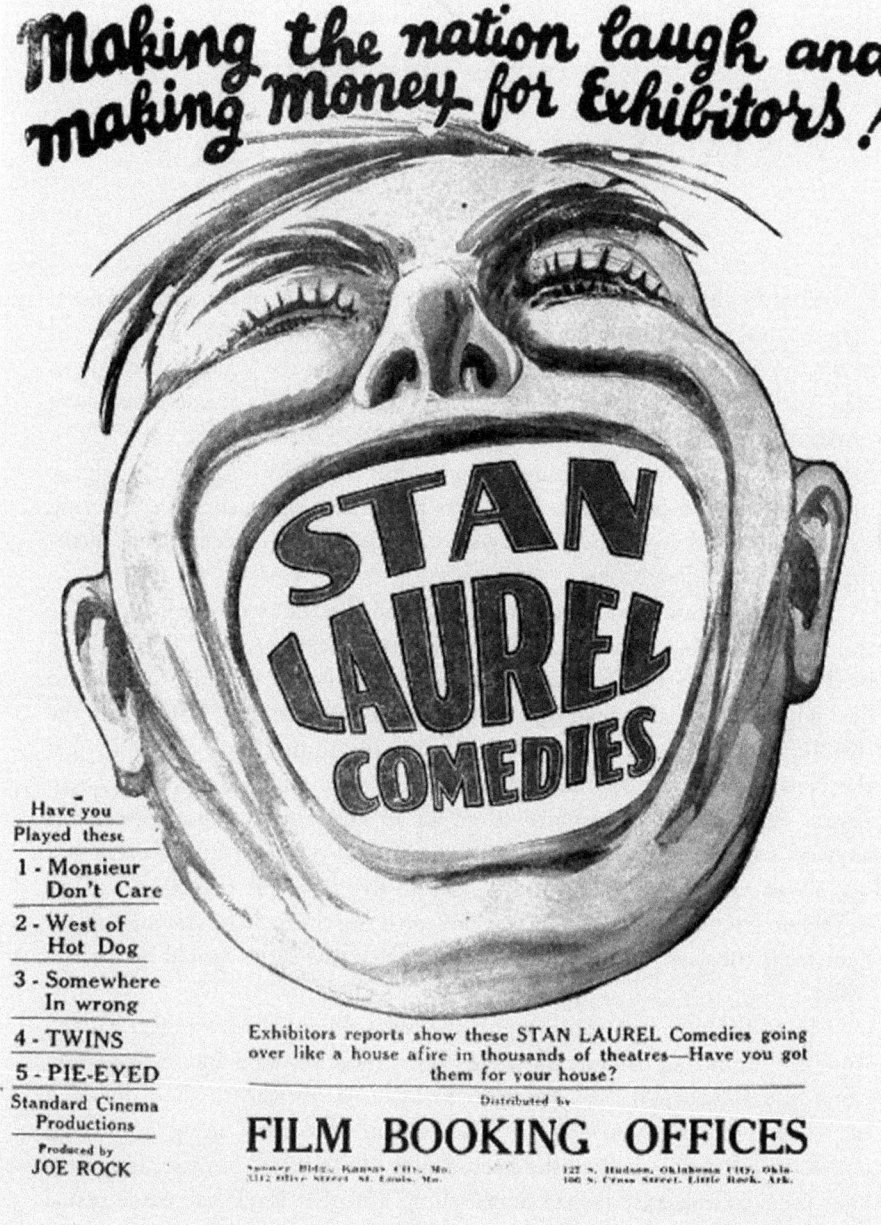

Joe Rock heavily advertised his Stan Laurel productions.

Between stints for Hal Roach, Stan starred in 12 comedies for independent producer Joe Rock.

proving that the alleged offense did not occur, and Stan soon ended his relationship with his former partner.

Despite his personal difficulties, Stan was a popular comedian, and theater owners were happy to book his short comedies. Laurel had also benefited from Roach's willingness to allow his comedians opportunities for creative input in front of and behind the camera, and his films for Rock were now billed as Stan Laurel Productions. Percy Pembroke was usually the credited director, but it was clear that it was Laurel who supervised these films. Laurel retained the premises he had developed at Roach, from working-class comedies to burlesques of popular pictures, honing his presentation and his performance with each production. Over the run of 12 films, facets of the evolving Stanley character would become increasingly apparent.

Detained

Cast

Stan Laurel .... The wrong convict
Julie Leonard .... The warden's daughter

Credits

"Perc" (Percy) Pembroke .... Director
Murray Rock .... Assistant director
Edgar Lyons .... Cinematographer
Tay Garnett .... Titles

A Stan Laurel production presented by Joe Rock.
No copyright registered.*
Production date: February 1924.
Released October 30, 1924, by Standard Cinema Corporation/Selznick Distributing Corporation.
Two reels.

Laurel's initial effort for producer Joe Rock is noteworthy for Stan's display of character traits that would evolve into the Stanley persona of the Laurel and Hardy era. Some of the shameless mugging seen in earlier films is still in evidence, but the developmental strides of his screen character distinguish this otherwise routine farce.

Stan (whose character isn't given a name) is subdued by an escaped convict who switches clothes with him. Now clad in conspicuously striped garb, Stan is hauled away by a prison guard. The new convict causes disruption everywhere; even a simple task like washing up results in a guard getting doused with soapy water. A tough inmate enlists Stan's assistance in an escape attempt but they wind up tunneling into a stockroom where explosives are stored.† Using a stick of dynamite to blow up one of the walls, they discover

---

*Stan's first two films for Joe Rock, Detained *and* Mandarin Mix-Up, *were not registered for copyright. Historian Rob Stone has speculated that they may have served as pilot films to secure financing and a distributor.*

　†*The tunneling sequence is reminiscent of scenes in an earlier Laurel comedy,* Pick and Shovel *(1923). Later, Laurel and Hardy would attempt similarly inept tunnel escapes in* The Second Hundred Years *(1927) and* The Flying Deuces *(1939).*

that the warden's office is on the other side. When he inadvertently renders his co-conspirator unconscious, Stan is proclaimed a hero and receives a pardon. As he departs, Stan weeps uncontrollably. His jail experience has made him a sadder but not particularly wiser individual: during a final embrace, Stan unwittingly steals the warden's watch and wallet.

Detained survives only in an abridged version (running 14 minutes; a home-movie edition, retitled *No Place Like Jail*, runs nine minutes),* so it may be impossible to offer an accurate assessment of the film.† Yet based on the footage that *does* exist, the gags have a random, off-the-cuff feel and Stan executes them with more restraint than usual. During the attempted escape, an inmate lights a stick of dynamite and hands it to Stan, who simply stands there in blank-faced bewilderment. In another sequence, Stan wanders into an execution chamber and watches a repairman work on an oversized switchboard, blissfully unaware that the man is trying to fix the electric chair in which Stan is sitting. However, none of this material is particularly inspired, and Stan doesn't have strong comic support (like James Finlayson) to play off.

For tried-and-true Laurel and Hardy fans, Stan's introductory scene is a revelation. Sporting a derby (which he wears throughout most of the picture), bow tie and rumpled suit, he has the essential appearance of his later Stanley character. And key Stanley traits are evident, if only in rough form: his blank stare coupled with his hands-behind-the-back stance; his ability to take hardship in stride; and his hope that flashing a smile will diffuse an uncomfortable situation. (His big, toothy smile comes across a bit forced here. Stan would later develop a wide, closed-mouthed grin that was much better suited to his character.)

Embryonic versions of the Laurel "cry," another key trait, are seen no less than three times. A tough inmate smashes the top of Laurel's derby, and Stan starts to cry (adding the clichéd theatrical gesture of covering his eyes with his arm) before quickly regaining his composure. As the same inmate and the warden engage in a violent struggle in the warden's office, Stan cries and runs around the room in a panic. (The aftermath of a dynamite explosion has given his sullied face a Pagliacciesque appearance.) Laurel's tearful farewell to the warden and his daughter is exaggerated for comic effect, although in retrospect it's odd to see Stan throwing his head back and bellowing his sorrow so excessively.

---

*Not to be confused with another Stan Laurel comedy, No Place Like Jail *(1918). There are no known surviving prints of this title.*

 †A hanging sequence described in the Kinematograph Weekly *review is not in surviving prints available for viewing. In this sequence, his neck is stretched way out of proportion, revealing Laurel's fondness for gags involving surreal physical deformity.*

The petulance inherent in many of Stan's previous performances is missing; Stan opts to portray his character as amiable and childlike, though not a complete innocent. He's still not above laughing derisively at others, as he does when he observes the soul of an electrocuted repairman winging his way to heaven.

Kinematograph Weekly had a higher opinion of Stan than the film itself: "Stan Laurel is a comedian with a personality fitted for better things than the desperate kind of slapstick. However, he gets over well in this undoubtedly amusing short set in a convict prison the like of which has unfortunately never been known. The fun is brisk and broad and with the exception of a rather unpleasant hanging gag, with an elongated neck, inoffensive."

Stan was definitely fitted for better things, and those better things would soon begin to take shape.

Mandarin Mix-Up

Cast
Stan Laurel . . . . Sum Sap

Credits
Percy Pembroke . . . . Director
Murray Rock . . . . Assistant director
Tay Garnett . . . . Titles

A Stan Laurel production presented by Joe Rock.
No copyright registered.
Production date: February 1924.
Released August 30, 1924, by Standard Cinema
Corporation/Selznick Distributing Corporation.
Two reels.

Produced immediately after *Detained* but released two months before it, *Mandarin Mix-Up* shows Stan working at a more deliberate pace and experimenting with intriguing ideas and imagery. Not all of these elements succeed, although Stan's desire to reach beyond stock comedy situations and try something different is admirable.

The arrival of a baby is hardly welcome news for his older brother, whose slovenly table manners prompt the housemaid to warn, "I'll throw you in with the dirty laundry!" Instead, the brother throws the baby into the laundry sack, which is carried away by a Chinese laundryman. Some 20 years pass and the baby, raised in Chinatown, has grown up to become Sum Sap, an "ace with the iron" who operates a laundry shop. Unaware of his true ancestry, he lives life as a Chinatown "dweller."

When Sum Sap strikes up an innocent conversation with a police officer, Sum Ting Wong, the leader of a Tong gang, mistakenly concludes that Sap is spilling the beans about the gang's criminal activities (though it is never

"Sum Sap" and his sweetheart in *Mandarin Mix-Up* (1924).

made clear what these activities might be, aside from hanging around the neighborhood, looking sinister). Marked for death by the Tongs, Sum Sap disguises himself as a policeman and avoids detection until Sum Ting Wong sees through the ruse. Running into a conveniently located costume shop, Sap emerges in Mandarin wardrobe, sporting a long (and patently fake) mustache, a disguise that fools Wong until he yanks off the mustache.

A young maiden named Lili gives Sum Sap a gun to protect himself and the inexperienced marksman fires a shot into a fireworks shop. The resulting explosions subdue the Tong gang; in gratitude, Sap decides to take Lili as his wife. The couple weds — Sap's laundry wagon is adorned with a "Just Married" sign — but Lili's long-lost mother suddenly turns up to reclaim her daughter. Then Sum Sap is informed that he's not really Chinese. Since he is also told that he has inherited an unexpected fortune, he is warmly received by his new mother-in-law.

Stan's training with the famed Fred Karno troupe is very much in evidence in *Mandarin Mix-Up*, as his pantomime and physical clowning are strikingly similar to Charlie Chaplin, another Karno veteran. Like Chaplin, Stan's gestures are subtle and precise, and often capped by sudden bursts of energetic movement. It isn't difficult to picture Chaplin behaving in the same manner when Stan ties two laundrymen's queues (ponytails) together for a makeshift clothesline. When Stan dons a policeman's uniform and intimidates the Tong gang, comparisons to police officer Chaplin cockily striding through the slums of *Easy Street* (1917) are unavoidable. However, it should be noted that Laurel isn't imitating Chaplin but rather relying on the same training that had an impact on the performing styles of both comedians. And some of the gags are purely cinematic, having no connection to Laurel's stage influence: when Sum Sap tries to climb to the top of a bunk bed, he steps on the head of a sleeping man who cries out in Chinese, the words conveyed via animation.

For a couple of set pieces, Stan reworks material from previous films. Playing a hyperactive infant in the opening scenes, Stan wears a bonnet, has his front teeth blackened out and has his hair arranged in a phony spit curl. He enhances his portrayal by sitting in an oversized high chair, an idea that expands upon the oversized-bassinet gags in *Mother's Joy* (1923) and *Brothers Under the Chin* (1924) and would reach fruition in the Laurel and Hardy short *Brats* (1930), in which elaborate, oversized sets made Stan and Ollie proportionately convincing children. (The high chair gag was later trotted out for Stan and Ollie's cameo as babies in *Wild Poses*, a 1933 Our Gang short.)

Stan repeats a routine he used in *The Egg* (1922) and *The Noon Whistle* (1923). After crashing through the skylight of a Buddhist temple, Sum Sap flees from Sum Ting Wong and comes across a row of four lockers. (Some might question why the temple has a locker room, although a better question to ponder is why no one ever challenges Laurel's unconvincing Chinese heritage.) Sap hides in the first locker, and as Wong locks the door, Sap pops out of the third locker, and so on. (This bit would turn up in animated cartoons, and Stan used a variation of it for *Swiss Miss* [1938], in which he and Ollie run in and out of kitchen lockers, pursued by an angry hotel chef.)

In the film's most inventive sequence, Sum Sap unconsciously inhales smoke from an opium pipe and, floating in a dreamlike state, he pursues an imaginary figure of his sweetheart. This was accomplished by simply photographing Stan in slow motion, but the results are quite effective, highlighting Stan's natural grace and timing. Even when Sum Sap trips over a curb and falls on his face, it looks like a ballet routine.

The final gag has Sum Sap, Lili and her kin piling into a taxi. When the taxi pulls away, we see Sum Sap sprawled in the street, having been pushed out the other side of the vehicle. (Stan would reuse the gag in *The Bullfighters* [1945], Laurel and Hardy's last American movie.)

The Chinatown scenes were filmed at the Universal Studios lot. The standing sets, built for other studio productions, give *Mandarin Mix-Up* a slick polish that would have otherwise been beyond the budgetary scope for an independent producer like Joe Rock. The elaborate Buddhist temple set is particularly impressive.

As was common with other similarly themed films of the era, most of the Chinese characters are portrayed by non–Asian actors. Yet the role of Lili is played by an uncredited Asian actress (not Julie Leonard, as listed in other sources), which results in odd attempts to camouflage the interracial relationship. Despite being distinctly Asian, Lili is introduced as "a pretty American who lives in Chinatown, and wears clothes to match." Later, her mother is portrayed by a white actress (also uncredited) and a vague explanation is given as to how Lili's lost-child ancestry is just like Sum Sap's background. It would be decades before American movies depicted interracial relationships in a positive light, and this clumsy sidestepping around the issue was no doubt meant to diffuse any possible objections that this modest two-reeler might be condoning or endorsing the subject.

Kinematograph Weekly called *Mandarin Mix-Up* "an irresponsible [?] comedy ... with some quieter and even more effective touches." *Bioscope* felt that "Laurel does better in this than he has in some time. There is a lot of excitement and shooting but there are also some very nicely handled comedy bits."

Often underrated,* *Mandarin Mix-Up* is a pleasant and inventive outing. While it doesn't rank among Stan's very best solo efforts it certainly isn't one of his worst.

---

*For years, Mandarin Mix-Up *was only available in an overhauled reissue edition that contained overbearing sound effects and had a blabber-mouthed narrator commenting on every single gag. Regardless of what one thinks of the film, it didn't deserve this sort of treatment.*

Monsieur Don't Care

Cast

Stan Laurel .... Rhubarb Vaselino
With
Melba Brownrigg

Credits

Percy Pembroke .... Director
Murray Rock .... Assistant director
Reggie Lyons .... Cinematographer
Monte Brice, Lou Lipton .... Writers
Tay Garnett .... Titles

A Stan Laurel production presented by Joe Rock.
Copyrighted December 7, 1924.
Production Date: September 1924 (at Universal Studios).
Released December 1, 1924, by Standard Cinema
Corporation/Selznick Distributing Corporation.
Two reels.

As of this writing, there are no surviving copies of *Monsieur Don't Care*, making it the only one of the 12 shorts Laurel made for Joe Rock that falls into the "lost film" category.

In *Mud and Sand* (1922), Laurel parodied Rudolph Valentino in *Blood and Sand*. *Monsieur Don't Care* burlesqued another Valentino picture, *Monsieur Beaucaire* (1924). Set in 16th-century France, Stan plays Rhubarb Vaselino (he was Rhubarb Vaseline in *Mud and Sand*), the favorite courtier of King Louis XV. Vaselino is forced to flee to England, disguising himself as a barber, Monsieur Don't Care. He becomes involved with plenty of duels and court intrigue.

Monsieur Don't Care did not garner the same favorable response from critics that *Mud and Sand* received. *Kinematograph Weekly* stated, "The burlesque follows the main development of the original and at one or two points achieves its first purpose admirably. Too often, though, slapstick is used for its own sake than for the purpose of burlesque." *Bioscope* noted, "The action follows the main outline of the original pretty closely, but of course every incident and the character is broadly travestied. Apart from its burlesque value, the humor is not brilliant and even as burlesque the production lacks subtlety. The film however is elaborately staged and the slapstick business in which the fun mainly consists is capably executed."

Despite those contemporary opinions, it is a shame *Monsieur Don't Care* is currently unavailable for viewing, to let historians and fans judge for themselves. Laurel's films for Joe Rock were pivotal to his development as a screen comedian, and even the lesser efforts reveal his creative skills at work.

In *Monsieur Don't Care* (1924), Stan Laurel (left, with Syd Crossley) burlesqued Rudolph Valentino's *Monsieur Beaucaire*.

On November 18, 1924, shortly before the release of *Monsieur Don't Care*, bankruptcy forced the Selznick Distributing Corporation to transfer their film holdings to the Film Booking Office of America (FBO), who would distribute all of the subsequent Laurel/Rock comedies. (FBO also reissued the first three Laurel/Rock entries in 1925.)

West of Hot Dog

Cast
Stan Laurel . . . . Stan
Julie Leonard . . . . Little Mustard
Lew Meehan . . . . Bad Mike

Credits
Percy Pembroke . . . . Director
Murray Rock . . . . Assistant director
Edgar Lyons . . . . Cinematographer
Tay Garnett . . . . Titles

A Stan Laurel production presented by Joe Rock.
Copyrighted December 30, 1924.
Production date: circa October 1924.
Released December 29, 1924, by Standard Cinema
Corporation/Film Booking Office of America.
Two reels.

In *West of Hot Dog*, Stan portrays a meek tenderfoot who's entirely out of his element in the wild frontier. Appropriately, he scales back the brash aggressiveness of previous films and plays the role with childlike innocence, a characterization not too far removed from his later Stanley persona.

Stan is traveling to the Western town of Hot Dog to claim an inheritance. On the way, the stagecoach is held up by Bad Mike and his gang. During the robbery, Stan's cowardice earns him the scorn of another passenger, Little Mustard, who happens to be the sheriff's daughter.

Upon arriving at Hot Dog, Stan attends the reading of his uncle's will and is informed that he has inherited the entire estate, including the Last Chance Saloon. However, in the event of his death, everything will go to his cousins, who just happen to be Bad Mike and his main henchman.

Stan drops by the saloon and is horrified when Bad Mike kills a man during a poker game. Stan grabs Bad Mike's horse and tries to flee town but the horse instinctively brings him to the bandit's hideout. Bad Mike and his gang rob the saloon, as luck would have it, and head back to the hideout, where Stan is trembling in terror. Through a series of fortunate mishaps, the gang members wind up shooting each other. Hailing Stan as a hero, the sheriff and his posse allow him the honor of capturing Bad Mike, which Stan does, miraculously. Little Mustard is now smitten with the brave Stan, who chooses to ride off alone, into the sunset.

For Laurel and Hardy fans, the premise of Stan journeying West may bring to mind the team's classic feature *Way Out West* (1937). The similarities, however, are only superficial since the Laurel and Hardy film is infinitely richer in its characterizations and gags. Nevertheless, as a lampoon of Western clichés, *West of Hot Dog* contains some funny and clever passages.

At first, the prissy Easterner doesn't fully comprehend the danger he's in. When Bad Mike and his gang rob the stagecoach, Stan remains unperturbed, sneering at the gunman through a coach window — until Stan realizes there's no glass in the frame. After his suspenders are yanked off, Stan can't even raise his hands in surrender without his pants falling down.

Because of his character's timid, passive personality, Laurel's performance is fairly subdued and the comic set pieces have a more deliberate pace. Arriving in Hot Dog, Stan heads to the lawyer's second-floor office for the reading of

An early portrait of Stan Laurel as the kind of bespectacled character he would play in *West of Hot Dog* (1924), *Dr. Pyckle and Mr. Pride* (1925), *Half a Man* (1927) and *Now I'll Tell One* (1927).

his uncle's will. His outlaw cousins are there for the same reason and Stan is one heir too many for their liking, so they hurl him out of the second-floor window. (An obvious prop dummy is tossed out the window and just as it hits the ground it "becomes" Stan, thanks to simple but effective editing.) Shaken but undaunted, Stan returns to the office and closes the window, a preemptive move that proves futile when they hurl him through the window pane. He returns once again, but when the thugs make a threatening gesture, Stan throws himself out the window, figuring it will be the inevitable result.

In the film's most sustained set piece, Stan is trapped in Bad Mike's lair. As he runs from room to room in a state of frightened panic, the flying bullets narrowly miss him and strike the bandits, one by one, until Stan is the last man standing.

Stan's final confrontation with Bad Mike is a letdown, primarily because we never really witness it. Trembling with fear, Stan climbs up a ladder to the attic where Bad Mike is hiding. In an exterior shot, Bad Mike comes crashing through the attic window and onto the ground below. "He didn't fight fair!" Big Mike moans, as Stan emerges with an oversized mallet. This disappointing payoff never explains how the cowardly city slicker mustered up enough courage to subdue the villain. Considering the buildup to it, this final showdown is surprisingly unimaginative.

Having the Western hero ride off alone at the end of the movie was a cliché even by 1924, and Stan comes up with his own spin on it. Little Mustard had been contemptuous of Stan's cowardice, but now she's been won over by his bravery. This time, however, it's Stan turn to reject *her*, as he tips his hat and walks toward his trusty steed. He looks back at her to give one last open-armed gesture of regret and dries his tears with his handkerchief. In the meantime, the horse has wandered off and a cow has taken its place. Stan distractedly attempts to mount the cow and it runs off, dragging Stan along.

West of Hot Dog was shot on the Universal Studios back lot, and the studio's Western town gives the production a look of authenticity — at least in terms of *movie* authenticity. Thanks to numerous public-domain DVD collections, this is one of the most accessible Stan Laurel comedies. While not in the same league as the prime Laurel and Hardy films, it serves as an enjoyable introduction for those who are unfamiliar with Stan's solo work.

Somewhere in Wrong

Cast

Stan Laurel	Stan, a tramp
Julie Leonard	Farmer's daughter
Charles King	Grocery boy

Max Asher . . . . Stan's pal, a fellow tramp
Tige (a.k.a. Pete the Pup) . . . . Farmer's dog

Credits

"Perc" (Percy) Pembroke . . . . Director
Murray Rock . . . . Assistant director
Edgar Lyons . . . . Cinematographer
Tay Garnett . . . . Titles

A Stan Laurel production presented by Joe Rock.
Copyrighted January 30, 1925.
Released January 30, 1925, by Standard Cinema
Corporation/Film Booking Office of America.
Two reels.

Somewhere in Wrong is noteworthy for Stan's attempt to portray a character of greater depth than usual, free of the exaggerated, repetitive mugging upon which he frequently relied. The film represents a major step in his development as a screen comedian, although it is ultimately too derivative of the Chaplin movies it tries to emulate.

Stan and his pal are two tramps who can't resist the scent of the freshly made doughnuts that a farmer's daughter has just placed on her window sill. A vicious dog protects the front door of the farmhouse, so Stan tries to get the goodies by clinging to a clothesline. The irate farmer catches Stan sneaking onto the property but his sympathetic daughter takes pity on the starving tramp and invites him in for a meal. (In the meantime, Stan's pal has run off and is never seen again.)

Hired as a farmhand, Stan becomes smitten with the daughter, but her heart belongs to the grocery boy. The mortgage is due and the farmer assures the landlord that he will be able to make the payment. The landlord would rather seize control of the property; sneaking into the farmhouse in the middle of the night, he steals the money from the safe. To help his benefactors, Stan sneaks into the landlord's office, steals money from *his* safe, and hands it to the landlord to pay off the mortgage. Then Stan picks the landlord's pocket and puts the money back in the landlord's safe. Stan is devastated when he sees the daughter in the arms of the grocery boy. Not even a plateful of doughnuts can assuage his sorrow.

By this time, any comedic portrayal of a tramp was considered Chaplinesque, regardless if the Chaplin influence was evident. In this case, however, the label applies, as Stan appropriates Charlie's screen persona (particularly from Chaplin's Essanay period) and adds his own comic sensibilities. *Somewhere in Wrong* desperately wants to be a Chaplin comedy, specifically *The Tramp* (1915). Although Stan's tramp looks nothing like Charlie's, both films have identical plotlines: a tramp is taken in by a farmer and his daughter; the tramp saves the day but loses the girl to another man. Yet for all its crude humor, *The Tramp* has moments of heart-wrenching emotion, whereas the pathos in *Somewhere in Wrong* seems hollow and contrived.

Somewhere in Wrong is at its best when it sticks to visual comedy. As the film opens, Stan ("a fierce, fiery, fearless, two-fisted loafer") and a fellow tramp are lazily sitting by a stream. Stan decides to wash his feet, so he unties his shoe laces then raises his pants legs — and the shoes along with it, revealing they have no soles and the bottom of his feet were exposed anyway. When Stan tries to steal doughnuts left to cool on a window sill, he grabs hold of a convenient clothesline as his buddy reels him closer to the target. Once inside the house, Stan spies a wall safe and tries to open it, only to be baffled by its flat, impenetrable surface. Then he discovers it's actually a mirror reflecting the image of a safe on the opposite wall! This gag turned up again in *Moonlight and Noses* (Hal Roach, 1925), a Clyde Cook two-reeler directed and co-written by Laurel.

When the landlord tries to exit the house after cracking the safe, Stan is awakened from his slumber and mistakes his bare foot for an intruder's hand. After issuing a stern warning, he winds up shooting himself in the foot. This gag was reworked in the Laurel and Hardy comedy *Oliver the Eighth* (1934) and again by The Three Stooges in *Dizzy Detectives* (1942).

Commendably, Stan stays in character throughout the film, without relying upon such tiresome habits as laughing uproariously to punctuate individual gags. He's still energetic, but his reactions are slower paced and more deliberate. When he sees the farmer's daughter in a transparent negligee (a racy bit to which the censors objected), he stands there transfixed rather than coyly smiling at her or the audience. Even a burst of melodramatic gesticulating (he wants to rob the farmer's safe but his conscience gets the better of him) is in character.

It's when *Somewhere in Wrong* goes for pathos that the film falters and, by comparison, illustrates how unerring Chaplin's artistic instincts were. In *The Tramp*, Charlie's infatuation with the farmer's daughter (Edna Purviance) is shattered when she introduces him to her new beau. Realizing that his love would never be reciprocated, Charlie politely excuses himself, goes into the kitchen and writes a farewell note. Spotting her hat, he gently kisses it then pauses to wipe his tears on a window shade. By the time Edna reads the note, Charlie is already headed down the country road that had been his path of introduction.

In *Somewhere in Wrong*, Stan, having saved the farm from financial ruin, writes the girl a love note and rehearses a passionate declaration of his tender feelings. But when he sees her locked in an embrace with the grocery boy, he crumples the note and staggers away, weeping uncontrollably. Exiting the house, Stan is so distraught that he momentarily contemplates shooting himself in the head. He decides instead to seek comfort in a plate of doughnuts.

There's a world of difference between these sequences. Chaplin uses his sad eyes and defeated body language to convey his sorrow, subtly underplaying his emotions. (When he kisses Edna's hat, Charlie effectively performs this bit with his back to the camera.) By contrast, Stan overplays his scene with overwrought sobbing, repeatedly letting loose with a cavern-mouthed wail. The result is neither poignant nor amusing and comes off as a soulless, misfired attempt to tug at the audience's heartstrings.

Nevertheless, *Somewhere in Wrong* was a step in the right direction, as Stan was refining the interrelationship between character, gags and plot. But he still had a way to go before he blossomed into Stanley, a character audiences would embrace as affectionately as they did Chaplin's tramp.

Twins

Cast

Stan Laurel . . . . Stan and his twin brother
Julie Leonard . . . . Stan's girl
Alberta Vaughn . . . . Brother's wife

Credits

"Perc" (Percy) Pembroke . . . . Director
Murray Rock . . . . Assistant director
Edgar Lyons . . . . Cinematography
Tay Garnett . . . . Titles

A Stan Laurel production presented by Joe Rock.
Copyrighted June 2, 1925.
Released February 28, 1925, by Standard Cinema
Corporation/Film Booking Office.
Two reels.

A far-fetched, somewhat predictable but very funny comedy, *Twins* anticipates the twin brother/mistaken identity premise that would be used for *Our Relations* (1936), one of Laurel and Hardy's most polished feature-length films.

Engaged to be married, Stan runs into his identical twin brother, who is heading for Seattle on business. Stan is invited to stay at his brother's home, although for reasons never made clear, the brother has never told his shrewish wife about Stan's existence. When the wife meets Stan's fiancée, she sees a picture of the girl with Stan and immediately concludes that her husband is cheating on her. The wife goes back home, where she encounters Stan, whom she mistakes for her spouse. Stan, on the other hand, has no idea who this irate woman is. (Apparently, the twin brother doesn't confide much in anybody.) Accusations soon become physical and there is a wild slapstick brawl. Stan attempts to fight back, leaping, scissors-kicking, and wildly swinging, but missing every time. The wife gives Stan a pretty sound pummeling, but when the police arrive and look in the window, she quickly puts Stan's hands over her throat, causing them to believe he is the instigator. Stan is hauled into court but manages to escape. Things are finally cleared up when the brother returns from his trip.

In *Twins*, Laurel further hones his screen characterization by presenting an alternate persona. While Stan remains the same bubbly, giggling character he had been in most of his previous solo efforts, his twin counterpart (whose footage is limited) is not too far removed from the beloved Stanley of the Laurel and Hardy years. The twin brother is meek and henpecked, yet oddly comfortable in his own skin, despite the subordinate status he maintains in his marriage. In nearly all of the films in which Stan is a married man, he is subordinate to his wife (as his character would be to Oliver Hardy).

One can only speculate whether Stan's volatile relationship with Mae Laurel was the catalyst for this sort of character, especially since *Twins* contains a conclusion in which the wife soundly trounces the man she believes to be her husband. Joe Rock stated in later interviews that he made it very clear to Stan that Mae would not be hired by his company and was to have nothing to do with the production of the films. Stan's personal life was his own, but Rock also clarified that disciplinary action would be taken if any problems with Mae affected his work.

Whereas *Twins* offers no explanation as to why the brother has never told his wife about Stan, *Our Relations* makes it clear from the start that Stan and Ollie don't want news about their long-lost twin brothers, Alf and Bert, to stain their reputations as upright citizens. (They receive word that sailors Alf and Bert were hanged at sea during a mutiny, but they're very much alive and create a lot of confusion when they arrive in town.) The brother is only dealt with peripherally in *Twins*, and "his" scenes are limited. In *Our Relations*, both sets of twins share equal screen time, although special-effects shots of all four together are minimal.

While *Our Relations* was the only Laurel and Hardy film to repeat the twin-brother premise, the dual-role theme would turn up in *Brats* (1930; where they play their own children), *Twice Two* (1933; they play their own sisters and each other's wives), and *The Bullfighters* (1945; Stan is mistaken for a lookalike matador named Don Sebastian). The concluding scenes of *A Chump at Oxford* (1940) dealt with dual personality, as a blow to the head transforms simple-minded Stanley into Lord Paddington, a brilliant scholar and athlete.

Twins is great fun, if a bit unremarkable, and shows Laurel continuing to explore the possibilities of a tangible screen persona.

Pie-Eyed

Cast

Stan Laurel .... Stanley
Glen Cavender .... Jack Tinney (Firewater Club manager)
Thelma Hill .... Mrs. Tinney
William Irving .... Trombone player

Credits

Percy Pembroke, Joe Rock .... Directors
Murray Rock .... Assistant director
Edgar Lyons .... Cinematography
Tay Garnett .... Titles

A Stan Laurel production presented by Joe Rock.
Copyrighted March 20, 1925.
Released March 30, 1925, by Standard Cinema
Corporation/Film Booking Office.
Two reels.

A fast-paced exercise in sustained comic inebriation, *Pie-Eyed* is an interesting and often underrated Laurel effort. The film has been compared to Charlie Chaplin's classic *One A.M.* (Mutual, 1916), although it is closer in style and content to another Chaplin short, *A Night Out* (Essanay, 1915).

Stanley, a member of the temperance society, is conducting field research on the evils of drink — by whooping it up at hotspot called the Firewater Club, managed by Jack Tinney, a former heavyweight boxing champ (Glen Cavender, who played comic heavies in other Laurel comedies). Stanley's liquor-fueled revelry gets out of hand, and Tinney punches him in the eye and warns him to settle down. But Stanley's behavior is still out of control, as he tangles with other club patrons and members of the jazz band. When he makes a play for a club dancer, who happens to be the boss's wife (Thelma Hill, who later turned up in the Laurel and Hardy comedy *Two Tars* [1928]), Tinney knocks him to the floor with one punch, then hands him his business card ("If you ever need a boxing teacher," he advises).

Stanley is ejected from the club and wanders the streets in a drunken stupor. A cop intervenes and when Stanley presents Tinney's card, the helpful officer takes him back "home" and puts him to bed. Upon returning to their apartment, the Tinneys are flabbergasted to discover the unruly patron has invaded their privacy and Stanley beats a hasty exit, with an irate Jack Tinney in hot pursuit.

Stan Laurel is a study in comic inebriation in *Pie-Eyed* (1925).

Made during the Prohibition era, *Pie-Eyed* begins by identifying Stan as a member of the temperance movement — an anti-drinking crusade that sprang up during those years — then reveals him to be completely intoxicated. In one of the film's best gags, Stan is shown celebrating with his "friends" — two superimposed images of himself! The reference to the temperance society is merely used to set up Stan's character, but it also serves to indicate a general disdain for self-appointed do-gooders and their "moral" campaigns. (The recent HBO series *Boardwalk Empire*, also set during Prohibition, exposes the hypocrisy of private conduct and public image in dramatic fashion, as gangster "Nucky" Thompson [played by Steve Buscemi] poses as a member of the temperance society to mask his criminal activity in supplying bootleg liquor to speakeasies.)

While some feel that Laurel's drunk routine quickly becomes tiresome and redundant, the portrayal is more complex than that and manages to sustain interest throughout the film's two-reel running time. Stan explores both the giddy and hostile nature of his character's boozy personality. He's in high spirits (literally) while he's wreaking havoc, but when he meets with opposition, his mood turns aggressive. He takes it upon himself to lead the jazz band, but after getting hit with a trombone slide, he starts to pick a fight with the trombone player (William Irving, a familiar foil in comedy shorts from the silent era through the 1930s). Stan is even brazen enough to challenge the tough nightclub manager and winds up with a black eye. (Stan orders a steak to ease his wound.)

This injury doesn't calm Stan down. A couple at the next table amuse themselves by trying to flip spoons into a drinking glass. Stan attempts to execute the trick but his spoon flies off his table and slides down the back of a woman's dress. He retrieves the utensil and the angry woman shoves him into the band, where he lands directly on his trombone-playing nemesis. After yet another warning from the manager, Stan tries to consume a bowl of soup but is interrupted when loud notes (depicted via crude but clever animation) emitting from the trombone bounce off the back of his head. One of these notes lands directly in the bowl, causing its muddy contents to splash all over another patron. When the club dancer (the manager's wife) begins her act, Stan joins in, slipping on the paper streamers covering the floor, and dragging her down with him. As he embraces the shaken dancer, the manager intercedes once again.

Some may find Laurel's behavior in *Pie-Eyed* off-putting, and this criticism is valid. His character is unsympathetic, and his repeated rudeness might make viewers sympathize with his exasperated victims instead. Yet most humor is fundamentally based on social impropriety, and comic depictions of drunkenness are no exception. Of course, there is nothing inherently funny about alcoholism in real life, but in motion pictures (and on television), inebriation was often used as a method of releasing a character's inhibitions for comic effect. Character actors like Arthur Housman, Jack Norton and Hal Smith built careers on portraying amiable drunks, while Joe E. Lewis, Dean Martin and Foster Brooks created booze-swilling personas that audiences found endearing. Stan's eagerness to fight, his lack of inhibition, and his base sexual impulses are all at the surface of his personality in *Pie-Eyed*. On its own modest terms, it is a noteworthy performance, and Laurel seems to relish the opportunity of exploring a character with almost no sense of shame or protocol.

Thrown out of the club, Stan interacts with inanimate objects, as Chaplin did in *One A.M.* The difference is that these scenes constitute only a portion of *Pie-Eyed*, while Chaplin devoted two reels to stumbling around the house, trying to get to bed, and displaying brilliant comedic invention in the process. In *One A.M.*, inanimate objects take on a life of their own, becoming humanistic foes. In *Pie-Eyed*, inanimate objects remain objects, as Stan mistakes a tree cage for a jail cell, loses his hat under an automobile, and gets sprayed with water from a passing street-cleaning vehicle as he attempts to retrieve the hat. One memorable gag has Stan leaning against a lamppost while he puts on his overcoat. But as he slides his arms through coat sleeves, he wraps the coat around the post, so he is unable to move from the spot until a helpful cop yanks him away — and splits the overcoat in two. (In these scenes, Laurel carries an umbrella, which approximates Chaplin's trademark cane.)

The key difference between *One A.M.* and *Pie-Eyed* is that Chaplin deals exclusively with inanimate objects (table, rug, staircase, Murphy bed) while Laurel interacts with other people. In Chaplin's tour-de-force, these objects are imaginary opponents. Laurel's opponents, on the other hand, are genuine, the product of his insensitive behavior.

Pie-Eyed is actually closer in spirit to Chaplin's *A Night Out*, in which Charlie and Ben Turpin's drunken roughhousing causes a run-in with a restaurant headwaiter. Charlie is also caught in a compromising situation with the headwaiter's wife, similar to the nightclub manager finding Stan in bed in *Pie-Eyed*.

The climactic chase, with the enraged husband chasing Stanley all over the apartment building, is loaded with energy as they run through corridors, jump through windows and scale the fire escape. But there are no memorable gags, and Stan indulges in the sort of exaggerated arm-flailing that silent-era comedians often fell back on in an effort to compensate for the paucity of material. One odd gag has Stan leaping from a window and falling, in slow motion, several stories to the pavement below, where he lands upright and unharmed.

Stan's aggressively obnoxious demeanor in *Pie-Eyed* provides a sharp contrast to his blissful state of inebriation in Laurel and Hardy films such as *Blotto* (1930), *The Devil's Brother* (1933), *The Bohemian Girl* (1936) and *Swiss Miss* (1938). In *Blotto* and *The Devil's Brother*, intoxication leads to uncontrollable laughing jags. When Stan and Ollie unwittingly get drunk on moonshine liquor in *Them That Hills* (1934), they maintain their jovial spirits, even after an irate husband (Charlie Hall) starts a fight with them.

Laurel would reuse the taken-to-the-wrong-home premise for the Laurel and Hardy two-reelers *Scram!* (1932) and *The Fixer Uppers* (1935), where they would also incur the wrath of jealous husbands. (In *Scram!*, they wind up at the wrong house first, then inadvertently get the homeowner's wife intoxicated.)

While it isn't one of Laurel's best solo efforts, *Pie-Eyed* is a fascinating attempt to put his own spin on established situations and themes. Not all of it works (a lot of it doesn't, in fact), but the film contains a number of solid gags in addition to ideas that he would refine in later films, to much better effect.

The Snow Hawk

Cast
Stan Laurel .... Stan
Glen Cavender .... Midnight Mike
Julie Leonard .... Storekeeper's daughter

Credits
Percy Pembroke .... Director
Murray Rock .... Assistant director
Edgar Lyons .... Cinematographer
Tay Garnett .... Titles
A Stan Laurel production presented by Joe Rock.
Copyrighted April 30, 1925.
Released April 30, 1925, by Standard Cinema
Corporation/Film Booking Office of America.
Two reels.

Several sequences for *The Snow Hawk* were shot on location at Lake Arrowhead (in California's San Bernardo Mountains) and considering the extra time and effort put into this production, it's a shame the results aren't better.

Stan is an all-purpose employee at a general store in the Great Northwest wilderness. He's hopelessly in love with the storekeeper's daughter but she only has eyes for a dashing Royal Canadian Mountie, which prompts Stan to run off and join the Mounties. Midnight Mike, a notorious thief and murderer, is on the loose and he turns out to be none other than the Mountie who has been romancing the girl. After he robs the safe, Midnight Mike's escape plan is foiled when Stan tags along to help track down the culprit. Stan discovers his rival's true identity (not through any deductive reasoning on his part — Midnight Mike blurts out an angry confession) and brings him back to the store, where the criminal tries to turn the tables by claiming that Stan is the guilty party. But another arresting officer recognizes Midnight Mike, leaving Stan free to embrace his now-impressed sweetheart.

Despite a few amusing bits, *The Snow Hawk* is flat and uninspired, lacking the satiric brilliance of Buster Keaton's *The Frozen North* (1922) or the lunatic gusto of Ben Turpin's *Yukon Jake* (1924), to cite two similarly themed comedies. Perhaps to compensate for the paucity of material, Stan reverts to some high-octane mugging, which only serves to emphasize the film's creative shortcomings. His blatant attempts to engage the audience often has the opposite effect.

Early on, Stan injects a rare note of pathos. He slips the storekeeper's daughter a letter containing his marriage proposal. She tears up the note and hands the pieces back to him, shaking her head in refusal. Stan sighs and tries to take the rejection in stride, then breaks down sobbing. This sort of unre-

Stan Laurel and Anita Garvin in a publicity shot for *The Snow Hawk* (1925), taken before Garvin became ill and was replaced by Julie Leonard.

quited love was portrayed more effectively by Charlie Chaplin and Harold Lloyd. Though Stan performs the scene well, there isn't enough depth of character for it to have the impact intended. More notable is the comic payoff, in which Stan leans his head against the store counter and the storekeeper mistakes his raccoon-skin hat for a live critter. The storekeeper grabs a rifle and blasts the hat, with Stan's resulting "fright wig" appearance looking very close to the unruly mop he had in the Laurel and Hardy films.

Even the better passages in *The Snow Hawk* will remind viewers of superior work done by other comedians, as when the storekeeper's daughter offers the Mountie a piece of candy. To get even, Stan places mothballs in the candy box, but the Mountie declines any further samplings. The girl then offers a piece to Stan, who makes sure that it isn't a mothball before he closes his eyes and opens his mouth in anticipation. But she decides to eat it herself and reaches into the box for another piece, which turns out to be one of the mothballs. Stan struggles to conceal his disgust as she playfully pops yet another one into his mouth. In Laurel's hands, this bit is reasonably amusing, yet it's too derivative of a similar and much funnier sequence in Harold Lloyd's *Grandma's Boy* (1922) to come off as anything other than recycled goods.

The outdoor scenes are beautifully photographed (by Edgar Lyons), which makes the climactic manhunt all the more disappointing since there are no memorable gags to take advantage of the setting. Instead, all sense of characterization flies out the window as Stan romps around in the snow like a hyperactive puppy, treating his once-hated rival as a convivial companion. Stan's mugging is particularly excessive in this sequence, and that doesn't help matters.

A common complaint about Laurel's films for Joe Rock is the lack of strong supporting players who appeared in the Hal Roach productions (e.g., James Finlayson, George Rowe). It's unfortunate that Anita Garvin, originally cast as the storekeeper's daughter, became ill and had to be replaced by Julie Leonard, Stan's regular leading lady in the Rock films. Garvin was a gifted comedienne whose rapport with Stan is obvious in several movies (*From Soup to Nuts, Their Purple Moment, Blotto* and *Be Big*, to name a few) and it's always a treat to watch them interact, no matter how weak the material may be. As a substitute, Julie Leonard is adequate but clearly not in Garvin's league.

The Snow Hawk could have featured any nondescript comedian and yielded the same results. Stan Laurel, however, wasn't just *any* comedian, yet this unmemorable vehicle offers little evidence of his true comedic genius.

Navy Blue Days

Cast

Stan Laurel . . . . Stan
Julie Leonard . . . . Little Grenadine
Glen Cavender . . . . Peter Vermicelli

Credits

Percy Pembroke . . . . Director
Murray Rock . . . . Assistant director
Edgar Lyons . . . . Cinematographer
Tay Garnett . . . . Titles
A Stan Laurel production presented by Joe Rock.
Copyrighted May 30, 1925.
Released May 30, 1925, by Standard Cinema
Corporation/Film Booking Office of America.
Two reels.

In *Navy Blue Days*, Stan once again takes a single idea and builds an entire two-reeler around it. There are a few good gags plus a concentrated effort to stay in character (as limited as the characterization may be), although the overall result is one of Laurel's lesser solo comedies.

Stan is a first-class gob whose ship is stationed in an unspecified Latin American country. During mail call, other sailors get letters but there's nothing for lonesome Stan. The chief petty officer receives a dinner invitation from his girlfriend, Little Grenadine, who instructs the officer to bring a friend along. Stan desperately tries to become the invited guest, but after his attempts to cajole the officer fail, he simply follows him to the house. Stan is instantly smitten with Grenadine, and she takes an immediate liking to him (as she does with all servicemen). As Stan gets familiar with his new sweetheart, her boyfriend, Peter Vermicelli, the local tough guy, shows up, forcing poor Stan to flee for his life.

Unlike some of Stan's other gag-driven comedies in which he frantically hits the ground running from the get-go, *Navy Blue Days* opens promisingly with a deliberately paced scene with Stan performing laundry duty. As fellow crew members toss their soiled garments into an enormous pile, Stan washes a single sock. Realizing he doesn't have the matching one, he burrows into the mountain of clothes — we see various sections "rippling" as he searches through the entire stack — and emerges at the summit, triumphantly holding the errant sock. Another memorable bit has Stan carrying kegs out of a supply room, narrowly avoiding a large swinging crate each time he walks in and out of the door.

Stan's usually brash screen personality is modified into a lonely sad sack who simply won't take "no" for an answer. While that's enough to get the dinner-invitation premise started, it's not enough to carry the film. The chief petty officer, played by an uncredited actor, is a cardboard comic foil, and Stan's character has done nothing to earn our sympathy, so his dogged attempts to engage the officer become a bit exasperating. (The viewer begins to empathize with the officer, which was hardly the intention here.)

For those who are familiar with silent-era comedies, one gag will strike a note of déjà vu. At dinner, a famished Stan sits down at the table with the officer, Grenadine and members of her family. As Grenadine's father says grace, everyone lowers their eyes and raises a fist, grasping a fork, to their foreheads. The moment that grace is finished, everyone but Stan skewers the food with their forks, leaving Stan with an empty plate and empty stomach. This is a repeat of an identical gag in Buster Keaton's *My Wife's Relations* (1922), where it came off better since Buster used it as one of several dinner-table gags and not as the primary punchline as Stan does here.

The climactic chase, with Stan chased throughout the village by Vermicelli and his crew (comprised of nearly every male in town) is full of energy and quick throwaways gags. But this finale, as well as the overall film, is difficult to properly assess since the available version of *Navy Blue Days* is missing the concluding scenes (in which the chief petty officer beats up Vermicelli and his gang but Stan gets credit for their defeat). The abruptness of what now passes for a conclusion negates the few merits that preceded it.

Reviewers who had the opportunity to see the film in its entirety didn't hold it in high regard. *Motion Picture Today* called it "a rather inane comedy ... which has very little to offer in the way of entertainment. The gags are as old as the proverbial hills." *Moving Picture World* was more to the point: "There is not enough material to hold up for two reels."

Navy Blue Days is a misfire, but it also represents a small step in the right direction. In time, Stan would learn how to take a simple premise and flesh it out with inventive gags rooted in finely tuned comic characterizations.

The Sleuth

Cast

Stan Laurel	Webster Dingle
Glen Cavender	The husband
Alberta Vaughn	The wife
Anita Garvin	Female crook
Dick Gilbert	Crook

Credits

Harry Sweet	Director
Murray Rock	Assistant director
Edgar Lyons	Cinematographer
Tay Garnett	Titles

A Stan Laurel production presented by Joe Rock.
Copyrighted June 30, 1925.
Released June 30, 1925, by Standard Cinema
Corporation/Film Booking Office of America.
Two reels.

The Sleuth is a mess, a conglomeration of random, crazy gags resulting in what is arguably the weakest of Laurel's films for Joe Rock. Some isolated moments are funny, but they don't have any cumulative effect, despite Stan's formidable exuberance. The proceedings have the delirium of a dream sequence and, had it been framed that way, it would be easier to account for the odd inconsistencies.

Detective Webster Dingle ("I Solve Your Puzzles") is hired by a woman to trap her cheating husband who is also consorting with a gang of crooks. Dingle arrives at their home disguised as the new maid, and the husband makes a play for "her." Later, Dingle dons a series of different disguises in an effort to crack the case. Finally, masquerading as a sultry vamp, Dingle rounds up the husband and his crew.

Glen Cavender (far left), Stan Laurel (dangling), Alberta Vaughn (center), Anita Garvin (far right) and assorted crooks in *The Sleuth* (1925).

The Sleuth was the first of two Laurel-Rock productions directed by Harry Sweet, and it is odd that the film has such a weak structure, given that Rock praised Sweet for being an efficient director who storyboarded (illustrating the progression of scenes in comic-strip fashion) all of his movies. Rock was particularly impressed with this aspect of Sweet's direction, but if Sweet did indeed map out his scenes, his technique was ineffective in this instance. *The Sleuth* is surprisingly haphazard and lacks any semblance of cinematic structure, though director Gil Pratt reportedly shot additional footage (the fact that Dick Gilbert's character is played by another actor in the final scenes would seem to confirm this), so Sweet may not be entirely to blame. On the other hand, *Half a Man* (see separate entry), the second Sweet-directed Laurel comedy, exhibits some of the same shortcomings found here, and this is probably not a coincidence.

Further compounding the difficulty in properly assessing the film, the DVD edition of *The Sleuth* derives from at least two different sources, as evidenced by the variance in print quality and condition, and at times it is hard to ascertain whether the sloppy continuity is due to missing scenes or slapdash filmmaking — or both. When the woman comes to Dingle's office to plead her case, she recounts, in flashback, how her young daughter alerted her that Daddy and his crooked friends were up to no good. Yet it's never explained exactly what the husband is up to, and who the gang of thugs are. There are indications that the husband has hired them to steal his wife's valuables, but since there are no intertitles during these scenes, this is just conjecture. There's a hint that the relationship between the husband and the female member of the gang (Anita Garvin) may be more than just a professional one, yet this is another vague plot point.

Missing footage or not, the film's lack of continuity is off-putting. In one scene, Dingle is in drag as the maid; suddenly, in the next scene, the husband is chasing another maid — a real female — while Dingle dusts for fingerprints upstairs. There is no transition, leaving the viewer perplexed and rendering the previous buildup pointless.

Nevertheless, there are some amusing scenes, starting with the introduction to Webster Dingle, who is first seen toying with a blacksmith puzzle. As Dingle struggles to figure it out, a delivery boy enters the office and, grabbing the puzzle, quickly separates the interlocked metal pieces, then puts them together again and hands it back to the dumbfounded detective. Frustrated, Dingle tries to do it himself, to no avail. (In the Laurel and Hardy films, Stan was the one who could easily play simple games while Ollie would get flummoxed trying to accomplish the same moves, e. g. the "kneesie-earsie-nosie" and "finger wiggle" bits in *The Devil's Brother* or the peewee game in *Babes in Toyland*.) When a stranger enters the room, Dingle grabs the telephone and pretends to make an important call to impress the potential client. But the charade is exposed when the stranger turns out to be the telephone repairman, who reconnects the dead phone line.

The Sleuth marks the only known time Stan did two female impersonations in the same picture. As the flirty housemaid, Stan does a dry run for his roles in the Laurel and Hardy films *Duck Soup* (1927) and its remake, *Another Fine Mess* (1930). He opts for a slinkier approach in his second masquerade, playing an alluring vamp who raises the blood pressure of the husband and his henchmen. Laurel was often quite funny doing his drag routines, something that he originated in British music hall productions and did in vaudeville before incorporating it into his movies. He would perform the bit in a number of the Laurel and Hardy films, including one of their last efforts, *Jitterbugs* (1943).

Despite the paucity of good material, Laurel's timing is sharp and precise. The best running gag involves Dingle's skill as a quick-change artist, and every time a hat is snatched from his head, he's got another one to quickly replace it. Ironically, Stan's performance in this frenetically paced comedy reveals glimpses of the slow-thinking Stanley-to-come, especially in moments when his reaction to the mayhem is a simple blank stare.

Unfortunately, a lot of the gags are unremarkable (Dingle, as the maid, breaking vases over the amorous husband's head; Dingle leaving powdery white footprints on the floor where he is dusting for fingerprints, etc.), although plenty of energy is expended trying to pump life into them. Dingle smokes an outlandishly oversized pipe in an early scene; while it's a reasonably amusing sight the first time around, Laurel relies on the prop a little too much. Even the concluding fight scenes are uninspired and come across as a rather desperate way to wrap things up.

Anita Garvin (1906–1994) is curiously underused in an ill-defined role. This expert comedienne would continue to work with Stan through the Laurel and Hardy partnership, making her final appearance with the team in the six-reel version of *A Chump at Oxford* (1940). In later years, Garvin would recall (with uncanny accuracy) details from her career. She remembered Laurel being the creative force behind his solo films during this period, and also indicated that he directed some of the Rock-produced Jimmy Aubrey comedies. There is no record of this, but Garvin's memory was so reliable that Laurel may have indeed directed these pictures without receiving credit for them.

The Sleuth is a misfire, but the basic premise is a good one. Laurel evidently thought so, because after leaving Joe Rock's employ and re-signing with Hal Roach, he reworked it for his first credit as writer-director, *Chasing the Chaser* (1925), which repeated some of the same gags.

Dr. Pyckle and Mr. Pride

Cast

Stan Laurel	Dr. Stanislaus Pyckle/Mr. Pride
Julie Leonard	English Miss (Pyckle's assistant)
Tige (a.k.a. Pete the Pup)	Pyckle's dog
Syd Crossley	Victorian gentleman
Dot Farley	Townswoman

Credits

Percy Pembroke	Director
Murray Rock	Assistant director
Edgar Lyons	Cinematographer
Tay Garnett	Titles

A Joe Rock production. Copyrighted July 30, 1925.
Released July 30, 1925, by Standard Cinema Corporation.
Two reels.

Stan Laurel turns into a fiendish practical joker in *Dr. Pyckle and Mr. Pride* (1925).

Based on Robert Louis Stevenson's novella *The Strange Case of Dr. Jekyll and Mr. Hyde* (1886) — and more specifically, the 1920 movie adaptation starring John Barrymore — *Dr. Pyckle and Mr. Pride* (often listed incorrectly as *Dr. Pyckle and Mr. Pryde*) is a delightful parody that ranks among the best of Stan Laurel's solo comedies. The dual-personality theme gives Stan plenty of elbow room to flex his comedic muscles, and the results are hilarious, if atypical of his usual style.

The setting is 19th-century London. Dr. Stanislaus Pyckle tells his colleagues that he wants to discover a way "to separate the Good from Evil in the human mind." To this end, he proclaims, "I'll get it if it takes a life — Any life but my own!" In his laboratory, Pyckle mixes chemicals until he concocts a formula that transforms him into Mr. Pride,* a wild-eyed, shaggy-haired fiend who runs around town pulling mischievous practical

---

*None of the onscreen characters refer to Pyckle's alter ego as "Mr. Pride." The only reference to the name is in the film's title.

jokes. An angry mob chases back to Pyckle's laboratory, where he takes an antidote and, as the good doctor, sends the crowd away. But Pyckle continues to experiment with the potion and Pride's reign of terror continues, resulting in yet another mob storming his home. He drinks the antidote once more, but has become immune to its effect and turns back into Pride. He makes a play for his assistant, who subdues him by smashing a bottle over his head.

The version of the film available on DVD by Kino On Video fades out at this point. It's apparent the concluding scene is missing, since the mob rushes back into the house after the assistant screams, but we never see any follow-up to this. In *Laurel or Hardy: The Solo Films of Stan Laurel and Oliver "Babe" Hardy*, Rob Stone fills in the blanks: "Dr. Pyckle is found out. He attempts to poison himself, but drinks castor oil by mistake."

Even without the original ending, *Dr. Pyckle and Mr. Pride* is an inventive and funny two-reeler that shows what an accomplished farceur Stan had become. In some of his previous work, his portrayals would waver from frantic hyper-action to deliberate subtlety, often within the same film. Here, the Pyckle-Pride framework allows Stan to indulge in both styles of humor and still remain completely in character — or, in this case, *characters*.

As Dr. Pyckle, Stan deftly lampoons John Barrymore's performance as the dedicated but tormented Dr. Jekyll. Wisely, Stan gesticulates only when necessary (his expressions and mannerisms are exaggerated enough to emphasize the farcical elements), yet Stan delivers a performance that is impressive on its own terms. When Pyckle stares at his mutating hand and realizes he can no longer rely on the antidote, Laurel gives dramatic intensity to his cries of anguish — which is certainly more than one would expect to find in a free-wheeling satire.

As Mr. Pride, Stan is a study in methodical mayhem. He energetically leaps and jumps about as he had done in other films, but here these tactics are part of the character's personality, conveying his unbridled glee over the havoc he's wreaked and providing a contrast to Pyckle's staid demeanor. While the Mr. Hyde of the original story indulged in his basest desires, Pride's crimes against humanity include snatching an ice cream cone from a child, cheating at marbles, blowing a party favor into the face of a kindly old woman, popping a paper bag behind an unsuspecting passerby, placing a distinguished gentleman's digits in a Chinese finger trap, and assaulting hapless citizens with his pea-shooter. The addition of a fright wig and severe make-up to Laurel's long face and infectious grin gives Pride a comically sinister appearance, making his "offenses" seem all the more outlandish. The mere sight of Pride scampering through the streets in search of his next victim is good for a laugh.

Stan gives the initial transformation sequence a nice balance of earnestness and lunacy. Alone in his laboratory, pacing the floor, inspiration (in the form of a fallen vase) strikes Pyckle and he sits down to concoct his new formula. With each added chemical, his eyes widen with excitement until he proclaims, "AT LAST! I'll call it Dr. Pyckle's 58th Variety!"* Agonizing over the next step ("I must not take it — I would make a fiend of me!"), he hesitantly raises the beaker to his lips, only to tumble backwards out of an open window, swallowing the potion on impact. Back inside the lab, the mixture kicks in, as Pyckle rolls, leaps, and thrashes around wildly before falling on the floor and transforming into the evil Mr. Pride. (A conveniently placed cabinet obscures Pyckle's face, so we never see the metamorphosis, only the end result.) Laurel's bravura execution of this sequence provides evidence, if any is required, of a fine actor and superb physical comedian.

In one very funny set piece, Pyckle's dog (Tige, a.k.a. Pete the Pup from Hal Roach's Our Gang comedies) laps up some of the potion that has accidentally spilled onto his food plate. As Pyckle assures an angry mob that he hasn't seen the "vicious fiend" they've been pursuing, the dog emerges from the laboratory, now transformed into his evil canine counterpart — illustrated by the fright wig he's wearing! The demonic pooch grabs Pyckle by the seat of the pants and drags him back into the lab, where he goes berserk on his master.

Dr. Pyckle and Mr. Pride was shot on pre-existing sets on the Universal Studios lot, which gives the film a production polish far beyond its moderate budget. The studio wardrobe and set design also adds to the verisimilitude, which in turn heightens the comedic aspects of the picture.

The reviews for *Dr. Pyckle and Mr. Pride* were generally favorable, though some felt, surprisingly, it was not up to Laurel's usual standards. *Film Daily* stated, "It has been extremely well produced, but the story is not one that lends itself particularly to comedy, although Laurel does fine work.... The scenes in which 'Pride' roams the streets and wreaks his evil deeds are the funniest in the picture." *Moving Picture World* reported, "There are several amusing moments and while not as uproarious as some of the star's previous burlesques and lacking in more subtle touches it nevertheless should prove entertaining especially to patrons who like to see burlesques of familiar stories." But the *Exhibitors Trade Review* noted, "Stan does mighty good work in the burlesque of Robert Louis Stevenson's weird mystery tale. The transition scenes where Stan changes from Dr. Pyckle to Mr. Pride are very well done, and are worthy of a more ambitious picture."

---

*This is a reference to the "57 Varieties" slogan the Heinz Company used to promote their food products. (Today, it's been shortened to "Heinz 57.")

For years, *Dr. Pyckle and Mr. Pride* was thought to be a lost film. Actually, it wasn't lost, just difficult to see. Archivist Raymond Rohauer, a controversial figure in the film-collecting community, owned a print but didn't make it accessible to the general public. Yet when he supplied material for Jay Ward's *Fractured Flickers* TV series (1963), clips from *Dr. Pyckle* were used for a recurring "Minute Mystery" segment in which Laurel was presented as master detective "Sherman Oaks." Rohauer was fanatical about guarding his property and *Dr. Pyckle and Mr. Pride* was just one of many titles he kept under wraps. Stan Laurel fans who were intrigued by the brief excerpts on *Fractured Flickers* had to wait years to see the entire film (or at least an approximation of it), and even then it wasn't the Rohauer print but an inferior-quality French edition.

Robert Louis Stevenson's tale would inspire future movie sendups, resulting in numerous clunkers (including *Jekyll and Hyde ... Together Again*, *Dr. Jekyll and Ms. Hyde*, and *Dr. Heckyl and Mr. Hype*), and a certifiable gem: Jerry Lewis's *The Nutty Professor* (1963).

Half a Man

Cast

Stan Laurel	Winchell McSweeny
Blanche Payson	A dainty French Ma'm'selle
Julie Leonard	The girl
Tui Lorraine Bow	Bow Female castaway
Murray Rock	Boat crew member

Credits

Harry Sweet	Director
Murray Rock	Assistant director
Edgar Lyons	Cinematographer
Tay Garnett	Titles

Also known as *No Sleep on the Deep*
A Stan Laurel production presented by Joe Rock.
Copyrighted August 30, 1925.
Released August 30, 1925, by Standard Cinema
Corporation/Film Booking Office of America.
Two reels.

Half a Man is not a very consistent or imaginative comedy. There are some pleasantly amusing moments, but not enough to sustain its relatively brief running time. It does, however, allow Laurel to explore playing a meek, sexless character with at least some basic qualities of the Stanley persona for which he would become legendary.

After his father, a fisherman, goes broke, Winchell McSweeny is sent out

Murray Rock (left, Joe Rock's brother) and Stan Laurel in *Half a Man* (1925).

into the world to fend for himself. Winchell's mother makes her inexperienced son promise to stay away from women ("I'll fight 'em off," he swears), but he winds up stumbling aboard a fishing boat filled with female passengers. Winchell carefully avoids all contact with the women, but does agree to photograph them. (When did he suddenly develop photographic skills?) The explosive flash powder sets fire to the ship and the ladies are loaded onto life boats, while the men — all but Winchell — bravely take their chances by diving into the water.

Stranded on a desert isle (actually, Santa Catalina Island in California), the women are pining for male companionship when waterlogged Winchell washes ashore and becomes their collective object of desire. Panic-stricken,

Winchell fights off their advances until he discovers his newfound desirability gives him power over the castaways. His reign comes to a halt when the male crew members wash ashore and the women begin pursuing them. This leaves Winchell free to dally with a pretty young woman with whom he had become smitten, but his freedom is short-lived. The other men throw themselves back into the surf and the man-hungry femmes start chasing Winchell all over again.

Half a Man takes a trite, one-joke premise and does little with it. Harold Lloyd explored his character's fear of females in *Girl Shy* (1924) with hilarious results, and Jerry Lewis used the theme for his brilliant farce, *The Ladies Man* (1961). But this unremarkable two-reel comedy can't even muster up a fraction of the laughs evoked by those two feature-length films.

It does begin promisingly, as the opening scene establishes Laurel's wimpy character as an inept simpleton. As Winchell sets off on his own, his father consoles his weeping spouse: "Don't worry mother — The child can take care of himself," and we see Winchell entangled in a fishing net, staggering along while trying to extricate himself. It is a neat visual image (although it can be argued that Laurel lets it run too long), and sets the premise in motion with a solid gag.

Once Winchell is aboard the female-laden boat, the main premise is shunted aside for a series of protracted and tiresome gags involving seasickness. Having the island inhabited by love-starved women gets the film back on track. Winchell cannot avoid the situation, especially since the leader of the females is Blanche Payson, an Amazonian comedienne who was already a veteran at playing such domineering roles. (A few years later, she would work with Laurel and Hardy in *Below Zero, Our Wife* and *Helpmates*.) However, the comedy gives us a twist by having Winchell realize that his status as the sole love object gives him power and authority over these women. They are willing to do whatever he asks, and this gives the meek Winchell the sort of power and authority he had never experienced in the past. Whenever the situation gets out of hand, Winchell threatens to jump off a cliff, and the women bow to his every command. (Unfortunately, this ploy backfires when Payson sees the other men washing ashore, prompting her to grab Winchell and hurl him off the cliff.)

In a funny role reversal of melodramatic damsel-in-distress scenes, Payson can no longer suppress her carnal urges and creeps up behind the carefree Winchell, like a lioness stalking her prey. When he finally notices her, it's too late, and the other women look on in horror as poor Winchell is nearly ravaged by his oversized attacker.

It is curious that this second Laurel film directed by Harry Sweet is uneven in the same manner as *The Sleuth* had been. Joe Rock's later recalling of Sweet carefully storyboarding his directorial efforts is belied by the examples presented with the two Laurel films he helmed. Both lack the structure that Percy Pembroke managed apparently without the use of Sweet's storyboard method. (Before his untimely death in 1933, Sweet went on to direct Edgar Kennedy two-reelers at RKO.)

Half a Man was the last of the 12 Laurel productions that Joe Rock had promised his distributors. Rob Stone reported that Rock shot the films within seven months, but indicated it took 12 months to complete them, allowing the producer to pocket the five months of extra-budgeted money. This left Laurel without a paycheck for extended periods of time, and his percentage was allegedly withheld as well. Stan found employment back at the Roach Studios.

8

Laurel Returns to Hal Roach Again

It has been claimed that when he signed with Hal Roach in 1925, for the third time, Stan Laurel expressed that he no longer wanted to act, preferring instead to spend his time writing and directing. However, the decision to keep Laurel behind the scenes was more convoluted than that, a result of a contractual stipulation imposed by Joe Rock.

Laurel was now an established star comedian and Roach wanted him to continue in this vein. But Rock still had several Laurel comedies to release and did not want his distributors to know they were already completed. Rock had finished 12 Laurel comedies in seven months, but told his distributor that the pictures would take a full 12 months to produce. While this practice would allow Rock to keep the extra budgeted money, it left Laurel without any income during the five months he waited for the films to be sold. So when Laurel accepted an offer to rejoin Roach, Rock stipulated that Laurel not appear onscreen, so his distributor would not catch on that the Rock-produced Laurel comedies were no longer in production.

Writing and directing were hardly new responsibilities to Laurel, who had been working in these capacities, sans credit, for some time. The challenge of creating films for other comedians was something that interested Laurel a great deal, so he was eager to go back to work at the Roach Studios.

Oliver Hardy, still a freelance actor, was working on the Roach lot with increasing frequency, though not as a contract player. Hardy's expert performances enhanced any production in which he appeared, and his services were much in demand by directors and star comedians. Laurel stated in later years that he tried to use Hardy as often as he could on the films he directed, little realizing that their onscreen partnership was imminent.

This was a particularly good time in Stan Laurel's life. He was happily married to Lois Neilson, gainfully employed, established as a popular comedian, and respected in the movie industry as a talented writer and director. He was not yet a star of the caliber of Chaplin, Keaton or Lloyd, but he was on the verge of joining their ranks.

Laurel Films Without Laurel (The writer-director period)

Laurel was on the Roach staff for fewer than five days before he was given a directorial assignment, helming a script he had written for comedian James Finlayson. Fin had worked frequently with Laurel, and was a veteran of both the Mack Sennett and Hal Roach comedy factories. Fin had already completed two starring pictures for other directors, but with this third venture, Stan had the task of helping to groom Finlayson into a comedy star. Roach's attempt to establish Fin as the star of his own series was not the success everyone hoped for, but Finlayson would lend able support in many comedies at the studio for the next 15 years.

The first Finlayson vehicle Laurel directed from his own script was *Chasing the Chaser* (filmed May 11–14, 1925), a two-reeler released July 5, 1925. Stan's previous working relationship with Finlayson gave them an immediate and comfortable rapport, and the resulting film is quite funny. Laurel realized Fin's capacity for exhibiting bluster and embarrassment, so he cast him as a husband with a roving eye whose wife hires a private investigator to catch him cheating. The thing is, Fin's flirtations

Laurel returned to Roach as a writer and director with no plans to be on screen, in 1925.

are all rather innocent, so he has to be trapped into an impending tryst. The detective his wife hires is a female impersonator who poses as the new maid and flirts with Fin until the two are in a compromising position. At that point, the wife is summoned from another room. However, when Fin discovers the ruse, he asserts his manhood and reclaims control of the household.

This story allows Laurel to present Fin in his best light. The short, bald, plain-looking man is hardly the lady-killer type, but he considers himself to be a handsome rogue. While nothing comes of these flirtations, perhaps Fin merely wants to feed his delusional ego.

In the first shot, Fin keeps trying to walk quickly in front of women so he can see if they are pretty; he then sets himself up to be noticed by them. It is staged perfectly by Laurel, who uses several edits, cutting from different angles, and changing from a moving camera to one that is stationary to capture the action. This keeps the pace brisk and allows us to look at Fin from every angle, showing his tenacity as well as his skewed self-perception.

Rather than use one of the Roach regulars as the detective, Laurel recruited Fredrick Ko Vert, a professional female impersonator, for the role. Ko Vert is as plain and balding as Fin, but with expert use of makeup, clothing, and a wig, he could transform himself into an attractive woman, which is perfect for his scenes with Fin. Their comical dance to a phonograph record concludes with the maid fainting, which forces Fin into the compromising position that will prove his dalliances to the wife and earn the detective his fee.

James Finlayson starred in several films written and directed by Laurel, circa 1925.

When Fin discovers

the maid is a man, he chases him away with a gun and rants to his sobbing and apologetic wife. He sits her on his lap, promising to never look at another woman again, then sees an attractive girl boarding a streetcar outside his home. He immediately rushes to the window, throwing his wife off of his lap, as the film concludes. Laurel, choosing to end this short with a gag, also reasserts how Fin has no intention of changing.

For his first script, rather hastily assembled, and his initial directorial assignment at Roach, Laurel presents a keen eye for his star and his attempt at helping the studio to groom Finlayson into the breakout comedy star they wanted. By 1925, Roach wanted a comedian at the level former employee Harold Lloyd had become, or as popular as Buster Keaton. Maybe even as popular as Charlie Chaplin himself. Now, in retrospect, it seems silly that James Finlayson, funny though he is, was considered as a possibility to reach that lofty level. He does not have the creative capacity of Lloyd, Keaton, or Chaplin. However, Laurel did, and Roach recognized the possibilities. (It should be noted that a nursemaid with a baby buggy whom Fin notices early in *Chasing the Chaser* is 18-year-old Fay Wray, who would achieve screen immortality for her role in *King Kong* [1933], which would define her career until her death at age 96 in 2003.)

Using the staple of military comedy for the next Finlayson vehicle, Laurel, interestingly enough, investigates a possible team dynamic. *Unfriendly Enemies* (filmed May 19–23, 1925, released September 13, 1925, has Fin and George Rowe (who appeared in Laurel's solo comedies) teamed as cameramen covering the war. While *Unfriendly Enemies* is not quite as amusing as *Chasing the Chaser*, it was already evident that Laurel's films for Roach were uniformly the funniest comedies the studio was releasing, judging by critical responses and exhibitor comments. Laurel was astutely aware of how to best utilize Finlayson's talent, and gave him a co-star to bounce his reactive style of comedy off. Fin's inability to achieve Harold Lloyd's level of popularity notwithstanding, it was clear that Laurel was working hard to properly showcase Fin.

Laurel's third attempt to make Fin a lead comedian, *Yes, Yes, Nanette* (co-directed by Clarence Hennecke and filmed May 28–June 2, 1925, and released July 19, 1925), is also a very funny one-reeler, and further benefits from the presence of Oliver Hardy as a jealous boyfriend. *Yes, Yes, Nanette* has historical significance of Laurel and Hardy working together (as director and actor) for the first time at the Hal Roach Studios. (That Stan and Ollie would be teamed in less than two years never entered anyone's mind at this point.)

In *Yes, Yes, Nanette* (the title references the popular stage play *No, No, Nanette*), Laurel continues to zero in on Finlayson's strengths as a comedian.

Brought home to meet his new bride's family, Fin gets to react in his inimitable style to an overbearing father, a disappointed mother, a giggly and flirtatious sister, and a pesky brother. Oliver Hardy is the bride's old boyfriend, still attracted to his former flame and itching for a fight.

As demonstrated in *Chasing the Chaser*, Laurel liked worm-turns scenarios where Fin reasserts his manhood at the conclusion. *Yes, Yes, Nanette* ends this way as well, with Fin trouncing the much larger Hardy after a reel's worth of humiliation, winning the respect of all.

The Laurel-Finlayson collaborations are quite funny and demonstrate Laurel's capacity to intertwine characters and gags for maximum effect. But since the Finlayson comedies hadn't caught on with the public, Roach still searched for a breakout star. Laurel was reassigned to work with Clyde Cook, an Australian-born comedian whose wiry dexterity onstage had earned him the nickname "Kangaroo Boy."

Laurel's first film with Cook, *Moonlight and Noses* (filmed June 9–20, 1925, with retakes on July 6), released October 4, 1925, survives only in partial form. Judging by the extant first reel, we see Laurel's modification in his approach to Cook, as opposed to Finlayson. Laurel seemed to perceive the genesis of the Laurel-Hardy partnership without realizing it. In *Moonlight and Noses*, he teams diminutive Cook with hulking Noah Young as they play a couple of cat burglars hired by a doctor (Finlayson, back to supporting roles) to steal a body from a graveyard. The doctor is accused of misdiagnosing a patient who later died, so he wants to exhume the body to prove his innocence.

Anyone familiar with the Laurel and Hardy films will recognize ideas in *Moonlight and Noses* that Laurel would later use in *Habeas Corpus* (1928; directed by James Parrott, supervised by Leo McCarey) and *Night Owls* (1930; directed by Parrott). Even the dynamic between Cook and Young has overtones of Stan and Ollie. Cook is expected to do the dirty work while Young waits outside. Young is effectively frightened enough to join him. Cook is clearly the subordinate, but will still stand up to Young on occasion.

Cook seemed to click more effectively than Fin, and a series followed. Critics at the time indicated that scare comedies had already become standard fare and that many were not funny and fewer still were spooky. *Moonlight and Noses*, however, was applauded for being both funny and spooky.

Laurel directed Cook again in *Wandering Papas* (filmed July 13–August 1, 1925, with retakes on September 5), released February 21, 1926, which also featured Oliver Hardy. While Cook is not teamed with Hardy, the experience did allow Laurel once again to be impressed with the bigger man's deft skills as an actor and comedian. A funny (if predictable) comedy, *Wandering Papas* is set in a lumber camp and recalls earlier Laurel films such as *The Noon*

Whistle (1923) and *Smithy* (1924), as well as two later Laurel and Hardy pictures, *The Finishing Touch* (1928) and *Busy Bodies* (1933). It is also reminiscent of Larry Semon's *The Sawmill* (1922), with Hardy as a lumber-camp foreman.

This idea of teaming Cook with a larger co-star continued with *Starvation Blues* (filmed September 14–29, 1925), released December 13, 1925. Richard Wallace and James W. Horne directed from a script on which Laurel was merely one of the four credited writers (the others being Richard Wallace, Frank Terry and Sherbourne Shields). Cook and Syd Crossley are cast as street musicians playing out in the cold, a premise Laurel would reuse for the Laurel and Hardy two-reeler *Below Zero* (1930; directed by James Parrott).

At this point it appears Laurel was exploring what could be done with a team situation, apparently feeling Cook's talents were best suited to having a partner. Laurel also had opportunities to direct Oliver Hardy and assess his formidable skills as a comic actor. All of these factors would certainly later shape his perspective as he and Hardy found themselves appearing together in films as their careers at the Roach studio continued. While the Cook series did not eventually pan out any better than the Finlayson one had, Cook

Clyde Cook (far right) starred in *Starvation Blues* (1925), which was co-written by Stan Laurel. Next to Cook is Syd Crossley.

retained very fond memories of working with Laurel. In a 1980 interview with the authors, Cook stated:

> Stan Laurel was the most creative person I worked with. Of all the pictures I did for Mr. Roach, the ones with Laurel are the funniest. We just had a basic scenario back then. We pretty much worked out the picture as we shot it. Laurel always came up with such wonderful ideas. And he would laugh as he told us, and we would laugh with him. It was a terrific association.

Laurel continued to write and direct, often in collaboration with others, enjoying his steady employment at Roach and the freedom to tap into his creativity on the other side of the camera. There is no record of him missing acting for the camera and, by all accounts, this was an extremely satisfying and productive period.

In an interview with Boyd Verb for *Films in Review* (March 1959 issue), Laurel recalled the off-the-cuff nature of working from a so-called script:

> We did have a script, but it didn't consist of the routines and gags. It outlined the basic story idea and just a plan for us to follow. But when it came to each scene, we and the gagmen would work out ideas. Oh, a few gags were mentioned here and there in the script, but they were always *worked out* on the set. We'd rehearse them a few times and then shoot them.

With this sort of working method, it is difficult to ascertain the exact nature of Laurel's contributions to these collaborations. For instance, Laurel was one of ten writers who devised gags for *Don Key (Son of Burro)*, released May 23, 1926. He also collaborated with others on the scripts of *Your Husband's Past* (released February 7, 1926), *What's the World Coming To?* (January 17, 1926), *Dizzy Daddies* (which he also co-directed; March 14, 1926), *Wife Tamers* (March 28, 1926), *Never Too Old* (co-directed; June 27, 1926), *Along Came Auntie* (July 25, 1926) and *Should Husbands Pay?* (co-directed; September 5, 1926).

With Richard Wallace, Laurel co-directed *Madame Mystery* (filmed December 10–24, 1925), released April 18, 1926, a vehicle for fading movie vamp Theda Bara, co-starring Oliver Hardy. Laurel also worked on the script with four other writers (Grover Jones, Krag Johnston, Hal Yates, Carl Harbaugh). *The Merry Widower* (filmed February 19–March 9, 1926), released August 1, 1926, was another Wallace-Laurel directorial collaboration.

Wallace and Laurel were the credited co-directors (under the supervision of F. Richard Jones) of *Raggedy Rose* (filmed March 15–April 2, 1926; retakes April 15–17; released November 7, 1926), a three-reeler starring Mabel Normand, formerly one of Mack Sennett's leading players. (A five-reel version of *Raggedy Rose* also exists, although how and where it was distributed remains unclear.) However, Rob Stone has uncovered paperwork indicating that it was Laurel who was most responsible for the direction of this film (he also co-wrote the script). At the time, Normand's name had been tarnished by scandal (director William Desmond Taylor was murdered and Normand had been a suspect) and years of drug abuse had taken its toll. According to co-star Anita Garvin, Normand was trying to make a comeback, and a sympathetic Roach believed in her. Garvin also stated that Normand's mind was "pretty far shot" when she made the picture. Nevertheless, the reception to *Raggedy Rose* was positive — it received a standing ovation at a preview — and Roach followed it up with another Normand three-reeler, *The Nickel Hopper*, released December 5, 1926, co-written by Laurel and co-starring Oliver Hardy as a hopped-up jazz drummer. Mabel Normand made three more short comedies for Roach: *Anything Once!*, *Should Men Walk Home?* and *One Hour Married*, all 1927 releases. They were her last film appearances; her health declined and she died of tuberculosis on February 22, 1930.

Laurel's last solo directorial effort was *Wise Guys Prefer Brunettes* (filmed May 14–June 2, 1926; additional scenes June 7), released October 3, 1926. Ostensibly a vehicle for Helen Chadwick, it devotes more footage to the antics of James Finlayson as the harried Dean of an undisciplined college. The supporting cast includes Ted Healy, of Ted Healy and His Stooges fame. (His Stooges, of course, being The Three Stooges.) Laurel and Hardy would later appear with Healy, though not in the same scenes, in *Hollywood Party* (1934). Later, Stan would cast Betty Healy, Ted's former wife, as Mrs. Laurel in *Our Relations* (1936).

It seemed inevitable that Laurel would return to onscreen acting full-time and this eventually transpired strictly by accident. Or, more precisely, because of an accident. Laurel wound up as a last-minute replacement for an injured Oliver Hardy, who was set to play a role originally intended for Syd Crossley. It was not only Stan Laurel's official return to the screen, but it was one more small step in the direction of his teaming with Hardy.

Get 'Em Young

Cast

Harry Myers	Orvid Joy
Stan Laurel	Summers, the butler*
Eugenia Gilbert	Gloria
Max Davidson	Isaac Goldberg
Charlotte Mineau	The hired Mrs. Joy
Fred Malatesta	The executor of the will
Ernie Wood	Female impersonator†

*The character is referred to as "Stan" in the version available on DVD from Kino On Video.
 †Sources list the character as "Lawrence Lavender Virgin," although he is unnamed in the DVD edition.

Credits

Fred Guiol (and Stan Laurel, uncredited) . . . . Director
F. Richard Jones . . . . Production supervisor
Sherbourne Shields, Jean Yarbrough . . . . Assistant directors
Stan Laurel, James Parrott, Hal Yates . . . . Writers
Harry Gersted . . . . Cinematographer
Frank Young, Alvin Lange . . . . Assistant cinematographers
LeRoy Lodwig, Harry Lieb . . . . Editors
H. M. Walker . . . . Titles
Leo Samwell, William Wessling . . . . Props
Elva Nelson . . . . Teacher

A Hal Roach production. Copyrighted October 26, 1926.
Production dates: June 19–July 2, 1926.
Miniature photography: August 5, 1926.
Released October 31, 1926, by Pathé Exchange.
Two reels.

Among longtime Laurel and Hardy enthusiasts, the reputation of *Get'Em Young* rests not on artistic merit — the film was not widely available for viewing until recently — but on its historical importance as a pivotal (if not immediately obvious) step toward bringing Stan and Ollie together as a screen team.

Stan was assigned to direct *Get 'Em Young* with Oliver Hardy slated for a supporting role as the butler.* With Stan at the helm, filming began on Saturday, June 19, 1926. During that weekend, Hardy, preparing a meal at home, burned his arm when he spilled hot gravy from a leg of lamb. The injury prevented Hardy from starting his participation in the picture the following Monday, and with no other performer available to fill the sudden vacancy, production supervisor F. Richard Jones recruited Laurel to replace Hardy. Laurel was reluctant to return to acting — his legal issues with Joe Rock were still ongoing — but a raise in salary (an additional $100 per week) erased his opposition to the idea. Fred Guiol assumed the directing chores, and Stan was back in front of the cameras once again.

A vehicle for faded star Harry Myers (who, five years later, would have a prominent supporting role as the drunken millionaire in Chaplin's masterpiece, *City Lights*), *Get 'Em Young* employs the time-honored premise of a man who must be wed by a certain date and time in order to collect an inheritance. During an ocean voyage, Orvid Joy meets Gloria, another passenger, and impulsively marries her. Orvid is returning to the U.S. to collect a million-dollar inheritance that is contingent upon him having a wife, although his love for Gloria is genuine. Unaware of his client's newlywed status, Isaac

---

Rob Stone has noted that in the original outline for Get 'Em Young, *Syd Crossley was slated for the role of the butler while Oliver Hardy was to play the part of the female impersonator.*

Goldberg, Orvid's lawyer, hires a woman to pose as Mrs. Joy in name only, to satisfy the demands of the executor of the will. Gloria sees Isaac's telegram referring to Orvid's "wife" and when the faux Mrs. Joy rushes up to Orvid after the boat docks, Gloria storms off.

Required to hold a marriage ceremony in the presence of a notary, Orvid hires a female impersonator to fill in for the missing bride. But the persnickety drag performer refuses to wear the shabby wedding dress, so Summers, the butler, is recruited for the masquerade. Summers winds up getting drunk and reduces the ceremony to chaos. Fortunately, Gloria materializes in the nick of time to prove Orvid is really married after all.

Stan's official return to the screen (discounting his cameos in *Seeing the World* and *45 Minutes from Hollywood*) is not the unqualified success one would have hoped for. For the first two-thirds of the film, his character cries over *everything*, and the incessant whining quickly becomes tiresome. (In later years, Laurel would single out *Get 'Em Young* as the origin of his famous cry, even though he had performed the bit in previous films. The crying routine was much funnier in the Laurel and Hardy comedies, where it was used more judiciously.) Stan's performance is also hampered by his appearance: for whatever reason, his nose is darkened, giving it a perpetual glow. This curious, ill-advised affectation is needlessly distracting and completely at odds with the appearance of the other cast members.

Despite these drawbacks, Stan does deliver some solid laughs during the final third, when he becomes an unwilling substitute for the missing bride. His awkward attempts to emulate a feminine walk foreshadow similar scenes in the Laurel and Hardy comedies *That's My Wife* (1929) and *Jitterbugs* (1943).*

Things kick into high gear once Stan, attempting to calm his nerves, downs a bottle of alcohol and gets roaring drunk. His character *finally* stops crying and his inebriated assertiveness showcases Stan's gift for physical comedy. (Although Harry Myers wasn't in the same league as physical comic, he establishes a good rapport with Stan and proves to be an effective foil.)

All told, *Get 'Em Young* is a mediocre knockabout farce, though the *Exhibitors Trade Review* was charitable: "This is broad burlesque so well handled by director and performers it can not fail to evoke genuinely hardy laughs." The *Kinematograph Weekly* hit closer to home: "More conspicuous for the hard work of its cast than its humor. Slapstick scenes are most effective, others being forced and occasionally in execrable taste."

---

*Stan also appeared in drag in other Laurel and Hardy comedies, including Why Girls Love Sailors *(1927),* Duck Soup *(1927),* Sugar Daddies *(1927),* Another Fine Mess *(1930) and* Twice Two *(1933).*

Stan may have considered the overly frantic *Get 'Em Young* to be a missed opportunity because he later revamped the spouse-impersonation premise as *That's My Wife* (1929), a hilarious Laurel and Hardy two-reeler in which clever gags are complemented by nuanced performances — illustrating the creative strides Stan would make in three short years.

On the Front Page

Cast

Lillian Rich	Countess Polasky*
Tyler Brooke	Young Hornby
Stan Laurel	Dangerfield
Bull Montana	Polasky's private secretary
Edwards Davis	James W. Hornby†
Edgar Dearing	Motorcycle cop
Leo White	Beauty expert
Rolfe Sedan	Beauty expert
William Courtright	J. W. Hornby's assistant
Bill Brokaw	Party guest

Credits

James Parrott (and Fred Guiol, uncredited‡)	Director
F. Richard Jones	Production supervisor
Jean Yarbrough	Assistant director
James Parrott, Stan Laurel	Writers
Frank Young	Cinematographer
Alvin Lange	Assistant cinematographer
Harry Lieb	Editor
R. O. Sanders, Sherbourne Shields	Props

A Hal Roach production. Copyrighted October 26, 1926.
Production dates: August 23–September 4, 1926.
Released November 28, 1926, by Pathé Exchange.
Two reels.

On the Front Page reworks the basic set-up of *Get 'Em Young*, with Stan in a supporting role as a butler who helps his employer get out of a predicament. In both films, Stan outshines the top-billed stars, even with imperfect material. This time, however, he gives a better-modulated performance that brings him within hailing distance of his soon-to-be familiar Stanley persona.

---

*Also spelled Polaski in the film.

†An in-joke reference to James W. Horne, a contract director at the Hal Roach Studios. Horne would later direct several Laurel and Hardy films, including *Big Business* (1929), *Chickens Come Home* (1931), *Beau Hunks* (1931; in which Horne also co-starred), *Thicker Than Water* (1935), and *Way Out West* (1937).

‡Fred Guiol, the original director, was replaced by James Parrott four days into the production.

8. Stan Returns to Hal Roach Again

European vamp Countess Polansky, notorious for her scandalous reputation ("five ex-husbands and countless lawyers"), arrives in America and causes an immediate sensation in the tabloids. James W. Hornby, publisher and chief mud-slinger of the *Daily Squawk*, is furious that the *Daily Gazette*, a rival newspaper, has scooped him on a story about the countess's affair with an unnamed American billionaire. Hornby's ne'er-do-well son, one of the staff members, promises to uncover all the details surrounding the rumors.

Young Hornby hits upon the bright idea of having his butler, Dangerfield, pose as a wealthy suitor so he can snap a photo of the countess in a compromising situation. The reluctant Dangerfield puts on a tuxedo belonging to Hornby's father and goes to the hotel where the countess is staying. But the countess gets wind of the ruse and decides to teach them a lesson by pretending to seduce Dangerfield. Her amorous advances stir the libido of the normally girl-shy butler and he begins chasing her around the room. To ensure a newsworthy scandal, young Hornby telephones the police to report that the countess is hosting a wild party.

The countess's bulldog-like private secretary attempts to throw Dangerfield out of the apartment. Dangerfield manages to get away but his jacket and trousers are torn off in the process. After the police break down the door, reporters identify the mysterious suitor by a name sewn into the lining of the jacket: J. W. Hornby. The next morning, the headlines declare "PROMINENT NEWSPAPER PUBLISHER ESCAPES RAID, BUT LEAVES HIS CLOTHES BEHIND," as a golf-club-wielding Hornby chases his son and the butler down the street.

Stan Laurel is a girl-shy butler who tries to seduce a vamp (Lillian Rich) in *On the Front Page* (1926).

Comparing Stan's performance here to the one he gave in *Get 'Em Young*, it's amazing to realize these films were made less than two months apart. The desperate, relentless mugging has been replaced with a surer sense of characterization; there is also better plot development. As a *veddy* proper English butler, Stan's deportment is appropriately formal ("Your evening weed, sir," he says while placing a humidor before the young Hornby), so there's none of the exaggerated gesticulating that often undermined earlier performances. As the plot complications mount, his behavior reveals traits that we would come to associate with Stanley: the dazed, blank-faced puzzlement as his mind slowly processes information, and the shedding of tears out of fear or hopelessness (as opposed to incessantly crying for little reason). However, he isn't quite Stanley yet, particularly during the reverse-seduction scene in which Dangerfield aggressively pursues the countess. The skirt-chasing aspect of Laurel's early persona is at odds with the child-man he would become, and in the Laurel and Hardy films, Stanley's romantic pursuits usually involved a shy smile and a hand wave. (An exception is *Putting Pants on Philip*, an atypical but funny L and H effort.)

As he did in *Get 'Em Young*, Stan steals the picture. Tyler Brooke isn't distinctive enough to make much of an impression as a lead comedian. His shot at stardom was short-lived and he was soon reduced to minor supporting roles.* Top-billed Lillian Rich is also no competition for Stan, although she does as well in her relatively limited femme-fatale role. (The outrageously lavish set design of Countess Polansky's apartment—complete with spider-web curtains—compliments the lovely Rich's spirited performance.)

Some of the film's funniest sequences involve a running gag with young Hornby encountering motorcycle cop Edgar Dearing at the worst possible moments. Dearing was a real-life motorcycle patrolman who started playing supporting roles in Hal Roach comedies, supplying his own uniform and motorcycle. Dearing appeared in a few Laurel and Hardy comedies, most notably *Two Tars* (1928), before becoming a full-time actor. He worked with the boys as late as 1944, turning up briefly (as a motorcycle cop) in *The Big Noise*.

Brooke and Laurel have the lead roles in the picture, and the *Motion Picture News* pointed out this discrepancy: "Lillian Rich is starred in this comedy although the real work done by Stan Laurel and Tyler Brooke of her supporting company would seem to entitle them to the stellar honors ... but [the premise's]

**In 1929, Tyler Brooke sued Oliver Hardy after an alleged altercation during a billiards game. Although he appeared in several comedy shorts produced by Hal Roach during the mid-to-late 1920s, Brooke's association with the studio ended at this point. He was not seen in another Roach production until* Two Mugs from Brooklyn *(1942), made after Laurel and Hardy severed their connection with Roach. Brooke committed suicide in 1943.*

possibilities are hardly realized. Strenuous work by capable players somewhat wasted."

On the Front Page is hardly an unsung comedy classic, but it's a good example of the type of slapstick drawing-room farces that were so prevalent during the era. Better yet, glimpses of an emerging Stanley provide amusing hints of the comic brilliance that would soon follow.

Postscript: *On the Front Page* was put into production after another project, slated for Stan and Oliver Hardy, was shelved. For more on this aborted project, see the entry on *Why Girls Love Sailors*.

9

LAUREL WITH HARDY

The initial Hal Roach productions that featured Stan Laurel and Oliver Hardy were not true Laurel and Hardy movies. In the first one, *45 Minutes From Hollywood* (1926), they don't even share any scenes together. (Hardy has a prominent supporting role, while a barely recognizable Laurel makes a fleeting appearance.) The very next effort, *Duck Soup* (1927), presented them as a full-fledged team, revealing traces of the rapport they would soon refine into a unique screen partnership. But the potential of their union was not immediately seized upon and the next few films that followed were essentially solo Laurel comedies that Hardy just happened to be in. With the exceptions of *Duck Soup* and *Do Detectives Think?* (1927) — which came even closer to capturing the familiar Stan and Ollie characters — Laurel is the lead comedian or shares the spotlight with old crony James Finlayson, while Hardy provides able if limited support.

These early entries have been criticized for failing to take full advantage of Laurel and Hardy's combined talents. It's understandable that fans and historians would grow impatient with the prolonged development, particularly in light of the seemingly mystifying regressions that occurred whenever the team was on the verge of a legitimate partnership. However, their ultimate teaming only seems obvious in hindsight. At the time these pictures were made, they were still being approached as Stan Laurel vehicles. Having Laurel share the spotlight with Finlayson was a holdover from Stan's previous stay at the Roach Studios (of course, Laurel's admiration for Fin's talent had a lot to do with it, too). It's far too easy to second-guess and criticize the decision-makers for not teaming Stan with Ollie sooner, especially from a viewpoint several decades after the fact. The fact that Laurel and Hardy eventually *were* teamed is what counts the most.

Categorizing these early outings as "Laurel and Hardy" comedies can lead to confusion and disappointment, especially for uninitiated fans. Or, for that matter, even diehard fans. But to collectively dismiss these films is to overlook their virtues, if not as bona fide L and H efforts then as examples of '20s-era silent comedy. If the lessons learned from these pictures were necessary factors in the evolution of Stan and Ollie's beautifully cultivated screen personalities, then their existence is justified, regardless of how unsatisfying the results may seem by comparison.

Some Supporting Appearances

In 1926, just as he was about to begin using Oliver Hardy more frequently as a supporting player in his solo comedies, Stan Laurel made a couple of fleeting appearances in Hal Roach productions. The first was in *Seeing the World*, released February 13, 1927, an Our Gang comedy that utilized footage shot during a European vacation taken by James Finlayson and director Robert McGowan. With a cameraman along, they filmed many sites with Finlayson appearing on camera in some scenes.

Upon returning to the States, Fin and McGowan gave their footage to Roach, who had his staff construct an Our Gang comedy around it. Scenes with the gang were filmed at the studio from October 29 to November 15, 1926, and combined with the European material to make it look like they had traveled overseas. Stan Laurel's contribution is a cameo appearance with Frank Butler, set in front of a London fish and chips shop. (This scene was shot on the Roach lot and was not part of the authentic European footage.)

Laurel also appeared briefly in the aforementioned *45 Minutes From Hollywood*, released December 26, 1926, in a role likely intended for James Finlayson, since Stan is made up to look like Fin, right down to his prominent mustache. The fact that Oliver Hardy appears in this film, in a larger supporting role, has identified it as a Laurel and Hardy comedy, even though Stan and Ollie have no interaction.

Finally, Laurel and Hardy both appear, separately, in the Charley Chase comedy *Now I'll Tell One* (filmed April 20–25, 1927), released October 5, 1927. At this writing, only the second reel survives, and for years it was believed that only Laurel had a supporting role in the picture. But the rediscovery of this footage has shown us that Hardy also appears, although not in any scenes with Laurel. (Stan plays Charley's lawyer in the main courtroom scenes, and Ollie is seen as a policeman in a flashback.) While by some criteria this categorizes *Now I'll Tell One* as a Laurel and Hardy film, it is technically a starring vehicle for Charley Chase.

We did not believe these titles warranted separate sections in our discussion of Laurel's starring films, but they are certainly worth mentioning.

Duck Soup

Cast

Stan Laurel	Mr. Laurel / "Agnes"
Oliver Hardy	Mr. Hardy
James Marcus	Colonel Buckshot
Madeline Hurlock	Lady Plumtree
William Austin	Lord Plumtree
Bob Kortman	Forest Ranger
Stuart Holmes	Forest Ranger
William Courtright	Colonel's butler

The character names are taken from the English-translated intertitles of the U.S. DVD edition, which were translated from a surviving European print that had French and Dutch titles. As originally written, Laurel's character name was James Hives and Hardy's was Marmaduke Maltravers. In the DVD edition released in Europe by KirchGroup, Laurel's character is Hives, Hardy's is unspecified, and the names of supporting characters differ: Colonel Buckshot is Colonel Blood, and Lord and Lady Plumtree are Lord and Lady Tarbotham.

Credits

Fred L. Guiol	Director
Leo McCarey	Supervising director
Richard Currier	Film Editor
Arthur J. Jefferson	Story ("Home From the Honeymoon")
H. M. Walker	Titles

A Hal Roach production. Copyrighted January 13, 1927.
Production dates: September 20–October 2, 1926.
Released March 13, 1927, by Pathé.
Two reels.

For nearly five decades *Duck Soup* was considered a lost film, leaving fans and historians to speculate about its contents and merits. In *The Films of Laurel and Hardy* (1967), William K. Everson echoed the commonly held belief that it was essentially a solo Laurel comedy, with Hardy's footage severely limited. When a surviving print was uncovered in a European archive in 1974, it was a revelation to find that Laurel and Hardy appear as a full-fledged team—not quite Stanley and Ollie, perhaps, but much closer to those characters than anyone expected.

Laurel and Hardy are hoboes accosted by a forest ranger recruiting volunteers to put out wildfires. Recoiling in horror at the though of hard (and hazardous) labor, the boys scurry away on a bicycle, with a group of angry rangers in hot pursuit. The duo hides out in the luxurious mansion of Colonel Buckshot, who is away on safari. His servants are away for the weekend, so Stan and Oliver decide to spend some time living as the other half do. But the mansion has been advertised for rent during the colonel's absence, so when honeymooners Lord and Lady Plumtree show up to look over the place, the boys pose as master and maid. The masquerade works well enough until the colonel arrives home unexpectedly and finds a houseful of strangers — two of whom are trying to beat a hasty retreat with a truckload of valuables.

Based on "Home from the Honeymoon," a sketch written by Stan's father, Arthur J. Jefferson, *Duck Soup* was originally conceived as a vehicle for Laurel and another Hal Roach contract player, Syd Crossley. The reasons behind replacing Crossley with Oliver Hardy remain unclear, but the film undoubtedly benefits from the substitution. The most interesting aspect of *Duck Soup* is that Laurel and Hardy are working as a bona fide team, already displaying many of the hallmarks that would come to be associated with their inimitable personalities. Cast as vagrants, as they would often be in later films, Hardy assumes the role of the pompous leader with Laurel as the meek follower. (Hardy's overbearing nature must be held in check, or it can stimulate Laurel's rebellious nature.) In time-honored L and H tradition, they use their wits (such as they are) to create a situation that momentarily shields them from trouble, until their ruse is (inevitably) exposed.

The Laurel and Hardy seen in *Duck Soup* are, understandably, a little rough around the edges. As hoboes, their wardrobe is tattered, especially Hardy's suit and atypical top hat. (Laurel wears a derby that makes him look like the Stanley he would become, although he's not wearing his trademark bow tie.) Hardy is further hampered by his grubby, unshaven appearance, which not only minimizes the effectiveness of his delicate pantomime but makes his charade as the master of the house seem unconvincing, even by the relaxed standards of a humble two-reel comedy. Nevertheless, their interplay is surprisingly sharp, giving the impression that they had been partners for years. Yet it is nothing more than a coincidence that the duo operates as a cohesive unit here, as they naturally had no idea they would soon be marketed as an official team. The film's structure is the same basic structure that would define Laurel and Hardy's relationship and modus operandi. There are a few harbingers in the Laurel solo films discussed previously, while Hardy was paired with smaller-statured comedians during his early career (e.g., the Plump and Runt series with Billy Ruge, and Hardy's teaming with diminutive Bobby Ray). So in *Duck Soup*, Stan and Ollie are simply responding in the same manner as they had in several earlier situations where they were a part of a team dynamic. Only now, for the first time, each had found a partner that was not a mere foil, but someone who would bring out the other's best. Hardy's domineering persona forces Laurel to scale back the frantic excesses that undermined some of his earlier screen performances (broadly mugging to the camera, needless repetition of certain bits, and so forth).

Duck Soup was remade as *Another Fine Mess* (1930), after Stan and Ollie had refined their screen personalities and interaction to a much greater extent. Ironically, although *Another Fine Mess* contains superior elements, *Duck Soup* is arguably a funnier film. The biggest advantage *Duck Soup* has over the remake is its running time: at two reels, *Duck Soup* speeds merrily along while *Another Fine Mess* moves noticeably slower at its three-reel length. *Another Fine Mess* uses dialogue to flesh out Stan and Ollie's childlike characters, and shifts the focus to situational humor. The remake also features a better supporting cast. Madeline Hurlock is spirited in the silent version but she lacks the effortless charisma Thelma Todd exhibited in the same role. (Todd's double-entendre laden "girl-talk" session with "Agnes" is one of the highlights of the remake.) And certainly James Marcus is no match for James Finlayson's riotous interpretation of Colonel Buckshot.

Yet *Duck Soup* still emerges as the tighter, more amusing of the two movies. It touches upon the plot points in a more efficient manner and, as a silent film, places greater emphasis on physical comedy. An early sequence in *Duck Soup* finds Hardy furiously peddling a bicycle, with Laurel riding on the handle bars, careening through the streets of Hollywood. It's a very funny set piece, heightened by the fact that Stan and Ollie are performing the stunt themselves. In *Another Fine Mess*, the bicycle chase is used for the climax, as the boys flee from Colonel Buckshot and the arresting officers. (The forest-ranger angle was dropped from the remake.) This time, however, the boys are (supposedly) hidden inside an animal skin, and the sequence is clearly executed by two stunt men instead. It's still amusing, but the real Stan and Ollie don't even appear in the finale of their own film.

As Stan and Ollie reverted to being non-equal co-stars in their very next film (*Slipping Wives*, with Hardy in support of Laurel), *Duck Soup* can only be considered an aberration rather than a serious attempt to create a new team. That it is their first film together since *The Lucky Dog* (discounting their separate supporting roles in *45 Minutes From Hollywood*) makes it even more intriguing that they are working in tandem here. While it isn't an unsung comedy classic, *Duck Soup* represents the first true Laurel *and* Hardy movie, which is enough to rank it as a motion-picture milestone.

Slipping Wives
Cast

Priscilla Dean	The wife
Herbert Rawlinson	Leon
Stan Laurel	Ferdinand Flamingo/Lionel Ironsides
Oliver Hardy	Jarvis the butler
Albert Conti	Hon. Winchester Squirtz

Credits

Fred L. Guiol .... Director
Lewis R. Foster .... Assistant director
F. Richard Jones .... Supervising director
George Stevens .... Cinematographer
Richard Currier .... Film Editor
Hal Roach .... Story
H. M. Walker .... Titles
William Lambert .... Costume Designer
Working title: "Her House Sheik."
A Hal Roach production. Copyrighted January 17, 1927
Production dates: October 20–November 3, 1926.
Released April 3, 1927, by Pathé.
Two reels.

After filming *Duck Soup* with nearly all of the rudiments of the familiar Laurel and Hardy traits recognizable, Stan Laurel and Oliver Hardy were next cast in the same film, although not as a team. This certainly proves that their pairing in the previous film was simply academic, and while there was already a buzz about the Hal Roach studios that the two worked well together, the idea of their possibly making magic as a duo was yet to be explored.

Hal Roach seemed to favor stories involving marital mix-ups, with husbands and wives suspecting their spouses of real or imagined philandering. Infidelity was an edgy and daring topic in the 1920s, despite the decade's reputation for permissiveness (flappers, jazz, speakeasies). The same moviegoing public that chose to convict an innocent Roscoe Arbuckle (after he was acquitted by an apologetic jury for the 1921 rape and murder of actress Virginia Rappé) would react more prudishly to the idea of marital affairs. When used as a plot device in a mere two-reel comedy, the subject of infidelity might have seemed titillating and naughty.

Priscilla Dean, the top-billed star of *Slipping Wives*, had been the "Queen of the Universal Lot," starring in such productions as *Outside the Law* (1921; with Lon Chaney), *Under Two Flags* (1922; parodied by Laurel as *Under Two Jags*) and *The White Tiger* (1923), all three directed by Tod Browning. By the late 1920s, Dean was another faded actress (like Theda Bara and Agnes Ayres) signed by Hal Roach to appear in his "All-Star" comedy shorts. Herbert Rawlinson was a leading man in feature films who was now relegated to lower-prestige roles.

In *Slipping Wives*, Priscilla is upset because the passion has gone out of her marriage. She suspects (wrongfully) that her husband, Leon, an artist, has a roving eye for his pretty models. Her friend Winchester Squirtz suggests that she find someone to act as her lover to make hubby jealous. When simple-minded Ferdinand Flamingo comes to the door with buckets of paint to do some handy work in the house, he is immediately recruited for the "position." During a party that evening, Ferdinand poses as novelist Lionel Ironsides ("the famous writer of fairy stories") and does his best to essay his hired role as a flirtatious lothario. Leon sees through the inept charade but makes an effort to make his wife think he really is jealous in order to rekindle their romance. In the meantime, Ferdinand further complicates matters by mistaking Squirtz for Priscilla's husband and Leon for her gigolo.

Priscilla Dean and Herbert Rawlinson do the best they can to set up the basic premise and keep it going, although it's obvious they were just being used for whatever name value they still had, with the real comedic chores assigned to Laurel and Hardy (and, to a lesser extent, Albert Conti). Nevertheless, Dean delivers a charming performance and proves to be a surprisingly good foil for Stan.

The dynamic between Laurel and Hardy is adversarial. Hardy, clean-shaven and very funny in a supporting turn as a staid butler, takes an immediate dislike to the delivery man, who refuses to enter through the servants' quarters as instructed, and, after some roughhousing, manages to drench Hardy with a bucket of paint. While Laurel spent most of his career searching for a solid character to play consistently, Hardy seemed to find at least some of the rudiments of the beloved Ollie quite early on. Little bits like the long stare, the tie-twiddle, and other special Ollie-isms were added as his character evolved, and most of these mannerisms during this formative period during which he was essentially subservient to Stan. During their first confrontation in *Slipping Wives*, Laurel causes Hardy to wind up on the receiving end of the abuse — something that would define their style after they became an official team.

Much of the humor is situational and, overall, less effective than many of Laurel's other solo efforts. Perhaps Hardy's presence is a distraction. We naturally wait for the two to share a scene, to see how their relationship will be presented, and to watch them play off each other in this embryonic stage of their partnership. Even as we attempt to objectively assess this as a Laurel solo film with Hardy in support, Hardy's presence forces us to acknowledge the duo's scenes together more closely.

The few times Laurel and Hardy do share the screen, they are seen physically battling over something or other. For instance, Hardy the butler insists Laurel the guest take a bath, and another bout of roughhousing results in both of them getting dunked in the tub water. Had the duo never made *Duck Soup* (that film's unavailability until the mid–1970s hampered previous studies of the team), it would be perfectly understandable to accept Laurel and Hardy as adversaries with little screen time together in what is essentially a Stan Laurel solo outing with Hardy in support. Since they portrayed a team in *Duck Soup*, *Slipping Wives* is generally perceived to be a huge step backward. But *Duck Soup* was an aberration. It created a spark of notice from the Roach staff as to Laurel and Hardy's ability to work together, and there may have been a series of experiments to have Hardy support Laurel in the latter's starring comedies. The team would evolve from here, making further strides in *Do Detectives Think?* a bit later on, before becoming an official team beginning with *The Second Hundred Years*. At the time of *Slipping Wives*, however, they were merely two actors appearing in the same film, and the fact that they shared only a few brief, frantic scenes together simply shows the genesis of their development as co-stars.

The highlight of *Slipping Wives* is Laurel's wonderful pantomime of the Samson and Delilah tale, which he enacts when Lionel Ironsides is called upon to describe his latest story. Mussing his hair and squaring his shoulders, Stan launches into a series of athletic poses while relating the exploits of "this gink Samson." Stan begins to sashay as he depicts Delilah, a "lady barber" who trips over the sleeping Samson and trims the mighty man's long locks, snapping her fingers contemptuously after the betrayal. Samson awakens to discover his hair missing and his strength depleted (Stan does a hilarious rubber-leg bit to convey Samson's weakened condition) as "forty thousand Philadelphians" poke his eyes out in corkscrew fashion. When Samson regains his strength, Stan uses long-stemmed flower-pot holders to depict Samson's destruction of temple pillars. This set piece, punctuated by Priscilla Dean's mortified reaction shots and Oliver Hardy's attempts to physically attack Stan, is brilliantly executed by Laurel, providing ample opportunity for him to indulge his gifts as a physical comedian. In the later Laurel and Hardy films, Stan's pantomimic interludes — such as the wine-bottling routine in *The Bohemian Girl* (1936) and his attempt to get a dutiful St. Bernard to relinquish a barrel of brandy in *Swiss Miss* (1938) — were more genteel in nature, in keeping with Stanley's childlike persona. In *Slipping Wives*, however, Stan's Samson-Delilah pantomime contains the zestful energy and sadism evident in much of his solo work.

The premise of *Slipping Wives* was revamped for *The Fixer-Uppers* (1935), a second-echelon (albeit still enjoyable) Laurel and Hardy two-reeler, and one of the team's last shorts before switching exclusively to feature film production. The same plot was also refashioned by The Three Stooges in *Boobs in Arms* (1940), a disjointed two-reeler that switches from marital farce to service comedy with little rhyme or reason.

Slipping Wives is an amusing but decidedly run-of-the-mill two-reeler, no better than other similarly themed comedies the Roach Studio was churning out at the time. Subsequent Laurel and Hardy films employing marital infidelity as a central plot device (e.g., *Their Purple Moment, We Faw Down, Unaccustomed As We Are, Chickens Come Home*) were subtler and more character driven, which made the comic complications much funnier.

Eve's Love Letters

Cast

Agnes Ayres	Eve
Forrest Stanley	Adam
Stan Laurel	Anatole the butler
Jerry Mandy	Mr. X
Fred Malatesta	Sir Oliver Hardy
Charlie Hall	Taxi driver

Credits

Leo McCarey	Director
George Stevens	Cinematographer
Richard Currier	Film Editor
Stan Laurel	Story
H. M. Walker	Titles

A Hal Roach production. Copyrighted April 11, 1927.
Production dates: January 17–28, 1927.
Released May 29, 1927, by Pathé.
Two reels.

An entire study could probably be written on just the Hal Roach productions that involve flirting husbands and wives whose dalliances really mean no harm, but spark the jealousy of the mate. *Eve's Love Letters* once again investigates whatever humor can be derived from this frequently mined theme. Perhaps the ways and mores of the 1920s were such that this particular plot idea was especially titillating to average moviegoers.

This is another Hal Roach "All-Star" comedy showcasing a star whose career was faltering. Top-billed Agnes Ayres, who had appeared in *The Sheik* (1921) and *The Son of the Sheik* (1926), two iconic Rudolph Valentino films, was signed by Roach in hopes that her name would give the picture added marquee value. Ayres and co-star Forrest Stanley were the ones singled out by reviewers, with an occasional nod to Stan Laurel, who was the one who really handled the bulk of the comedic chores.

While Laurel had already appeared with Oliver Hardy in some comedies, Hardy is absent from *Eve's Love Letters*, although Fred Malatesta plays a character named Sir Oliver Hardy. (Rob Stone opines that Hardy was slated for the role but was still working on the feature *No Man's Law*.) Since *Eve's Love*

Letters was made after Stan and Ollie had been appearing together, it was listed in early Laurel and Hardy filmographies, with the reference to "Sir Oliver Hardy" causing further confusion.

Eve and Adam's idyllic existence is threatened when Eve receives a mysterious note: "The burning letters you wrote to Sir Oliver Hardy before your marriage will be turned over to your husband unless you pay $10,000 for them." She enlists the aid of Anatole the butler to recover the incriminating love letters. They break into Sir Hardy's mansion and during a tussle with Hardy and his henchman, Mr. X, they manage to destroy the evidence. But when an intoxicated and irate Adam shows up, Anatole and Eve don matching hats and capes in order to flee, unrecognized.

The tipsy Adam flirts with Anatole-in-drag, so Eve decides to teach him a lesson. Back home, Eve encourages Anatole to continue the dame charade, and the faithful servant alternates between playing himself and a flirtatious vamp as a panic-stricken Adam desperately tries to get the mystery "woman" out of the house. Eve also puts on the hat and cape to further confuse and torment her spouse, as the film settles into a series of rapid-fire exits and entrances from room to room, and deftly timed costume changes.

As far as the oft-used jealousy/philandering angle goes, *Eve's Love Letters* is a hit-and-miss affair, with some interesting ideas blending with pretty standard ones. Agnes Ayres and Forrest Stanley get into the spirit of things and deliver energetic performances, although one can't avoid thinking how much more mileage Roach stalwarts like Anita Garvin and James Finlayson could have gotten out of the same material. Fortunately, Laurel's pantomimic skills shine in a sequence where Adam believes Anatole has been shot. Stan mimics a detailed death scene, complete with bullet trajectory, rapture and an ascent to Heaven, and it comes off as one of the funniest set pieces in the movie.

One particularly fun visual is really a director's gag, but may have been devised by Laurel. The despondent husband is home, wondering as to his wife's whereabouts. There is a close shot of a full liquor bottle, as the husband's hand picks it up out of the frame. Seconds later, the hand comes down with an empty liquor bottle being put back in its place. While the gag did not show up again in Laurel's later work, it is the sort of clever visual he would enjoy using when assuming even greater control of his own product. Of course, an argument can also be made in favor of Leo McCarey, who would soon prove to be one of the best comedy directors of his time, with such films as *Duck Soup* (1933), *Ruggles of Red Gap* (1935) and *The Awful Truth* (1937) to his credit.

After retrieving the love letters from Sir Hardy's safe, Laurel and Ayres frantically dodge the former suitor's attempts to get the letters back, resulting in a fast-paced and nicely choreographed series of keep-away tactics, including Laurel bending over and "hiking" the letters through his legs to a receiving Ayres. This bit of business would be expanded to greater effect in the Laurel and Hardy feature *Way Out West* (1937) when a mining deed is retrieved from swindlers in the same manner.

It is difficult to determine whether or not Oliver Hardy's presence would have made any difference to the overall quality of *Eve's Love Letters*. The Sir Oliver Hardy character is ill-defined and underdeveloped, and while Hardy's comedic know-how could have invested it with more depth, he may not have had enough screen time to do so. Nevertheless, it would have been fun to see him as part of the keep-away sequence that is the portent to what he would later do with Stan in *Way Out West*.

Upon completion of *Eve's Love Letters*, Laurel went right back to work with Hardy in support. Sometimes Hardy would have only minor roles, such as in *Love 'Em and Weep*, but often the role was bigger, further honing the evolution of cinema's greatest comedy duo.

Love 'Em and Weep

Cast

Mae Busch	Peaches
Stan Laurel	Romaine Ricketts
Jimmie (James) Finlayson	Titus Tillsbury
Oliver Hardy	Judge Chigger
Charlotte Mineau	Mrs. Aggie Tillsbury
Vivien Oakland	Mrs. Ricketts
Gale Henry	Old Lady Scandal
Charlie Hall	Butler
May Wallace	Mrs. Chigger
Ed Brandenburg	Waiter

Credits

Fred L. Guiol	Director
F. Richard Jones	Supervising director
Floyd Jackman	Cinematographer
Richard Currier	Film editor
Hal Roach, Stan Laurel, Fred L. Guiol	Writers
H. M. Walker	Titles
William Lambert	Costume designer

Working title: "Better Husbands Week."
A Hal Roach production. Copyrighted April 11, 1927.
Production dates: November 26–December 7, 1926.
Retakes: January 12–13, 1927.
Released June 12, 1927, by Pathé.
Two reels.

Another in a procession of Hal Roach comedies dealing with marital jealousy and philandering, *Love 'Em and Weep* has been completely overshadowed by its superior remake, *Chickens Come Home* (1931), one of Laurel and Hardy's best efforts. While the original comes across even more frenetic by comparison, it is fairly entertaining on its own modest terms.

In *Love 'Em and Weep*, Titus Tillsbury, a respectable businessman, is visited by Peaches, an old flame who blackmails him with an incriminating photo of their romantic fling, which occurred years before Tillsbury was married to his wife, Aggie. Romaine Ricketts, Tillsbury's assistant, tries to prevent Peaches from crashing a dinner party hosted by the Tillsburys, but when she shows up anyway, she's introduced as Romaine's wife. To complicate matters, the town gossip alerts the real Mrs. Ricketts that her husband is up to no good, and before long, Tillsbury's cover-up scheme unravels spectacularly.

Love 'Em and Weep is a fun-though-standard marital farce from the period, showcasing a fine performance by the top-billed Mae Busch as the aggressive gold-digger. Unlike other Roach "fallen stars" (Priscilla Dean, Theda Bara), Busch had a background in physical comedy and her sharp timing is completely in sync with Laurel and Finlayson's performances. Although Busch never achieved full-fledged stardom at Roach, she proved to be a marvelous comic foil for Laurel, who continued to rely on her during the Laurel and Hardy years.

Stan is a bit more subdued than he is in his earlier efforts, though he isn't quite Stanley yet. He's still too reactionary to be the slow-witted persona he would soon develop. Nevertheless, he's just as intimated by women as he would be in the later Laurel and Hardy films, as confrontations and setbacks bring him to the verge of tears.

Although *Love 'Em and Weep* and *Chickens Come Home* share identical storylines and a number of the same gags, the artistic differences between them are pretty significant. *Love 'Em and Weep* is actually a Stan Laurel-James Finlayson comedy, with Oliver Hardy barely making an impression in a thankless supporting role as one of Finlayson's party guests. (Stan and Ollie have no interaction, and during the fleeting occasions when they're in the same scene, Hardy is either way off in the background or standing off to the side.) In its haste to establish the plot, the film defines the characters in very shallow terms: Finlayson is a businessman but it is never made clear what the nature of his business is; Laurel is Finlayson's assistant but we're never sure what his duties are or whether his loyalty stems from friendship or the need to protect his job; and Charlotte Mineau is a standard-issue jealous spouse.

On every level, *Chickens Come Home* improves upon the original. The remake runs three reels instead of two, utilizing the extra time to introduce its characters properly. Ollie, the co-owner of a successful fertilizer company (!), is a mayoral candidate, which gives more weight to the blackmail angle. While Finlayson did a nice job of conveying his character's fear of exposure, his broad, blatant mannerisms stand in stark contrast to Hardy's textured performance. Hardy adopts a more subtle approach, registering his internal stress through a series of nervous gestures and verbal fluctuations. Stan is Ollie's friend as well as business partner, thus establishing why he goes to extreme lengths to help his pal.

The supporting roles also have greater depth. Mae Busch's gold-digger becomes even more of a menace, thanks in large part to the coarseness and sheer volume of Busch's voice. Charlotte Mineau was amusing as Finlayson's wife, but she pales in comparison to the elegant and gifted Thelma Todd, who makes every suspicious glance count. Finlayson plays Hardy's butler, assuming a role played by Charlie Hall, who was Fin's butler in the original. In *Love 'Em and Weep*, when Fin received suspicious phone calls, Hall was a confidante. But in *Chickens Come Home*, Fin the butler knows something peculiar is going on and uses this knowledge to further blackmail an increasingly flustered Hardy, who keeps slipping Fin money to keep him quiet. Even as a servant, Fin holds the upper hand over Ollie.

The best gag in *Love 'Em and Weep* has an unconscious Mae Busch perched on Finlayson's back as Stan tries to "walk" her past a skeptical Charlotte Mineau and her startled guests. It's an inventive sight gag that plays even funnier in *Chickens Come Home*, where it benefited from better pacing and reaction shots. (It was also the primary running gag in *Sugar Daddies*.)

Virtually every scene in *Love 'Em and Weep* can be found in *Chickens Come Home*, with the exception of a sequence at a restaurant where Ricketts takes Peaches, to stall for time. Wisely, this extraneous set piece was jettisoned for the remake.

Love 'Em and Weep is invariably a disappointing experience for those who see Laurel and Hardy's names in the credits and expect a full-fledged team effort. For these viewers, Hardy's limited participation negates whatever enjoyment can be gleaned from this energetic (albeit meant undeniably minor) farce.

While we would still argue that Stan Laurel would have been a formidable solo comedian had he never teamed with Oliver Hardy, it is obvious that their partnership brought out the best in Stan's creative instincts, allowing him to mature as an artist. The difference between the Laurel in *Love 'Em and Weep* and the Laurel in *Chickens Come Home* is the difference between a talented comic and a comic genius.

Why Girls Love Sailors

Cast

Stan Laurel . . . . Willie Brisling
Oliver Hardy . . . . First mate
Viola Richard . . . . Nellie
Malcolm Waite . . . . Captain of the *Merry Maiden*
Anita Garvin . . . . Captain's wife
Jerry Mandy . . . . Frightened sailor
Edgar Dearing . . . . Amorous sailor
Dick Gilbert . . . . Amorous sailor
Charles R. Althoff . . . . Grandpa Brisling
  Some sources claim Anna May Wong, Sojin, and Eric Mayne
   appeared in deleted scenes, but it is unconfirmed as to
     whether these scenes were actually filmed.

Credits

Fred L. Guiol . . . . Director
Floyd Jackman . . . . Cinematographer
Richard Currier . . . . Editor
Hal E. Roach . . . . Story
H. M. Walker . . . . Titles
Lambert . . . . Gowns
  A Hal Roach production. Copyrighted May 18, 1927.
    Production dates: January 31–February 19, 1927.
  Retakes (directed by Hal Yates): March 18 and 19, 1927.
           Released July 17, 1927, by Pathé.
                      Two reels.

Why Girls Love Sailors is clearly a solo Stan Laurel comedy, with all the other characters subservient to his. Stan hasn't completely forsaken the frantic behavior of earlier films and continues to overplay his hand by mugging directly to the camera and dancing a jig to punctuate triumphant moments. By comparison, Oliver Hardy gives a more textured performance despite his thankless supporting role, blending broad physical gestures with nuanced facial expressions. During their limited footage together, Hardy manages to act Laurel off the screen.

Willie Brisling, a happy-go-lucky gob, springs into action when his sweetheart Nellie is abducted by her former flame, a tough sea captain. Sneaking aboard the captain's ship, Willie disguises himself as a blonde temptress. The outlandish masquerade is convincing enough to attract the lustful attention of the first mate and the rest of the crew. After handily dispatching them, Willie begins flirting with the captain. When the captain's wife shows up and catches her husband with another "woman," Willie reveals his true identity and, freeing Nellie from a locked room, exposes the seaman as a philanderer. Willie and Nellie depart, leaving the captain to answer to his angry spouse.

Why Girls Love Sailors was long considered to be a lost film, and though its rediscovery was cause for elation, response to the actual movie was mixed. As it was common knowledge that this was a pre-team effort, no one expected to see the usual partnership, yet some expressed disappointment nevertheless. Contrary to popular belief, Hardy is not the primary villain of the piece (a standard menacing role assigned to Malcolm Waite) but a secondary heavy, so Stan and Ollie have much less interaction than anticipated. In a 1954 interview with John McCabe, Hardy cited *Why Girls Love Sailors* as the origin of his trademark tie-twiddle and slow-burn "camera look," but he was actually referring to *Sailors, Beware!*, another Laurel-Hardy entry that was shot a couple months later. (Ollie can hardly be faulted for confusing one similarly titled film for the other, especially when recalling events 27 years after the fact.)

For some, the disappointment over *Why Girls Love Sailors* was compounded by the discovery of an early version of the script found among the papers of director Fred Guiol that presents Stan and Ollie as a team, although the emphasis is still on Stan. In this scenario, Stan is a sailor whose Chinese sweetheart (a role slated for noted Asian actress Anna May Wong) is kidnapped by a villainous "money lender" (to be played by Sojin, a Japanese actor seen in numerous films of the era). With help from his petty-officer pal (Ollie), Stan heroically rescues his girlfriend. This project was abandoned because it would have been too cost-prohibitive to shoot as written; the exotic locale and action sequences would have required elaborate sets and an army of extras. To conform to a modest budget, the script was overhauled to the point where it bore faint resemblance to the original storyline, and the idea of teaming Laurel and Hardy was jettisoned entirely. (For a detailed description of the unfilmed script, see Randy Skredvedt's *Laurel and Hardy: The Magic Behind the Movies.*)

Stan's shallow character in *Why Girls Love Sailors* is amusing, but his personality lacks the depth that separates loveable performers from likeable ones. His introductory scene with Viola Richard is quite charming, as he shyly presents her with a necklace then steals a kiss, giddily stumbling across the room and innocently rolling around on her bed. But when he's bullied by the tough captain, Stan turns on the water works and can't stop weeping. Stan would use the crying routine judiciously in the later Laurel and Hardy films, where it was a surefire laugh-getter. In this instance, however, he leans on it too heavily and it wears out its welcome.

Stan fares better with his extended drag routine, although no explanation is offered as to why a female impersonator's wardrobe trunk is on the ship.

(This is the sort of lapse in logic that Laurel would studiously avoid in the future.) Usually this masquerade would call for Stan to be on his best behavior and try to emulate refined femininity, but here he goes for pure camp, brazenly sashaying around the deck to entice the crew members. One by one, he lures them to a secluded area where he knocks them unconscious, then contorts their hands and arms into rude gestures that prompt an irate Hardy to toss the insubordinate men overboard.

With the crew dispatched, Stan and Ollie share their only face-to-face moment in the film, with Stan flirting outrageously with the love-starved Ollie. Their rapport is instantaneous and Ollie displays his gifts as a masterful scene-stealer. Whenever he looks into the camera, it isn't gratuitous mugging but rather a silent method of sharing his surprise and disbelief with the audience. Their encounter is much too brief, though it builds up to Hardy's best scene in the picture: Stan quietly slips away, and Ollie doesn't realize the captain's wife has arrived. Chortling with roguish glee, Ollie repeatedly tickles her leg until he notices his mistake. As he would do countless times in later Laurel and Hardy movies, Ollie glances nervously into the camera and gulps, dreading the expected consequences.

Why Girls Love Sailors gets a tremendous boost from its female cast members. Viola Richard, one of the loveliest actresses under contract to the Hal Roach Studio, makes a charming leading lady. She would work with the boys again in *Do Detectives Think?* (1927), *Flying Elephants* (produced 1927, released 1928), *Leave 'Em Laughing* (1928), *Should Married Men Go Home?* (1928) and *Tit for Tat* (1935). Anita Garvin's undocumented appearance as the captain's wife was the most pleasant surprise regarding the film's rediscovery. Always a welcome presence, Garvin turns out to be the toughest character in the picture, kicking and punching Hardy for his impropriety, and shooting her husband for his infidelity.

For those who know in advance that it is far removed from a typical Laurel and Hardy movie, *Why Girls Love Sailors* might be passably entertaining. Its real value, however, is basically academic and we are thankful that this long-lost film was finally unearthed.

With Love and Hisses

Cast

Stan Laurel	Cuthbert Hope
Oliver Hardy	Top Sergeant Banner
Jimmie (James) Finlayson	Captain Bustle
Frank Brownlee	Major General Rohrer
Anita Garvin, Eve Southern	Captain's girlfriends at train station

Jerry Mandy .... Hungry soldier
Will Stanton .... Soldier sleeping next to Cuthbert
Chet Brandenberg .... Soldier
Frank Saputo .... Soldier
Charlie Hall .... Soldier
Josephine Dunn .... Soldier's girlfriend

Credits

Fred L. Guiol .... Director
Floyd Jackman .... Cinematographer
Richard Currier .... Editor
Hal Roach .... Story
Carl Harbaugh .... Writer (uncredited)
H. M. Walker .... Titles
Lambert .... Gowns

A Hal Roach production. Copyrighted May 18, 1927.
Production dates: March 14–March 30, 1927.
Released August 28, 1927, by Pathé.
Two reels.

While *With Love and Hisses* provides Stan and Ollie with more opportunities to interact than *Why Girl Love Sailors* did, their characters are still pitted against each other. It has been reported that gag writers had already noticed the chemistry between Stan and Ollie, yet like other early L and H collaborations, this is essentially a vehicle for Laurel, with Hardy in support. In *With Love and Hisses*, Stan is a lead comedian with two foils. In fact, Laurel spends as much screen time playing off James Finlayson as he does Hardy. Additionally, Laurel has just as strong a rapport with Finlayson as he does with Hardy. (And the same can be said for the rapport between Hardy and Finlayson.)

Among the recruits bound for Camp Klaxon is Cuthbert Hope, a dumb rookie who immediately runs afoul of tough Sergeant Banner. Both men are a source of great irritation for Captain Bustle, their no-nonsense superior officer. During a three-hour march led by Banner, the tired soldiers decide to take a dip in a lake they have stumbled upon during their maneuvers. Banner carelessly tosses a lit cigarette on the ground, and the resulting blaze destroys all of the discarded uniforms. Banner and the buck-naked privates hide behind a conveniently placed billboard (advertising Cecil B. DeMille's *The Volga Boatman*) to avoid being discovered by a pair of equestriennes. When they are accosted by a skunk, the recruits uproot the billboard (with their heads poking through holes in the sign, making their faces look like part of the artwork) and scurry down the road, trampling a couple of bees' nests along the way. A swarm of angry bees follow them back to camp, creating chaos during an inspection by Major General Rohrer. Later, Banner and the men continue to drill, despite their swollen, bee-stung posteriors.

Stan (left), in costume for *With Love and Hisses*, poses with Hal Roach contract players Viola Richard and Max Davidson on the Roach studio lot, 1927.

Often dismissed for not being enough of a "proper" Laurel and Hardy movie — a curious criticism, given its chronology — *With Love and Hisses* is quite amusing when approached as a solo Laurel effort. Cuthbert Hope is cut from the classic misfit mold, the type Stan had portrayed in many of his solo comedies. This time, however, he does not possess the rascally spirit he'd had as an equally inept Army private in *Smithy* (1924; which also featured James Finlayson as a flustered commander) and instead meekly accepts the redirection he receives from his superior officers.

In *With Love and Hisses*, Stan ventures even closer to the childlike Stanley character that would define his screen persona. There's no streak of the maliciousness found in earlier Laurel characterizations, and some of his reactions are slower, as Cuthbert Hope's bewildered, blank-faced stares reflect his inability to grasp the situations in which he finds himself. He also does plenty of grinning and crying, although these bits seem less intrusive here because this behavior fits the innocent character he's playing. (Unlike some previous films in which Laurel keeps repeating the crying routine until it has worn out its welcome.)

But he isn't quite Stanley yet. Some of the film's biggest laughs derive from Stan's effeminate poses during a drill formation, after he's been instructed to place his hand on his hip. The emphasis isn't necessarily on the sexual connotation — he's more like a playful child who takes what he feels is a silly command and exaggerates it to the extreme.

Stan's relationship with Ollie is not as adversarial as it had been in *Why Girls Love Sailors*, because here Stan has no reason to consciously defeat or undermine him. Private Hope is a simpleton without an agenda, aside from trying to adapt to military life, and his run-ins with Sergeant Banner stem from misunderstandings. At the train station, Hope spots a couple of women he thinks are blowing kisses at Banner and points them out to the sergeant. However, they were actually gesturing to Captain Bustle, and Banner lands in hot water when he's caught flirting with the girls. As would happen time and time again in later Laurel and Hardy films, Stan's helpfulness gets Ollie into another nice mess.

Like his later, more polished Ollie persona, Hardy's Sergeant Banner is capable of getting into trouble on his own, especially when he asserts his authority. Unable to find a vacant berth aboard the train, Private Hope sees an unoccupied luxury compartment and makes himself at home, unaware it's the captain's quarters. Banner pulls rank and throws the lowly rookie out of the compartment, claiming it for his own. By the time Captain Bustle shows up, Banner has devoured an entire fruit basket and made a general mess of the place. In what would become time-honored Laurel and Hardy tradition, Ollie doesn't assume responsibility for his own mistakes. Although his cigarette caused their uniforms to go up in flames, Banner still blames Hope for the calamity because Hope was supposed to be standing guard over the garments, not skinny-dipping with the rest of the troop.

Laurel exercised some degree of supervisory control over nearly all his films for Hal Roach from this time forward, regardless of the credited writers and directors. As with other early Laurel efforts, ideas and situations from *With Love and Hisses* would be repeated and revamped to greater effect in later L and H comedies. Hardy making a mess of the captain's quarters is a harbinger of a sequence in *A Chump at Oxford* (1940) in which the duo is duped into believing the dean's quarters are their own, and they proceed to make a similar shambles of the rooms. Stan's disruptive behavior during a drill foreshadows the bungled military routines in *Pack Up Your Troubles* (1932) and *The Flying Deuces* (1939) as well as their disastrous drill in *Great Guns* (1941). The soldiers' long, barely endurable march would later be recalled in *Beau Hunks* (1931) and the beehive gag was effectively expanded for the conclusion of *Bonnie Scotland* (1935). The final gag involving the troop's massively swollen posteriors is indicative of Stan's penchant for gags dealing with outlandish physical deformity, e.g., Stan getting a barrel-sized swollen stomach after drinking a barrel-full of water in *Below Zero* (1930); the boys with their broken legs wrapped around their necks in *Going Bye-Bye!* (1934); their distorted bodies in *The Bohemian Girl* (1936); and getting "skinned alive" in *The Bullfighters* (1945).

There's an undeniable crudeness to the humor in *With Love and Hisses* that some L and H purists find off-putting. Yet when placed in its historical context, the film is a funny (superficially, at least) chapter in the continuing evolution of Laurel and Hardy as a cohesive team.

Sailors, Beware!

Cast

Stan Laurel .... Chester Chaste
Oliver Hardy .... Purser Cryder
Anita Garvin .... Madame Ritz
Harry Earles .... Roger (the "baby")
Frank Brownlee .... Captain Bull
Lupe Velez .... Baroness Behr
Will Stanton .... Baron Behr
Viola Richard .... Pretty brunette bridge-player
Tiny (Stanley J.) Sandford .... Irate husband
Dorothy Coburn .... Brunette sitting in deck chair
Ed Brandenburg .... Cabdriver
May Wallace .... Society woman
Connie Evans .... Society woman
Barbara Pierce .... Society woman
Charley Young .... Man boarding S. S. *Mirimar*
(Contrary to the credits of the DVD edition, Edna Marian does not appear in the existing version of the film.)

Credits

Hal Yates (and Hal Roach, uncredited*) .... Director
Floyd Jackman .... Cinematographer
Richard Currier .... Editor

Studio records confirm that Hal Roach actually directed Sailors, Beware! *Hal Yates, who received sole director credit, only shot the retakes. Fred L. Guiol erroneously receives director's credit in the DVD edition.*

Hal E. Roach	Story
Frank Butler, Lige Conley	Writers
H. M. Walker	Titles

A Hal Roach production. Copyrighted June 9, 1927.
Production dates: April 4–April 14, 1927.
Retakes: April 18, 1927.
Released September 25, 1927, by Pathé.
Two reels.

As in *Why Girls Love Sailors* and *With Love and Hisses*, Stan and Ollie are pitted against each other in *Sailors, Beware!*, only this time Stan reverts to his earlier screen persona by being much more contentious and combative. Throughout, he refuses to be a flunky, remaining defiant in the face of repeated intimidation. He's also easily riled and given to sudden outbursts of temper, behavior that would be toned down and employed more judiciously in later Laurel and Hardy films.

Cabdriver Chester Chaste becomes a reluctant steward on the S. S. *Mirimar*, a luxury steamship, after his vehicle is mistaken for cargo and hoisted aboard. Cryder, the ship's purser, flirts with the ladies and tries to keep the obstinate Chester in line. Also on board is international crook Madame Ritz and her midget husband, Roger, who is posing as a baby, and the couple proceed to steal assorted valuables from the passengers. Chester becomes suspicious of the baby's oddly advanced demeanor and winds up exposing the pair as thieves.

Stan is no shy, mild-mannered innocent in *Sailors, Beware!* He's belligerent enough to chastise the ship's captain, cunning enough to fool the purser, and sharp enough to see through the con artists' charade. Since Chester feels he's been shanghaied, he is unwilling to accept a position as a steward, and only relents after the captain threatens to have him tossed overboard. Still, he doesn't feel duty-bound to any rules or regulations. Stan plays Chester as a man in a near-perpetual state of agitation. When Cryder throws a medicine ball at him, Chester hurls it back at full force. When the haughty Baroness Behr gives him a condescending look, Chester gives her an angry shove, pushing her into a swimming pool. (The Baroness is played by Lupe Velez, the future star of the Mexican Spitfire series, who would later engage in a memorable egg-breaking fight with Stan and Ollie in *Hollywood Party* [1934].) At other moments, Stan bursts into tears and the crying routine doesn't completely jibe with the aggressive character he's portraying. Though it's still amusing, the weeping is better suited for the childlike figure Laurel would later refine as his screen persona.

Once again, Laurel is the focal character while Hardy has a glorified supporting role. Although they only have a few scenes together, they share a

Although Lupe Velez and Oliver Hardy are also pictured, this poster for *Sailors, Beware!* (1927) makes it clear that Stan Laurel is the star of the film.

good, if atypical, rapport. As he was in *With Love and Hisses*, Ollie is Stan's superior, but this time Stan is not a willing subordinate. Their interaction is contentious, with Stan rebelling against Ollie's attempts to assert his authority. Their best shared moment comes when Chester gets entangled with a young woman jumping rope and in trying to extricate the newly assigned steward, Cryder becomes entangled himself. The trio (Laurel, Hardy and an uncredited actress) jumping rope in unison is a funny gag that succeeds because the performers are completely in sync with one another. Such expert timing would be a hallmark of Stan and Ollie's subsequent teaming.

Aside from his footage with Hardy, Laurel's best scenes involve Anita Garvin and Harry Earles as the crooked husband-and-wife duo. Garvin was a deft, sophisticated comedienne and, as always, she plays off of Laurel beautifully. In baby garb, the 25-year-old Earles makes a very convincing infant (as he did in the 1925 and 1930 versions of *The Unholy Three*) and his scenes opposite an increasingly skeptical Stan are all the more amusing because of it. At first, Stan suspects nothing and asks the "baby" if he wants to play. The tyke immediately pulls out a pair of dice and rolls them on the floor. Stan is bemused by this precocious behavior, but when the baby throws down some money and instructs Stan to do the same, he becomes wary of the baby's familiarity with gambling.

After the baby swindles him out his money, using loaded dice, Stan senses there's something amiss. Later, Garvin orders a still-rankled Stan to take the baby, resting comfortably in a carriage, down a flight of stairs. Stan complies by giving the carriage a hearty shove, causing it to barrel down the stairs at breakneck speed and crash into a closed door. (And at this point, Stan isn't even sure the baby is an adult!)

While Stan was still grappling with his screen persona, Ollie was inching closer to his familiar personality. In 1954, Hardy cited a scene from *Why Girls Love Sailors* (in which he got hit with a bucket of water) as the origin of his trademark tie-twiddle and slow-burn "camera look," but it turned out he was referring to *Sailors, Beware!* However, these claims don't even apply to this film, since he doesn't twiddle his tie (instead, he waves his fingers in embarrassment) and the camera look he gives is similar to ones he delivered in several previous comedies. (Ironically, Stan looks at the camera more often than Ollie does in this picture.)

What Ollie actually did in *Sailors, Beware!* was to further define his comic technique. The purser's uniform gives his character a self-imposed dignity that he carries with aplomb. Fancying himself a lady-killer, Purser Cryder (who has "only two things on his mind — Blondes and Brunettes") greets the boarding female passengers with a warm smile and an exchange of pleasantries, while male passengers are rudely hustled along. After Chester tricks him into thinking a pretty lady is awaiting his company, Cryder fastidiously adjusts his cap and brushes his sleeves before elegantly striding to the supposed rendezvous. When Cryder attempts to escort Madame Ritz up a staircase, he slips and falls flat on his face, in full view of a crowd of passengers. Deeply embarrassed, his sheepish smile barely masks his wounded pride. Worse yet, Cryder's tough-guy façade is undone after the midget, revealed to be a thief, beats him to a pulp.

Sailors, Beware! is often quite funny, though it has little in common with the later, more polished Laurel and Hardy efforts. It is best appreciated as a diverting showcase for two brilliant comedians on the verge of a historic partnership.

Do Detectives Think?

Cast

Stan Laurel	Ferdinand Finkleberry
Oliver Hardy	Sherlock Pinkham
Jimmie (James) Finlayson	Judge Foozle
Viola Richard	Mrs. Foozle
Noah Young	The Tipton Slasher

Frank Brownlee	Detective agency boss
Will Stanton	Tipton Slasher's pal
Wilson Benge	The new butler
Charles A. Bachman	Officer
Charley Young	Juror

Credits

Fred L. Guiol	Director
Hal Roach	Story
H. M. Walker	Titles

Working title: "Body Guards."
A Hal Roach production. Copyrighted July 8, 1927.
Production dates: April 25–May 6, 1927.
Released November 20, 1927, by Pathé.
Two reels.

The Laurel-Hardy comedy team hinted at in *Duck Soup* blossomed in *Do Detectives Think?*, a quantum leap in the evolution of their partnership. They still had a way to go to achieve their famed Stanley and Ollie personas, but at least they're a full-fledged duo, and not a lead comedian and a glorified supporting player as they had been (and would continue to be in a couple of subsequent films).

Judge Foozle sentences the Tipton Slasher to death by hanging, adding, "And I hope you choke!" The remark sends the murderer into a rage, and he vows to escape and cut out the judge's tonsils. When the Slasher does manage to break out, a panic-stricken Foozle instructs the head of a detective agency to send over two of his bravest men, who turn out to be Ferdinand Finkleberry and Sherlock Pinkham. As the fearless duo head to the Foozles' home, the Slasher accosts a butler scheduled to start a position with the judge and assumes his identity. (Conveniently, Mrs. Foozle greets the Slasher at the door, so the judge is unaware of his new servant's true identity.) After a harrowing attempt to retrieve their hats from a cemetery, Finkleberry and Pinkham reach their assigned destination and assure the Foozles that they are safe from danger. It takes a while for the shaky sleuths to realize the Slasher is under the same roof, and when they do, the killer decides to add them to his hit list. But Finkleberry is able to lock the Slasher inside a closet — where Pinkham is hiding — until arresting officers arrive.

Do Detectives Think? marked the first time the boys wore their trademark suits and derbies, which gave them the sort of genteel "half-assed dignity" that would define their characters. Yet their appearances still required some tweaking: Stan is too immaculately groomed to be completely convincing as an innocent child-man figure, and Ollie's scruffy mustache seems more appropriate for the comic heavies he portrayed in earlier pictures. The regulation-detective derbies they wear here would be altered slightly to make them look a little less dapper. (As Randy Skretvedt has noted, Stan wore an Irish children's derby in later films.)

Still, the rudiments of their onscreen relationship are in place. Stan forsakes the frantic mugging he used to rely upon so heavily, and there's none of the hot-tempered aggression found in some of his previous performances (although he has an oddly serious expression on his face during his introductory close-up) because he is willingly subservient to Ollie, who in turn envisions himself as the leader and brain trust of the team. Yet the intertitles make it clear right from the start that Ollie is more incompetent than Stan ("Ferdinand Finkleberry — The second worst detective in the whole world"; "Sherlock Pinkham — The worst"), which fits Hardy's own assessment that his screen character was actually dumber than Stan's because he always thought he was the smarter one.

Repetitive scared-reaction comedy dominates the film, as the boys shiver and fumble their way through one scene after another, so there is little opportunity for subtlety. That doesn't mean it isn't funny — this sort of spooky humor was a reliable format for all screen comedians — but by nature it revolves around the singular (and shallow) concept of having a performer scream in fear and run away. And Stan does plenty of screaming and crying. Though he's slow to grasp obvious perils (why does that butler look so familiar?), he's quick to react to imaginary ones, like the shadow of a goat that resembles a horned devil. In later Laurel and Hardy films with a "scare" theme (*Habeas Corpus*, *The Laurel-Hardy Murder Case*, *Oliver the Eighth*, *The Live Ghost*), the humor would spring from their characters' frightened reactions. In *Do Detectives Think?*, their characters have not been fully fleshed out, so we're left to laugh at the sight of them running about willy-nilly. Most of these shenanigans are still undeniably funny, but the gags don't have the same resonance they would have had there been identifiable characters to execute them. In other words, the majority of the gags in *Do Detectives Think?* would have been just as amusing had they been performed by nearly any other pair of comedians.

Nevertheless, there are signs of great things to come, as the appealing interaction between Laurel and Hardy becomes more apparent. Even at this early stage, they're getting their derbies mixed up, with Stan continually handing Ollie the wrong hat, much to Ollie's frustration. And Stan's good intentions only wind up putting his partner in harm's way, as when Stan attempts to handcuff Noah Young and slaps the cuffs around Ollie's wrists instead. What they haven't established yet, however, is the bond that would elevate them from being mere cohorts to inseparable friends. In *Do Detectives Think?*

there's an overriding sense of self-preservation, rather than camaraderie, especially on Ollie's part.

Do Detectives Think? signals a shift in the onscreen relationship between Laurel and James Finlayson. In previous Laurel comedies such as *A Man About Town* (1923) and *Near Dublin* (1924), Finlayson's participation was that of a near-equal partner. However, with the pairing of Laurel and Hardy, Finlayson's role was reduced to that of a supporting comic foil, albeit a reliable and hilarious one.

Do Detectives Think? was reworked as *Going Bye-Bye!* (1934), this time with Stan and Ollie as the targets of an escaped convict's wrath. The revamping benefited from a greater emphasis on character-driven humor and plot complications rather than stringing together a collection of frantic sight gags. Nevertheless, *Do Detectives Think?* is an underrated and very funny film that holds up surprisingly well when compared to the team's later, more accomplished efforts.

Flying Elephants

Cast

Stan Laurel	Little Twinkle Star
Oliver Hardy	A mighty giant
James Finlayson	Saxophonus
Viola Richard	Blushing Rose
Dorothy Coburn	Wrestling cavewoman
Leo Willis	Fishing caveman
Tiny (Stanley J.) Sandford	Hulking caveman
Budd Fine	Hulking caveman
Fay Lanphier	Cavewoman
Edna Marian	Cavewoman (scenes deleted*)

Credits

Frank Butler (and Hal Roach)†	Director
Hal Roach	Original story
H. M. Walker	Titles
Roy Seawright	Animation

Working titles: "Were Women Always Wild?" and "Do Cavemen Marry?"
A Hal Roach production.
Copyrighted September 2, 1927.
Production dates: May 9–May 14, 1927.

---

*Although featured prominently in publicity shots, Edna Marian does not have any scenes in the finished film.

†Studio records confirm that Hal Roach actually directed Flying Elephants. Frank Butler, who received sole director credit, only shot the retakes.

Retakes: June 9, 1927.
Released February 12, 1928, by Pathé.
Two reels.

If it had not been produced immediately after *Do Detectives Think?*, a film that should have cemented the Laurel-Hardy partnership once and for all, *Flying Elephants* might be easier to accept for its offbeat novelty value rather than being looked upon as a bewildering regression. Stan and Ollie have good solo scenes, but many L and H admirers are justifiably disappointed that their characters don't meet until the picture is nearly over — and when they do, they quickly become adversaries. This unsatisfying conclusion negates the amusing interludes that preceded it.

The setting is the Stone Age and omnipotent ruler King Ferdinand has decreed all males over the age of 13 and under 95 must marry within 24 hours "under penalty of banishment and death or both!" After a couple of failed attempts at securing a mate, Little Twinkle Star, "a merry swain in search of romance," falls for gorgeous Blushing Rose, daughter of Saxophonus, an aged wizard. ("He had been wizzing for years.") A mighty giant of a caveman comes along and sets his sights on Blushing Rose, so Little Twinkle Star tries to eliminate his competition. A wild goat conveniently butts the giant off a cliff, leaving our hero free to claim his lady love.

Beautifully photographed on location in Moapa, Nevada, *Flying Elephants* has the loose structure and impromptu feel of the early Keystone comedies. The entire cast is attired in the sort of animal-pelt wardrobe prevalent in cinematic depictions of the Stone Age. Stan, Ollie and most of the other male cast members wield oversized clubs and wear shaggy wigs (Stan's wig looks like it's on loan from a female impersonator) to further enhance their Neanderthal appearance, while the women are merely Jazz Age flappers with fur trimmings. This sort of 1920s anachronism is understandable and expected, but why several intertitles are written in Medieval-style text ("Wilt thou marry us?") is anyone's guess. Prehistoric beasts are represented by goats, bears, cartoon elephants and, in one brief shot, a Triceratops (a three-horned dinosaur) — or, more precisely, two men in a Triceratops costume, similar to the two-man horse costumes used for pantomimes and stage shows.*

For the most part, Laurel and Hardy operate separately, with Stan getting the lion's share of the spotlight. Stan's energetic performance as Little Twinkle Star owes more to his earlier solo comedies than it does to any of his recent efforts to scale back the hyperactive hopping and scissor-kicking. (Those

---

**The Triceratops costume also turned up in the Our Gang comedy* Playin' Hookey *(1928), where it was seen to greater advantage.*

trademarks are back with a vengeance.) Scampering across the landscape like a woodland sprite, the virginal caveman ("My mother hasn't told me everything") is shyly effeminate one minute then aggressively macho the next. When a cavewoman gives him the cold shoulder, Little Twinkle Star turns he-man and tries to carry her away. But she fends him off with a variety of wrestling moves, reducing the would-be warrior to tears.

In one of the film's funniest set pieces, Little Twinkle Star sets out to prove he'll be a worthy husband for Blushing Rose by exhibiting his skills as a fisherman. Wading into the river, he is unable to spear any fishes, so he resorts to a different technique: snatching a fly out of the air, he gently places it on the surface of the water then clubs the fish when it pops up, tossing it ashore. This procedure works well enough until he accidentally clubs another fisherman.

Stan's gift for physical comedy is evident in all of his scenes. Yet his personality is a bit too unfocused for an audience to grasp who his character is (other than a goofy young innocent), which makes Oliver Hardy's performance seem all the more assured by comparison.

Ollie, whose unnamed character is identified as "a mighty giant," takes what could have been a stock heavy role and, through his innate charm and finesse, becomes an appealing comic figure. In his solo scenes, he's a pompous oaf ("I can get five women in five minutes — And you ought to see me when I'm working fast") whose courtly demeanor and delicate gestures provide a humorous contrast to his hulking frame and scruffy appearance. Encountering a potential mate, he flashes a bashful smile and coyly waves his fingers before striking up a conversation: "Beautiful weather — The elephants are flying south." (And sure enough, we see winged pachyderms in flight via simple but charming animation.) But his self-confidence takes a beating when he attempts to woo seemingly eligible females and gets clobbered by their jealous mates. With expertly timed facial expressions, Hardy conveys surprise and resignation after he's clunked on the head by a rival's club.

Once "tagged" and twice shy, he tries to ignore the next potential conquest, and then stops to scan the horizon for rivals. Approaching the pretty cavewoman, he begins chatting amiably, only to get clunked by her unseen mate perched on a mountain ledge. Hardy doesn't bother to look up — he simply moves on, his frozen face masking a wounded pride striving to maintain its fragile dignity. A third girl is anxious to become his mate, but he's thoroughly disgusted by now. She begs him to reconsider and the minute he lets his guard down, a goat rams him in the posterior. Dejected, he slinks away, unaware of the true identity of his assailant. Hardy comes off so well in these scenes that the whole film goes awry when he is later pushed off a cliff and presumably falls to his death (even though Finlayson's character survived a similar spill).

When Stan and Ollie are finally introduced to one another, they engage in a friendly nose-rubbing, head-bashing greeting ritual. But they seem preordained to become rivals due to the dictates of the woman-hunt storyline. It may have been easier to have them square off instead of trying to establish a relationship so late in the picture, although seeing Ollie get bumped off (literally) is an unnecessarily brutal touch. Worse yet, it's not funny.

As the third-position comedian, James Finlayson's participation is limited to serving as a foil and go-between for Stan and Ollie. He's always amusing, but the role is not as showy as in previous collaborations with Laurel. Viola Richard makes a very fetching cave girl, and her physical beauty is matched by her willingness to embrace the spirit of the tomfoolery. She even devises a way to cure Finlayson's toothache: she attaches a string to the infected tooth and ties the other end around a boulder, then matter-of-factly instructs him to toss the boulder off the edge of a cliff! (Finlayson enlists Hardy's aid in executing the task; when the boulder is tossed off the cliff, it pulls the tooth — and Finlayson along with it.)

Flying Elephants went through changes during production. Existing publicity photos show Stan and Ollie clad in different cavemen costumes (less fur-laden than the ones they actually wear in the film) and wigs. Perky blonde Edna Marian, one of the "Hal Roach All-Stars," figures prominently in some of these photos, yet she does not have any scenes in existing prints.

Quite often, gags and routines were filmed and then, in the editing process, omitted from the final cut. A continuity gap in *Flying Elephants* indicates a jettisoned sequence: just as Little Twinkle Star seems to have made a conquest, a brawny caveman tosses the woman over his shoulder and carries her off. Undaunted, Little Twinkle Star throws his shoulders back and prepares to deal with the situation head-on. The scene abruptly cuts to our defeated hero, no longer holding the flowers he had in the previous shot, with no indication as to what occurred during the confrontation, except that he obviously lost the fight.

Flying Elephants was the final Laurel-Hardy film slated for release through the Pathé Exchange, which had been distributing Hal Roach productions for years. Roach had grown increasingly dissatisfied with Pathé's business practices; severing connections with them, Roach signed a more lucrative distribution deal with Metro-Goldwyn-Mayer. Pathé withheld *Do Detectives Think?* and *Flying Elephants* and released them months later, after the team had caught on with moviegoers. *Flying Elephants* was released on February 12, 1928, sandwiched between the superior Laurel and Hardy/M-G-M releases *Leave 'Em Laughing* (January 28) and *The Finishing Touch* (February 28). Audiences were undoubtedly confused as to why the two comedians had such limited interaction in this prehistoric farce.

The confusion would extend into the 1960s, when 8mm home-movie distributors marketed excerpts from *Flying Elephants* under its original title — which made no sense unless one had seen the picture — as well as pseudonyms like *Cave Men*, *The Amazons* and *The Fisherman*. Many consumers were baffled by these bizarre snippets that were packaged as "Laurel and Hardy" movies. (There is no footage of Hardy in *The Fisherman*.) It would take books such as William K. Everson's *The Films of Laurel and Hardy* to clear up the mystery by placing the film in its proper historical context.

Flying Elephants is best appreciated as a solo Stan Laurel comedy that just happens to feature Oliver Hardy in a key role. Or as an offbeat artifact that serves to illustrate that the true potential of the Laurel-Hardy pairing was not realized until their childlike characters became inseparable friends who faced life's hardships as a single unit.

Should Tall Men Marry?

Cast

Stan Laurel	Bill from Arkansas, a.k.a. Texas Tommy
Stuart Holmes	"Snake-tail" Sharkey
Jimmie (James) Finlayson	Joe Skittle
Martha Sleeper	Martha Skittle
Teddy (Theodore) von Eltz	Teddy
Edgar Dearing	Henchman
Lew Meehan	Henchman
Geraldine the mule	Herself

Credits

Clyde Bruckman (and Stan Laurel, uncredited)	Director
George Stevens	Cinematographer
Richard Currier	Film Editor
H. M. Walker	Titles

A Hal Roach production.
Copyrighted September 2, 1927.
Released January 15, 1928, by Pathé.
Two reels.

Stan Laurel's final comedy in which Hardy does not appear was not initially conceived as a vehicle to star him, nor were Clyde Bruckman and Stan (uncredited) the original directors. As such, it's more of a curio or footnote rather than being a representative example of Stan's work from this period.

On April 11, 1927, while Stan and Oliver Hardy were completing work on the two-reeler, *Sailors, Beware!*, Hal Roach's writing staff had completed

Stan (left), with assist from James Finlayson (right), handily subdues Stuart Holmes in this publicity shot for *Should Tall Men Marry?* (1928).

a script with the title *Why Cowboys Go Home*. Warren Doane, general manager of the Roach Studios, sent a telegram to Roach (who was in New York on business), suggesting Oliver Hardy for the role of "Paprika Pete." Roach wired back, stating that Hardy would not be right for the part, but offered no specific explanation as to why. The film was then shot with Eugene Pallette in the role originally meant for Hardy, with Louis Gasnier directing. It was previewed with the title *Cowboys Cry For It* on May 7, 1927. Hal Roach was so displeased by the results that he turned the project over to director Clyde Bruckman, with orders to recast the Pallette role with Stan Laurel and somehow to salvage the production.

Stan had just returned from location filming in Moapa, Nevada, shooting retakes for *Flying Elephants*. Beginning May 17, 1927, Stan and Bruckman spent a week revising *Cowboys Cry for It*, writing and directing new footage with most of the original cast members as well as excising footage of Eugene Pallette and inserting Stan into the proceedings. Although Stan received top billing in *Should Tall Men Marry?*, in the refurbished version of *Cowboys Cry for It* his character is merely a glorified supporting role. (Perhaps his prominent billing was compensation for not receiving a co-director's or writer's credit.)

In this Western farce, the action centers around the Arrowhead Ranch, where local baddie "Snake-tail" Sharkey ("so double-faced it took two barbers to shave him") asks wealthy rancher Joe Skittle for his daughter's hand in marriage. But Martha Skittle finds Sharkey repulsive — and besides, she's smitten with a mild-mannered cowboy named Teddy, who's the closest thing to a Greek god in Martha's eyes. None of this sits well with Sharkey; he and his henchman abduct the lovebirds, holding them captive in a barn. Joe and ranch hand Texas Tommy ride to the rescue, managing to thwart Sharkey and his gang.

While it isn't an unmitigated disaster, *Should Husbands Marry?* emerges as a slight, unmemorable two-reeler, despite Stan's handiwork. Stan, however, shouldn't be held accountable for this. He was confronted with the unenviable task of overhauling an already-completed film, one that had a basic, insurmountable flaw for a comedy: the central characters — the nominal hero, the damsel in distress, and the villain — were not designed to be funny. These characters could have derived from any standard-issue horse opera, and no amount of joke-laden title cards would have made them especially humorous. (It's a shame that Martha Sleeper wasn't given anything truly funny to do because she proved to be a capable comedienne when afforded the opportunity.) As a result, Stan and James Finlayson operate along the sidelines, valiantly trying to wring laughs from a plotline neither one has motivated. As always, the elfin Laurel and cantankerous Finlayson work well together, but they're at the mercy of a pre-existing framework and left to wiggle through the cracks in the screenplay (such as it is) and enliven the proceedings the best they can.

Had Stan been involved with this project from its inception, it's safe to assume that the resulting film would have been more cohesive, if not funnier. Laurel and Finlayson indulge in plenty of pratfalls, though their combined (and welcome) high spirits can't mask the dearth of comic inspiration. Watching a temperamental mule chase Finlayson is amusing at first, but the joke quickly wears out its welcome because no real set-up or rationale exists for it.

One set piece devised by Laurel is a comparative highlight: While Teddy awkwardly attempts to woo Martha, Texas Tommy covertly coaches the girl-shy cowpoke by demonstrating lovemaking techniques on a calf, putting his arm around the animal's neck and repeatedly kissing it on the lips. Unbeknownst to Tommy, Joe Skittle has witnessed these amorous antics and, in squinty-eyed wonder, he confronts Tommy: "How long has this been going on?" In short order, Tommy's shifting facial expressions convey an array of emotions, from stunned surprise to sheepish embarrassment to a look of disgust as the gravity of Joe's insinuation sinks in.

While this brief moment reflects Stan's growing subtlety as a screen comedian, his overall performance here is still laden with the familiar, broader mannerisms upon which he had come to rely, such as his triumphant hand-clapping jig whenever the tide turns in his favor, and the eruption of tears whenever he's injured (physically or emotionally) or frightened, a device that was often overused in his pre–Oliver Hardy efforts. (In the Laurel and Hardy films, Stan usually used the crying bit to punctuate a gag. In Stan's solo films, the crying bit was often *the* gag.)

Stan also continues to rely on "funny" garb to identify himself as the primary comic figure. Stan's elongated cowboy hat provides a perfect visual complement to his elongated face, yet Stan further hammers home the point by keeping the front of the floppy brim upturned at all times. And his loose chaps give him a baggy-pants Chaplinesque appearance, which may or may not have been intentional.

After the plot has been set up, the second half belongs to Laurel and Finlayson, and the pace picks up considerably during their attempts to rescue the romantic leads from the clutches of the villain and his gang. The gags may not be particularly memorable or inventive (how many times can an audience be expected to laugh at the sight of Stan falling off a horse?) but they're plentiful and energetic, and Stan should be given credit for providing a rousing finale to an otherwise lackluster effort.

Aside from its historical significance and a smattering of amusing scenes, *Should Tall Men Marry?* is not indicative of either Stan Laurel or Hal Roach at his best.

Sugar Daddies

Cast

Stan Laurel	Our hero
Jimmie (James) Finlayson	Cyrus Brittle
Oliver Hardy	The butler
Charlotte Mineau	The bride
Noah Young	Her brother
Edna Marian	The bride's daughter
Eugene Pallette	Portly man wearing derby
Sam Lufkin	Fun house ticket-taker
Dorothy Coburn	Brunette in fun house
Ray Cooke	Bellboy
Charlie Hall	Hotel extra
Jack Hill	Hotel extra
Jiggs	Dog

With
Jack Adams, Will Stanton

Credits

Fred L. Guiol . . . . Director
George Stevens . . . . Cinematographer
Richard Currier . . . . Film Editor
H. M. Walker . . . . Titles

A Hal Roach production. Copyrighted August 17, 1927.
Production dates: May 26–27, May 31–June 3, 1927.
Released September 10, 1927, by
Metro-Goldwyn-Mayer Distributing Corp.
Two reels.

Stan and Ollie had too few scenes together in *Flying Elephants*, a fundamental error corrected in *Sugar Daddies*. Yet sharing the same frame did not automatically make them a team either, and the film has little in common with the great Laurel and Hardy comedies that followed, which is why it is routinely dismissed by many fans and historians. However, for those willing to accept it as an atypical pre-partnership entry, *Sugar Daddies* is fast-paced, high-spirited fun, far more entertaining than previous efforts such as *Slipping Wives* and *Love 'Em and Weep*.

Oil tycoon Cyrus Brittle awakens after a night of drunken revelry to discover he's married to a hatchet-faced shrew with a brutish brother and wide-eyed daughter in tow. To extricate himself from this marital blunder, Brittle sends for his attorney, but to no avail — the new family demands a $50,000 payoff. Brittle, his butler and the attorney flee to a seaside hotel, and when the cutthroat in-laws track them down, Brittle and the attorney disguise themselves as the butler's exceptionally tall "wife." Sensing something fishy, the bride and her kin chase them all around a nearby amusement park.

One reason for the film's low reputation is that Stan and Ollie's characters, such as they are, have no depth or shading — they are merely gag-driven ciphers. In fact, they aren't even assigned names: Stan is singled out as "our hero," while Ollie is simply identified as "the butler." With his hair neatly slicked back, the bespectacled Stan basically repeats his role as the dutiful-but-inept lawyer from the Charley Chase short *Now I'll Tell One*. His byplay with Hardy is smoothly executed, as one would expect from two seasoned pros, but their familiar dynamic is lacking because Hardy's role doesn't permit him to dominate Laurel. Stan holds the upper hand, and his initial encounter with Ollie makes it quite clear: as the lawyer enters Brittle's home, he refuses to remove his hat and no amount of maneuvering on the butler's part can change this. In the later Laurel and Hardy comedies, the socially dense Stanley would immediately remove his headgear at Ollie's prompting, but here he will not relinquish his hat until he decides to.

There is not much comic invention on display in *Sugar Daddies*. The best gag is a variation of the best gag in *Love 'Em and Weep*: Donning a wig and long cape, Stan perches himself on Finlayson's back and they masquerade as a conspicuously tall woman (with a freakishly protruding abdomen!).*

But *Sugar Daddies* milks the joke for all its worth, and in the process brings Laurel and Hardy closer together, as James Finlayson literally goes undercover, hidden beneath the cape. Struggling to maintain the charade and remain one step ahead of their pursuers, Stan and Ollie cling to another as they race through the amusement park, with their panicked reactions foreshadowing scenes in later films in which the pair are pursued by angry spouses, police officers or assorted heavies. Ironically, once Laurel adopts the drag disguise, he looks more like Stanley than he did as the attorney. On the other hand, Hardy doesn't look exactly like Ollie because he's wearing the same parted-down-the-middle hairpiece he wore in *Love 'Em and Weep*.

Sugar Daddies turns into an energetic extended chase, and if the comic complications aren't particularly inspired, the location filming (at the Pike Amusement Park in Long Beach) is a tremendous asset, filled with nostalgic glimpses of the fun house and assorted rides, plus shots of boardwalk patrons watching the comedians' antics. George Stevens's occasionally shaky but nonetheless lively camerawork adds to the verisimilitude.

The film ends abruptly — a cop mistakes a tall woman for Laurel and Finlayson, and lifts her skirt in an attempt to expose the charade — and this lack of a plot resolution has led some to speculate that the existing source material is missing the original conclusion. While this may be a possibility, we hasten to point out that countless two-reel comedies have abrupt, inconclusive endings, so it is likely that a largely improvised trifle such as *Sugar Daddies* did not bother to offer a concrete ending.

Introducing James Finlayson as the focal character and then having him disappear for long stretches is an encapsulation of his career at the Hal Roach Studio. *Sugar Daddies* marked the last time Finlayson would be seen as a starring comedian alongside Stan and Ollie. As the Laurel-Hardy partnership solidified, Finlayson would be reduced to supporting-player status. Finlayson had showy roles in many later L and H comedies — most notably as a hapless homeowner in the reciprocal-destruction classic *Big Business* (1929) — but he would never again enjoy the same level of prominence as the rising comedy team.

By the time they filmed *Sugar Daddies*, the brass at the Hal Roach studio

---

*In Love 'Em and Weep, *an unconscious Mae Busch is perched on Finlayson's back. When the film was remade as* Chickens Come Home *(1931), Mae Busch repeated the role, with Stan and Ollie taking turns as her "support" crew.*

were listening to writer-director Leo McCarey, who kept pointing out how well Laurel and Hardy worked together. Their very next film, *The Second Hundred Years*, was produced as an official Laurel and Hardy comedy. They were now a bona fide team. While they would again experiment with separate roles (*Putting Pants on Philip*) and as adversaries (*Early To Bed*), from here on they are indeed a team and would continue as such. Laurel would never again make a film without Hardy. Hardy would make a couple of character appearances after Laurel retired from films, most notably opposite John Wayne in *The Fighting Kentuckian* (1949).

Oddly, some of the earlier films in which Laurel is the lead with Hardy in support were not released until well after their team tenure. Roach switched his production facility from Pathé to Metro-Goldwyn-Mayer studios in 1927. Pathé took its time releasing the Laurel and Hardy films they had, including *Flying Elephants*, which didn't come out until 1928. By this time, the duo was established with moviegoers, so their adversarial status here, especially since Hardy gets so much less footage, might have seemed a bit offbeat and less interesting. As we state in our chapter assessment, *Flying Elephants* is a funnier movie when approached from the proper perspective.

10

Laurel and Hardy

With the exception of *Putting Pants on Philip* (1927), *Sugar Daddies* marked the last time Stan Laurel and Oliver Hardy would be presented as anything but brothers-in-arms, who, despite petty squabbles, leaned on each other as they navigated their way through an often treacherous universe. In *The Second Hundred Years* (1927), the first "official" Laurel and Hardy comedy, the Stan-Ollie relationship is still rough around the edges, but the basic characters are in place and these personas would be developed and refined to perfection.

In previous years, Laurel rejected opportunities to work with Hardy onscreen, but not out of any personal animosity. Laurel simply felt that Hardy was not a traditional comic heavy; he once told Joe Rock, "[Hardy is] always trying to get a laugh. And if a heavy gets a laugh in the picture, it destroys his heaviness." Later, Laurel nearly turned down his destined partnership because he wanted to devote more time to writing and directing.

Yet once he teamed with Hardy, Laurel soon discovered that Ollie's character didn't compete with him, it completed him. The courtly, fastidious and pompous Ollie beautifully contrasted the slow-witted, sweet natured and obedient Stanley, and the interaction between these two childlike figures provided Laurel with a wealth of comic inspiration. As the personalities took shape, Laurel could now create gags driven by character not contrivance, transforming Stanley and Ollie into warm, loveable souls in whom audiences had a rooting interest. Ollie may see himself as Stanley's superior, but he also sees himself as Stanley's guardian and, when the going gets rough, his protector. Stanley, in turn, is devoted to Ollie, accepting his partner's boastful claims without question and willing to participate in whatever ill-conceived scheme is concocted. And both characters share an innate innocence that bonds them. For Laurel, as a comedy writer, this gave him the opportunity to devise material for two separate yet intertwined characters, and he made the most of it.

With Hardy providing the yin to his yang, Laurel would discover the

A publicity shot of Oliver Hardy (left) and Stan Laurel with Our Gang member Allen "Farina" Hoskins, circa 1928.

humanity of his own character and the freedom to set up a joke for his teammate. The beauty of the Laurel-Hardy pairing was that each one was equally funny in his own way. Hardy was every bit the comedian Laurel was and would routinely deliver the punchline to a gag, whether it was a spectacular pratfall or an exasperated look into the camera. When Stanley would launch into some flight of fancy, Ollie was there to react. When Stanley would do something dumb, Ollie would try to correct him — and prove, as Oliver Hardy would state in interviews, that he was really the dumb half of the team because he thought he was the smart one.

Laurel learned that a slower pace was better suited to the way Stanley and Ollie processed information (both were masters of the "delayed reaction" take). *We Faw Down* (1928), a funny but undervalued Laurel and Hardy comedy (it is seldom ranked among their best), is a prime example of how far Laurel's technique advanced in such a short span of time. In the film, Stan and Ollie want to sneak off to a poker game and tell their skeptical wives (Vivien Oakland, Bess Flowers) that they're going to meet Ollie's boss at the Orpheum Theatre. On the way to the game, they gallantly try to retrieve a woman's hat and get doused with a street sprinkler. The woman and her female roommate invite the boys back to their apartment to dry off, only to meet up with the woman's jealous boyfriend (George Kotsonaros), who just happens to be a prizefighter. Stan and Ollie jump out of the window — luckily, the apartment is on the ground floor — and make their getaway. Unluckily, they're spotted by their wives, who were rushing down to the Orpheum Theatre after receiving news that it burned down! Of course, Stan and Ollie are unaware of any of this, so when their wives ask them to describe the show they just sat through, they have to come up with the details in a hurry.

We Faw Down is propelled by the situation and characters, not stand-alone gags. It relies on the team's expert pantomime, as in their encounter with the two damsels in distress, and when Stan consults a newspaper advertisement then silently coaches Ollie as to which acts were on the theatre bill. In this later set piece, their rapport is particularly sharp, as their facial expressions and body language carry the humor. When Ollie tells one outlandish fib too many, Stanley can no longer hold back and dissolves into uncontrollable laughter. Ollie reprimands Stanley and valiantly tries to maintain his composure, but even he can't keep a straight face. The subtlety of this sequence is remarkable, particularly when one considers that Laurel had been prone to outrageous mugging only a couple years prior to this.

Once he teamed with Hardy, Laurel seemed to make great creative strides over a short period of time. While this is certainly true, it was also the end result of decades of honing his craft, first on stage and then in his solo work, in his capacity in front of and behind the camera. So the burst of creativity seen during the Laurel and Hardy years was merely the culmination of everything that came before it.

Laurel's character didn't stop evolving once Hardy entered the picture. The scrappiness he would exhibit in such silent-era L and H comedies as *The Finishing Touch* (1928), *You're Darn Tootin'* (1928), *Two Tars* (1928), *Big Business* (1929) and *Bacon Grabbers* (1929) would become less evident as time went on.

With the advent of "talkies," Laurel and Hardy made the transition more successfully than the majority of their silent-screen contemporaries because, as it turned out, their astute use of sound actually enhanced their humor. (Of course, a huge point in their favor was that their speaking voices perfectly matched their characters.) Right from the start, in the first all-talking comedy, *Unaccustomed As We Are* (1929), Laurel's inspired use of sound effects to convey offscreen action shows that he realized the potential of the new technology.

While some — including Laurel himself— preferred their output from the silent era, the duo continued to flourish during the sound era, turning out such enduring classics as *Brats* (1930), *Hog Wild* (1930), *Helpmates* (1932),

Stan Laurel and Oliver Hardy as bumbling burglars in *Night Owls* (1930).

The Music Box (1932; their only Academy Award-winning film), *Their First Mistake* (1932) and *Towed in a Hole* (1933). They began making feature-length films in 1931, alternating between features and shorts until 1935 when they switched exclusively to the longer format. Their best features include *Sons of the Desert* (1933; their most seamless effort), *Our Relations* (1936), *Way Out West* (1937) and *Block-Heads* (1938).

On November 18, 1932, at the Ambassador Hotel's Cocoanut Grove, Stan Laurel (left), Hal Roach and Oliver Hardy are all smiles after *The Music Box* was awarded an Oscar for Best Short Subject (Comedy) for 1931–32.

The sweet, slow-witted Stanley of the Laurel and Hardy years was a far cry from the hyperactive and often vindictive character Stan played in many of his solo efforts. By the time the silent era concluded, Laurel shed his tendencies to mug shamelessly and the more deliberately paced Stanley persona took shape. Whereas solo Stan could be a whirling dervish, Stanley reacted at a much slower rate, scratching his unruly mop of hair as he struggled to process information. With the coming of sound, Laurel's shrewd, economical use of dialogue further defined the Stanley character, as his limited powers of comprehension could now be conveyed through the hesitant delivery of a few select words. (Instinctively realizing that "all-talking" comedies didn't require wall-to-wall dialogue passages, Laurel learned to strike a perfect balance between spoken words and pantomime.) Ollie would ask Stanley a question, and before Stanley could even provide an answer, he'd grapple to understand the question, as Ollie fumed in silence, looking directly into the camera to express his frustration to the viewer.

On occasion, Stanley could organize his thoughts long enough to produce

Stan Laurel (left) and Oliver Hardy strike a pose at radio station KFVD, which was conveniently located on the Hal Roach lot, circa 1930.

Stan (left) and Oliver Hardy continued to entertain moviegoers during the World War II era, even in such imperfect vehicles as *Air Raid Wardens* (1943).

a coherent, often profound idea, but these moments of startling clarity were mercurial and were over as quickly as they began. In *Towed in a Hole*, Stanley tells Ollie that buying their own boat would be the best way to increase the profits of their fish-peddling enterprise. But when Ollie asks him to repeat the suggestion, Stanley's brief burst of ingenuity has evaporated, so he can only offer a garbled approximation of his original brainstorm. (No matter — Ollie is on the same wavelength: "I know exactly what you mean.")

Every so often, there were flashes of solo Stan in Stanley. An example that springs to mind is in *Blotto* (1930), in which Stanley wants to sneak out of the house to go to a swanky nightclub with his pal Ollie. But first Stanley has to come up with an airtight alibi that will appease his suspicious spouse, played by the always-welcome Anita Garvin. Ollie suggests that Stanley send himself a telegram ("important business") and Stanley chortles with conspiratorial glee. Stanley slips through an open window, plants the phony telegram, rings the doorbell, and sneaks back inside the house. Then he goes to the door and says, in a stilted, overly mannered tone, "Telegram for me? Now, who could have sent this?" Then he pretends to tip an imaginary messenger and steps back in the house, without the telegram. Within a split second, he realizes his mistake, steps outside again, hastily grabs the telegram and looks directly into the camera, making an open-mouthed "I almost blew it!" expression. This reaction — a throwback to the old Stan — is not an artistic regression. Rather, it's a playful and charming reminder of his earlier, rascally self.

After *Saps at Sea* (filmed 1939, released 1940), Laurel and Hardy parted company with Hal Roach and began making features for 20th Century–Fox. It may have been a more prestigious studio, but a major operation like Fox did not allow Laurel the same creative freedom he had enjoyed during most of his years at the Roach Studio. Plus, the team's style seemed a little old-fashioned compared to the slick, machine-gun delivery of newer, more contemporary comedians.

Nevertheless, the six films they did for Fox (plus two more for M-G-M) have their moments of fun, as imperfect as they are, and the box-office success of *Great Guns* (1941), *Air Raid Wardens* (1943), *The Dancing Masters* (1943) and *Nothing But Trouble* (1945; their all-time biggest hit!) confounds L and H purists who all but refuse to acknowledge the existence of these pictures.

Stan (left) and Oliver Hardy in their cinematic swan song, *Atoll K* (a.k.a., *Utopia,* 1951).

Even under less-than-ideal circumstances with less-than-ideal results, the enduring popularity of the team doesn't surprise historian Scott MacGillivray, as he explained in his superb study, *Laurel and Hardy: From the Forties Forward* (2nd ed., rev. and expanded, iUniverse, 2009):

> By 1945 Laurel & Hardy had been an indelible part of the American scene for almost 20 years. Very few performers could make that claim. This may be exactly the reason that so many Laurel & Hardy fans supported the "forties films" despite awkward scripts and strained situations. Moviegoers of the 1940s were enjoying Abbott & Costello, Danny Kaye, and Bob Hope on a superficial, ephemeral level: these were fast-talking, vaudevillian comedians doing topical, perishable jokes. The public enjoyed Laurel and Hardy on a more personal, nostalgic level. Stan and Ollie are old friends — and the fact that they have noticeably aged reminds us that they are *old* friends. A bit slower and milder than the current standard, set in their old routines, but still the same two funny fellows we've known from way back. And still jogging along at their own speed, despite being outrun by younger and faster competition.

It's a testament to Laurel and Hardy's enduring appeal that their lesser efforts were still able to entertain audiences. Emil Sitka, a veteran character actor/comedian best known for his appearances in numerous Three Stooges comedies, never had the opportunity to work with Laurel and Hardy but he was a great admirer of the duo and saw many of their movies first-run during the 1930s and '40s. He told the authors in 1989:

> I saw a lot of their Hal Roach movies when they were first released. I also saw the ones from the 1940s, the ones they made after they left Roach. I've read where those later ones are supposed to be awful, but I'll bet those critics never saw these films in a theater. Speaking as someone who actually saw these films in a theater — with a full audience — I can tell you that everybody laughed enthusiastically throughout all of those pictures. I never saw a Laurel and Hardy picture flop with an audience, and after I sat through a Laurel and Hardy picture, I always felt I got my money's worth — and more.

In recent years, it has come to light that Laurel was actually allowed to supervise and direct portions of *The Bullfighters* (1945), their last film for 20th Century–Fox (as well as their last American film), which no doubt explains why it's superior to the rest of Fox efforts. Under Laurel's guidance, Stan and Ollie seem more like the familiar Stan and Ollie than they do in any of their other post–Roach productions, and two set pieces Laurel personally contributed — a tit-for-tat water fight with Ed Gargan beside a hotel-lobby fountain and a reprise of their egg-breaking routine from *Hollywood Party* (1934) — compare favorably to their glory days.

For many Laurel and Hardy fans, it is unbearable to think that the abortive French-Italian production *Atoll K* (a.k.a. *Utopia* and *Robinson Cru-*

soeland, 1951) is Laurel's cinematic swansong. A poor culmination to such a rich legacy, *Atoll K* nevertheless contains some very funny scenes, despite the fact that Stan had to cope with illness and intolerable working conditions. As frail as he obviously was at the time, Stan still manages to rise to the occasion with moments, however fleeting, of glorious pantomime. That creative spirit and the honest desire to make people laugh are evident in all of Stan Laurel's movies.

Epilogue

Stan Laurel, Master of Comedy

After their Hollywood film career ended, Laurel and Hardy toured Europe, starred in the ill-fated *Atoll K* and planned a few projects that, unfortunately, never materialized. Plans for a proposed television series came to a halt when Hardy suffered a debilitating stroke in 1956. He died on August 7, 1957.

The Baby Boomer generation discovered Laurel and Hardy through television broadcasts of the team's '30s- and '40s- era films, the compilation *The Golden Age of Comedy* (1958), which excerpted some of their funniest silent comedies, and the 8mm prints of their movies made available to the home-movie market. As a result of the renewed interest, Stan received a slew of fan letters, which he graciously answered, and job offers, which he graciously turned down. Happily retired and living with his fourth wife, Ida, in Santa Monica, Stan

An out-of-character portrait of Stan Laurel from 1929.

spent his time relaxing and welcoming friends, fans, and assorted well-wishers to his Ocean Avenue apartment. He never lost his grand sense of humor or his interest in comedy, and after he passed away on February 23, 1965, he was eulogized as one of the greatest comedians of all time.

A plaque above his grave at the Hollywood Hills Forest Lawn Cemetery honors him with an epitaph that Stan would have been too modest to acknowledge, regardless of its accuracy:

> STAN LAUREL
> 1890–1965
> A MASTER OF COMEDY
> HIS GENIUS IN THE ART OF
> HUMOR BROUGHT GLADNESS
> TO THE WORLD HE LOVED.

Appendix: Compilations, Television Syndication, 8mm Movies and the Home-Video Market

Stan Laurel's solo comedies were generally forgotten in the wake of the more successful and artistically superior Laurel and Hardy films. By the time *The Bullfighters* was released in 1945, a younger generation raised on the team's pictures wasn't even aware that Stan had appeared in films without Ollie.

Laurel and Hardy didn't disappear from view after *The Bullfighters*. Far from it. Throughout the 1940s, their earlier sound-era comedies were reissued (sometimes under alternate or misspelled titles) by independent distributors such as Film Classics, Astor Pictures and Favorite Films. By the late 1940s, Laurel and Hardy movies were being broadcast on local television stations across the country.

These revivals only dealt with the Laurel and Hardy talkies.* Distributors and syndicators felt silent movies were too passé to appeal to modern audiences. One person who challenged this accepted belief was writer-producer Robert G. Youngson (1917–1974), who was preoccupied, if not obsessed, with silent cinema. During the 1940s, Youngson combed through historic newsreel footage in the Warner Bros. vaults and produced a series of one-reel shorts for the studio before graduating to a feature-length compilation *Fifty Years Before Your Eyes* (1951). One segment in *Fifty Years* focused on comedy films; a few years later Youngson would expand upon this concept with delightful results.

During this period, silent movies were often treated as outdated relics and objects of ridicule. The compilation feature Gaslight Follies *(1945) contained a re-edited version of* East Lynne *(1915), laced with sarcastic narration.*

The Golden Age of Comedy (1958) was Robert Youngson's heartfelt Valentine to the silent screen comedy of the 1920s. For one reason or another, Youngson wasn't able to include prime Charlie Chaplin, Buster Keaton or Harold Lloyd footage,* but he did showcase some of Laurel and Hardy's funniest sequences (from *Two Tars, You're Darn Tootin', The Battle of the Century, We Faw Down, Double Whoopee, Habeas Corpus*), plus memorable moments with Harry Langdon, Will Rogers, Ben Turpin, Jean Harlow, Carole Lombard, Billy Bevan and others.

The Golden Age of Comedy convulsed audiences everywhere it played and its remarkable success introduced Stan and Ollie to a whole new generation of fans. Youngson would continue to use footage from Laurel and Hardy silents for his subsequent compilations *When Comedy Was King* (1960), *Laurel and Hardy's Laughing 20's* (1965), *The Further Perils of Laurel and Hardy* (1967) and *4 Clowns* (1971).

But two other Youngson compilations, *Days of Thrills and Laughter* (1961) and *30 Years of Fun* (1963) traded upon the Laurel and Hardy brand name without delivering bona fide L&H footage. *Days of Thrills and Laughter* contains fleeting scenes of Stan and Ollie in their pre-team days. An excerpt of Stan in *Kill or Cure* (1923) came as a surprise to those unfamiliar with his solo career, but it proved disappointing to audiences who were expecting scenes of Laurel and Hardy together. Footage from *The Lucky Dog* (1921), revealing Stan and Ollie in their very first joint appearance (though they could hardly be called a team), was a major highlight of *30 Years of Fun*, yet it was a letdown for casual viewers who didn't care about the historical significance of this sequence and merely wanted to see trademark Laurel and Hardy antics.†

The Youngson compilations brought renewed attention to silent comedies in general and Laurel and Hardy in particular. In 1960, television syndicator National Telepix obtained a library of silent Our Gang two-reelers, with Mickey McGuire and Buster Brown shorts also tossed into the mix, and

---

Chaplin and Lloyd owned most of their major films outright and zealously protected the rights to them. The rights to Keaton's silent work were controlled by Raymond Rohauer, who was notoriously difficult. At the time, Chaplin's The Gold Rush *(1925) was not acknowledged to be in public domain. Keaton's* One Week *(1920),* Cops *(1922),* Daydreams *(1922),* The Balloonatic *(1923),* The General *(1926),* College *(1927) and* Steamboat Bill, Jr. *(1928) were in public domain, although Youngson apparently chose to pass on them for* The Golden Age of Comedy. Cops *was excerpted in another Youngson compilation,* When Comedy Was King *(1960), and footage from* Daydreams *was used for Youngson's* 30 Years of Fun *(1963). Producer-archivist Paul Killiam included an abridged version of* The General *in his silent-movie compilation,* The Great Chase *(1963).*

†*To illustrate Stan's solo career, different clips from* The Lucky Dog *and* Kill or Cure *were used for* Laurel and Hardy's Laughing 20's*. The clip from* The Lucky Dog *is only seconds long and does not feature any footage with Hardy.*

marketed them under the umbrella title *Mischief Makers*. National Telepix followed it up with a similar series, *Comedy Capers*, in 1961.

Like *Mischief Makers*, each "episode" of *Comedy Capers* was a two-reel short that had been whittled down to about 12 minutes in length. Original text and title dialogue cards were removed, rendering most of the storylines incoherent (gag-driven comedies survived better than those depending heavily upon plot), music scores were added, and each installment opened with the series' theme song. *Comedy Capers* and *Mischief Makers* were intended as kiddie fare, serving as a bridge between the animated cartoons (Popeye, Bugs Bunny) and live-action comedy shorts (Laurel and Hardy, The Three Stooges, Our Gang) that were currently enjoying great popularity on television. As such, they were hardly the best presentations for movie purists, yet during that pre-home video era, they made many hard-to-see films available for viewing. (The majority of these films never turned up in compilations or on the collector's market.)

While Laurel and Hardy were the top-billed stars of every *Comedy Capers* installment (the series consisted of 92 episodes), they were just two of several showcased performers; the others included Harry Langdon, Ben Turpin, Charley Chase, Larry Semon, Billy Bevan, Billy West, and the Keystone Cops. Stan and Ollie were seen in a few of the early films they made together as well as some of their solo efforts, though serious enthusiasts often had difficulty identifying what they were watching since all of the movies were retitled. Thus, Laurel and Hardy shorts such as *Do Detectives Think?* (1927), *Sailors, Beware!* (1927), *Flying Elephants* (1928) and *Liberty* (1929) were rechristened *The Bodyguards, Ship Ahooey, Cave Men* and *The Chase*, respectively. (An abridged version of *Slipping Wives* was also part of the package; research has not determined what the alternate title was.)

A handful of Stan's solo comedies (Hal Roach–Pathé silents from 1923) were also part of the *Comedy Capers* package: *White Wings* (retitled *The Painless Dentist*), *Pick and Shovel (The Miner), Collars and Cuffs (The Laundry), Short Orders (The Waiter), Save the Ship (The Houseboat), A Man About Town (The Gay Blade), Roughest Africa (The Hunter)* and *Under Two Jags (The Foreign Legion)*. While these truncated editions left a lot to be desired, they represented the widest exposure Stan's solo work had received since the films were first released. Viewers willing to overlook the limitations of the *Comedy Capers* format found themselves impressed by Stan's skills as a solo artist.

During the 1960s, silent-comedy enthusiasts who weren't content to wait for television broadcasts and theatrical compilations had the option to purchase 8mm (and 16mm) prints of select titles through various home-movie distributors. For Laurel and Hardy fans, Blackhawk Films in Davenport, Iowa, was *the* leading source for these movies, as this company had secured the license to reprint much of the team's output for Hal Roach. Blackhawk strove to supply film collectors with the most complete and best-quality prints possible, based on the material available to them. In addition to the Laurel and Hardy titles, which comprised a major portion of their catalog, Blackhawk sold a wide selection of comedies, dramas, Westerns, musicals and documentaries.

To supplement their Laurel and Hardy inventory, Blackhawk offered a sampling of Stan's solo efforts, including *Just Rambling Along* (1918), *White Wings* (1923), *Kill or Cure* (1923), *Oranges and Lemons* (1923), *Smithy* (1924), *West of Hot Dog* (1924) and *Half a Man* (1925).

Blackhawk had rivals in the 8mm marketplace, but few matched the quality of the Blackhawk line. At best, they were a way to obtain titles that Blackhawk didn't sell, such as Regent Films' edition of the solo Laurel comedy *On the Front Page* (1926). At worst, they were cheaply manufactured, bootlegged mini-reels containing incoherent chunks of murky-looking footage. Atlas Films, Coast Films and Carnival Films were three East Coast–based operations that specialized in churning out inexpensive product. Most of their releases were confusingly retitled (even for those familiar with the source movie) and sold in 50-foot abridgements, running approximately three minutes. Regardless, collectors who knew better frequently purchased these tacky little reels because they were an inexpensive (99¢ or less) way of getting a movie "fix" during those periods when the budget wouldn't allow for the higher-priced Blackhawk items. (Ironically, many former 8mm collectors, including the authors of this book, have retained their childhood affection for these bottom-of-the-barrel prints.)

In the United Kingdom, various home-movie distributors issued complete and condensed versions of Laurel's solo shorts under assorted alternate titles in the 9.5mm format. These releases included *The Noon Whistle* (retitled *Foreman Be Firm* and *Stick to Work*), *Collars and Cuffs* (as *Froth and Fury* and *Suds*), *Postage Due* (*Ghost in the Post, Penmanship* and *Stanley Is Forgetful*), *A Man About Town* (*Love at First Sight* and *Restless Romance*), *Roughest Africa* (*Oh Shoot*), *Pick and Shovel* (*Pick of the Miners*), *The Sleuth* (*Teatime Capers*) and *The Whole Truth* (*The Truth Tablet*).

By the early 1980s, the home-movie market was rendered obsolete with the advent of Beta and VHS videotape cassettes. (VHS would eventually emerge as the dominant format.) Since the Stan Laurel solo shorts were in "public domain" (a lapse in copyright status that makes the work in question available for free use to all), some titles turned up on bootleg-video volumes, often using Blackhawk Films prints for the video transfers.

As the DVD format supplanted videocassettes in the 1990s, some of Stan's solo films became ubiquitous selections on public-domain discs purporting to be Laurel and Hardy collections, when in fact these collections were primarily made up of solo Stan and Ollie efforts. The bulk of the bona fide L&H comedies are still under copyright, which makes them off limits to public-domain distributors. So unsuspecting consumers who think they've purchased a DVD collection of Laurel and Hardy movies are flabbergasted to find a Hardy-less Laurel in *Mud and Sand*, *Oranges and Lemons*, and *West of Hot Dog*, and Laurel *with* Hardy in *The Lucky Dog*.

Laurel's solo work finally received first-rate, respectful treatment in 2003 when Kino On Video released *The Stan Laurel Collection: Seventeen Comedy Shorts, 1923–1925* as part of their "Slapstick Symposium" series. Each title in this two-disc set was painstakingly restored by Lobster Films from the best archival material available. In 2008, Kino released a follow-up, *The Stan Laurel Collection Volume 2: Twenty-One Comedy Shorts: 1918–1926*, an equally impressive two-disc set also featuring restorations by Lobster Films.

Looser Than Loose, a DVD distributor that specializes in rare silent films, released several wonderful volumes entitled *The Larger World of Laurel and Hardy*, featuring many solo Laurel films that were not part of any other available collection, including some titles that had not seen American distribution in any format since their initial release. These collections also offered films in which Laurel did not appear, but did write and/or direct, some of them featuring Oliver Hardy.

There are still a number of Stan's solo movies that remain "lost," yet rather than bemoan their disappearance, we should celebrate the fact that so much of Stan's pre–Oliver Hardy work has been carefully preserved. These films represent a key chapter in the career of one of the screen's greatest comic geniuses. Today, this body of work is more accessible than ever.

BIBLIOGRAPHY

Books

Barr, Charles. *Laurel & Hardy*. Berkeley: University of California Press, 1968.
Cahn, William. *Harold Lloyd's World of Comedy*. New York: Duell, Sloan and Pearce, 1964.
Edmonds, I. G. *Big U: Universal in the Silent Days*. Cranbury, NJ: A. S. Barnes, 1977.
Everson, William K. *The Films of Laurel & Hardy*. New York: Citadel Press, 1967.
Guiles, Fred Lawrence. *Stan: The Life of Stan Laurel*. Briarcliff Manor, NY: Stein and Day, 1980.
Kerr, Walter. *The Silent Clowns*. New York: Alfred A. Knopf, 1975.
Lahue, Kalton C. *World of Laughter: The Motion Picture Comedy Short, 1910–1930*. Norman: University of Oklahoma Press, 1966.
_____, and Sam Gill. *Clown Princes and Court Jesters: Some Great Comics of the Silent Screen*. Cranbury, NJ: A. S. Barnes, 1970.
Louvish, Simon. *Stan and Ollie, The Roots of Comedy: The Double Life of Laurel and Hardy*. New York: Thomas Dunne, 2002.
MacGillivray, Scott. *Laurel & Hardy: From the Forties Forward*, 2nd ed., revised and expanded. Bloomington, IN: iUniverse, 2009.
McCabe, John. *Mr. Laurel and Mr. Hardy*. Garden City, NY: Doubleday, 1961.
_____. *The Comedy World of Stan Laurel*. Garden City, NY: Doubleday, 1973.
_____, Al Kilgore and Richard W. Bann. *Laurel & Hardy*. New York: E. P. Dutton, 1975.
Maltin, Leonard, ed. *The Laurel & Hardy Book*. New York: Curtis Books, 1973.
Mitchell, Glenn. *The Laurel & Hardy Encyclopedia*. United Kingdom: B. T. Batsford, 2003.
Scagnetti, Jack. *The Laurel & Hardy Scrapbook*. Middle Village, NY: Jonathan David, 1976.
Skretvedt, Randy. *Laurel and Hardy: The Magic Behind the Movies*, revised edition. Beverly Hills, CA: Past Times, 1994.
Stone, Rob. *Laurel or Hardy: The Solo Films of Stan Laurel and Oliver "Babe" Hardy*. California: Split Reel, 1996.

Articles

Kehr, Dave. "The Stan Laurel Collection, Volume 2." New York Times, July 8, 2008.
Sinnott, John. "The Stan Laurel Collection." DVD Talk, August 17, 2004.
Sinnott, John. "The Stan Laurel Collection 2." DVD Talk, June 3, 2008.
Verb, Boyd. "Laurel Without Hardy." Films in Review, March 1959.

INDEX

Numbers in *italics* indicate primary entries on Stan Laurel titles.
Numbers in ***bold italics*** indicate photographs or illustrations.

Abbott, Bud 4, 68, 76
Air Raid Wardens ***222***, 223
Along Came Auntie 172
Amalgamated Producing 38
Anderson, G.M. "Broncho Billy" 10, 38, 40, 48, 49, 51, 59, 60, 63
Another Fine Mess 157, 184
Anything Once! 173
Arbuckle, Roscoe "Fatty" 55, 81, 82, 121, 185
Armstrong, Billy 38
Artclass *see* Weiss Brothers
Astor Pictures 229
Atlas Films 232
Atoll K (Utopia) 43, ***223***, 224–226
Aubrey, Jimmy 129, 158
Ayres, Agnes 185, 188–190

Babes in Toyland 157
Bacon Grabbers 218
Baker, Eddie 80
Bann, Richard W. 104
Bara, Theda 17, 172, 185, 191
Barrymore, John 159, 160
The Battle of the Century 230
Be Big 153
Beach, Rex 98
Bears and Bad Men 31, *34*, *35*
Beau Hunks 65, 199
The Bellboy 2, ***3***
Below Zero 164, 171, 199
Berglund, Bo 40
Bernstein, Isadore 10
Bevan, Billy 230, 231
Big Business 66, 214, 218
Bischoff, Samuel 49
Blackhawk Films 11, 47, 231, 232
Blackton, J. Stuart 30
Block-Heads 20, 28, 219

Blood and Sand 54–56
Blotto 150, 153, 222
Boardman, True 38
Boardwalk Empire 148
The Bohemian Girl 150, 187, 199
Bonnie Scotland 18, 20, 199
Brats 20, 51, 103, 120, 136, 146, 218
British Pathé Exchange 112
Brooke, Tyler 178
Brooks, Foster 149
Brothers Under the Chin 119, *120*, 136
Browning, Tod 185
Bruckman, Clyde 209, 210
Bugs Bunny 231
The Bullfighters 70, 137, 146, 199, 224, 229
Bunny, John 30
Burlesque on Carmen 55
Burning Sands 91
Burns, Neal 13
Buscemi, Steve 148
Busch, Mae 191, 192
Bushman, Francis X. 38
Buster Brown 230
Busy Bodies 65, 110, 171
Butler, Frank 181

The Cabinet of Dr. Caligari 43
Carnival Films 232
Cavender, Glen 48, 147, ***156***
Cavett, Dick 41
Ceder, Ralph 92, 115
Chadwick, Helen 73
Chadwick Studios 76
The Champion 41
Chaplin, Charlie 1, 4, 5, 7–11, 16, 20, 24, 26, 27, 38, 41, 45, 48, 53, 55, 57, 72, 74, 75, 81, 94, 136, 143–145, 147, 149, 150, 152, 167, 169, 212, 230

235

Chase, Charley 5, 20, 23, 29, 64, 181, 213, 231
Chasing the Chaser 158, 167–169, 170
Chickens Come Home 66, 188, 191, 192
A Chump at Oxford 16, 49, 146, 158, 198
City Lights 174
Clark, Bobby 20
Clifford, Nat *see* Terry, Frank
The Cloudhopper 31
Clyde, Andy 20
Coast Films 232
Collars and Cuffs 70, *75–77*, 78, 91, 231, 232
Comedy Capers 90, 231
Conti, Albert 186
Cook, Clyde 144, 170, **171**, 172
Cooke, Alice 9
Cooke, Baldwin 9
Costello, Lou 4, 68, 76
Cowboys Cry for It 210
Crizer, T.J. 115
Crosby, Bing 20, 68
Crossley, Syd **139**, **171**, 173, 174, 183

Dahlberg, Mae Charlotte *see* Laurel, Mae
The Dancing Masters 223
Daniels, Mickey 128
Davidson, Max **197**
Davies, Marion 58
Days of Thrills and Laughter 43, 230
Dean, Priscilla 185–187, 191
Dearing, Edgar 178
DeMille, Cecil B. 196
Detained 26, 36, *132–134*
The Devil's Brother 66, 150, 157
Dirty Work in a Laundry 76
Dizzy Daddies 172
Dizzy Detectives 144
Do Detectives Think? 20, 180, 187, 195, *202–205*, 206, 208, 231
Do You Love Your Wife? 16, *17–20*, 21, 26, 28, 63
Doane, Warren 210
Dr. Heckyl and Mr. Hype 162
Dr. Jekyll and Mr. Hyde see *The Strange Case of Dr. Jekyll and Mr. Hyde*
Dr. Jekyll and Ms. Hyde 162
Dr. Pyckle and Mr. Pride 12, 125, *158*, **159**, *160–162*
A Dog's Life 41
The Dome Doctor 31
Don Key (Son of Burro) 172
Double Whoopee 230
Duck Soup 157, 180, *182–184*, 185–187, 203

Earles, Harry 201
Early to Bed 68, 215
Easy Street 136
The Egg 43–45, 65, 67, 70, 136
Engle, Billy **125**
Essanay Film Manufacturing Company 20, 22, 38, 41, 94, 143, 147
Everson, William K. 85, 182, 209
Eve's Love Letters 188–190

Fairbanks, Douglas 57
Favorite Films 229
Fields, W.C. 20
Fifty Years Before Your Eyes 229
The Fighting Kentuckian 215
Film Booking Office of America (FBO) 139
Film Classics 229
Films in Review 172
The Films of Laurel and Hardy 85, 182, 209
Finch, Flora 30
The Finishing Touch 44, 65, 67, 110, 171, 208, 218
Finlayson, James 65–69, 72, 85, 88, **89**, 91, 93, 97, 99, 100, **107**, 108, 110, 116, 118–120, **123**, 124, **125**, 127, 128, 133, 153, 167, **168**, 169–171, 173, 180, 181, 189, 191, 192, 196, 197, 205, 208, **210**, 211, 214
First National Pictures 41
The Fixer Uppers 20, 150, 187
Flicker Alley 47
Flowers, Bess 217
The Flying Deuces 18, 43, 65, 110, 199
Flying Elephants 35, 195, *205–209*, 210, 213, 215, 231
45 Minutes from Hollywood 175, 180, 181
4 Clowns 230
Fractured Flickers 162
Frauds and Frenzies 31, 32, *35–37*
Fries, Otto 52
From Soup to Nuts 153
Frozen Hearts 94, **95**, *96–98*
The Frozen North 151
Further Perils of Laurel and Hardy 230

Gargan, Ed 224
Garvin, Anita **152**, 153, **156**, 157, 158, 173, 189, 195, 201, 202, 222
Gas and Air 70, *77*, 78
Gasnier, Louis 210
Gavin, Jack 128
Get 'Em Young 173–176, 177, 178
Gierucki, Paul **8**, **95**

Gilbert, Dick 156
Gilmore, Helen 103
Girl Shy 164
Going Bye-Bye! 69, 199, 205
The Golden Age of Comedy 43, 226, 230
Gordon, Pete 35
Goulding, Alf 16
Grandma's Boy 153
Grant, Katherine 64, *71*, 72, 80, 90, 93, 97
Great Guns 67, 110, 199, 223
The Great Train Robbery 38, 120
Gregory, Ena 104, *107*, 108, 124, 127
Griffith, D.W. 24
Guiol, Fred 174, 194

Habeas Corpus 64, 170, 204, 230
Half a Man 156, 162, *163*, 164, 165, 232
Hall, Charlie 150, 192
The Handy Man 44, 52, 53, 59
Harbaugh, Carl 172
Hardly Working 77
Hardy, Oliver 1, 2, 4-7, 19, 20, 28, 32, 35-39, *40*, 41-44, 49, 51, 52, 56, 64-69, 72, 74, 79, 82, 89, 90, 96, 103, 104, 110, 113, 114, 116, 118, 132, 133, 136, 137, 140, 142, 144-146, 150, 157, 158, 164, 166, 170-176, 179-200, *201*, 202-210, 212-216, *217-223*, 224, 226, 229-233
Harlow, Jean 230
Hart, William S. 121
Hats Off 47
Healy, Betty 173
Healy, Ted 173
Helpmates 20, 23, 29, 164, 218
Hennecke, Clarence 169
Hickory Hiram 12, *13*
Hill, Thelma 147
Hog Wild 20, 110, 218
Hollywood Party 173, 200, 224
Holmes, Stuart 210
The Hoose-Gow 26, 72
Hoot Mon! 24, 25
Hope, Bob 68
Horne, James W. 171
Horsley, David 11
Hoskins, Allen "Farina" *217*
Housman, Arthur 149
Howard, Shemp 94
Huns and Hyphens 31, *32-34*, 35
The Hunter 90
Hunting Big Game in Africa with Gun and Camera 86

Hurlock, Madeline 184
Hustling for Health 26-29

Irving, William 149

Jamison, Bud 17-20, 22, 23, 26, 28
Jefferson, Arthur (Stan's father) 7, 183
Jefferson, Arthur Stanley (Stan Jefferson) 7, *8*, *9*, 10
Jekyll and Hyde ... Together Again 162
Jeske, George 66, 108
Jitterbugs 157, 175
Johnson, Mr. and Mrs. Martin E. 86
Johnston, Krag 172
Jones, F. Richard 174
Jones, Grover 172
Jones, Mark 76
Jungle Adventures 86
Just Rambling Along 20-24, 28, 50, 232

Karno, Fred 1, 7, *61*, 136
Keaton, Buster 4, 5, 7, 20, 31, 53, 75, 81, 82, 94, 109-111, 121, 151, 154, 167, 169, 230
Kennedy, Edgar 20, 113
Kennedy, Tom 45, 65
Keystone Cops 231
Keystone Studio 9, 20, 38, 68, 76
The Keystone Trio 9
Kill or Cure 47, *73-75*, 230, 232
Kino On Video (Kino International) 108, 111, 160, 233
Kornman, Mary 128
Kotsonaros, George 218
Ko Vert, Frederick 168

The Ladies Man 164
Laemmle, Carl 10, 11
Lahue, Kalton C. 31
Langdon, Harry 5, 75, 230, 231
The Larger World of Laurel and Hardy 233
Laurel, Ida 226
Laurel, Mae (Mae Charlotte Dahlberg) 9, 10, 56, 64, 97, 104, *107*, *123*, *125*, 128, 129, 146
Laurel and Hardy: From the Forties Forward 43
Laurel and Hardy: The Magic Behind the Movies 40, 194
Laurel and Hardy's Laughing 20's 230
The Laurel-Hardy Murder Case 204
Laurel or Hardy: The Solo Films of Stan Laurel and Oliver "Babe" Hardy 5, 12, 24, 40, 160

Leave 'Em Laughing 195, 208
Lehrman, Henry 11
Leonard, Julie 137, 153
Let's Face It 68
Lewis, Jerry 1, **3**, 5, 77, 162, 164
Lewis, Joe E. 149
Liberty 110, 231
Linthicum, Dan 16
The Live Ghost 69, 204
L-KO Motion Picture Kompany 11
Lloyd, Harold 5, 12, 16, 20, 26, 29, 53, 75, 92, 152, 153, 164, 167, 169, 230
Lobach, Marvin 69
Lobster Films 47, 108, 111, 233
Lombard, Carole 230
Lonesome Luke 16
Looser Than Loose 233
The Lost Films of Laurel and Hardy 92
Love 'Em and Weep 190–192, 213, 214
The Lucky Dog 38, 39, **40**, 41–43, 230, 233
Lyons, Edgar 153

Macdon Pictures 38
MacGillivray, Scott 43, 224
Madame Mystery 172
Malatesta, Fred 188
A Man About Town 83, 84–86, 205, 231, 232
Mandarin Mix-Up 44, 67, *134*, **135**, *136*, *137*
Marcus, James 184
Martin, Dean 2, 4, 149
McCabe, John 58, 59, 194
McCarey, Leo 42, 170, 189, 215
McCullough, Paul 20
McGowan, Robert 181
Me and My Pal 29
The Merry Widower 172
Metro-Goldwyn-Mayer 208, 215, 223
Metro Pictures Corporation 49, 58, 59
Mickey McGuire 230
The Midnight Patrol 29
Miller, Rube 14
Mineau, Charlotte 191, 192
Mischief Makers 231
Mr. Laurel and Mr. Hardy 58
Mixed Nuts 10, 21, 23, 48, **49**, 50
Modern Times 72, 81
Monsieur Beaucaire 138
Monsieur Don't Care 129, *138*, **139**
Montana, Bull 58
Montgomery, Earl 129
Monty Python and the Holy Grail 59
Moonlight and Noses 144, *170*

Moonshine 121
Mosquini, Marie 17, 28, 29, 82
Mother's Joy *102–105*, 120, 136
Mud and Sand 53, **54**, *55–57*, 63, 138, 233
The Music Box 20, 23, 47, 219, **220**
Mutual Film Corporation 147
My Wife's Relations 154
My Wonderful World of Slapstick 31
Myers, Harry 174, 175

National Telepix 230
Navy Blues 153–155
Near Dublin *105*, *106*, **107**, *108*, 205
Neilson, Lois 20, 167
Nestor Comedies 11
Never Too Old 172
The Nickel Hopper 173
A Night Out 147, 150
Night Owls 170, **219**
No Man's Law 188
No Place Like Jail 25, *26*, 133
The Noon Whistle 44, 65–67, 70, 91, 110, 136, 170, 232
Normand, Mabel 172, 173
Norton, Jack 149
Nothing But Trouble 223
Novello, Art *see* Toto
Now I'll Tell One 181, 213
Nuts in May 9, *10*, 12, 21, 48, 50, 91
The Nutty Professor 162

O, It's Great to Be Crazy 14, *15*
Oakland, Vivien 217
Oliver the Eighth 144, 204
On the Front Page 176, **177**, *178*, *179*, 232
One A.M. 147, 149, 150
One Hour Married 173
One Week 110
Oranges and Lemons 70, *78*, **79**, 80, 81, 232, 233
Our Gang 103, 128, 136, 161, 181, **217**, 230, 231
Our Relations 66, 145, 146, 173, 219
Our Wife 164

Pack Up Your Troubles 110, 199
Pallette, Eugene 210
Palma, Joe 94
Papyrus 112, 115
Pardon My Backfire 77
Pardon My Sarong 68
Pardon Us 26
Parrott, James 20, 23, 170, 171
Parrott, Paul 63

Pathé Exchange 16, 17, 108, 121, 208, 215, 231
Payson, Blanche 35, 164
Pembroke, Percy "Perc" 129, 132, 165
Perfect Day 20
The Pest 10, 45, **46**, 47, 48, 50, 73, 74
Pete the Pup (Tige) 161
Phoney Photos 12, 13
Pick and Shovel 70, **71**, 72, 73, 78, 231, 232
Pie-Eyed 147, **148**, 149, 150
Pollard, Harry "Snub" 16, 29, 69
Popeye 231
Porter, Edwin S. 38, 120
Postage Due 116, **117**, 118, 119, 232
Pratt, Gil 156
Purviance, Edna 144, 145
Putting Pants on Philip 25, 178, 215, 216

Raggedy Rose 172, 173
Rappé, Virginia 185
Rawlinson, Herbert 185, 186
Regent Films 232
Reynolds, Vera 48
Rich, Lillian **177**, 178
Richard, Viola 194, 195, **197**, 208
Richmond, Bill 2
Rio Rita 76
Roach, Hal 2, 3, 16, 17, 19, 20–22, 25, 26, 29, 42, 47, 59, 60, **61**, **62**, 63, 64, 66, 69, 72, 76, 77, 90, 92, 103, 118, 121, 127–129, 131, 132, 153, 158, 161, 165–167, 169, 171–173, 178, 180, 181, 185, 187–189, 191, 195, 198, 208, 210, 212, 214, 215, **220**, 223, 224, 231, 232
Road to Morocco 68
Robbins, Jess 40
Robin Hood 57
Rock, Joe 12, 121, 128, 129, **130**, **131**, 132, 137–139, 146, 153, 155, 156, 158, 165, 166, 174, 216, **217**
Rock, Murray **163**
Rogers, Will 29, 230
Rohauer, Raymond 162
Rolin Film Company 16, 21, 23, 26, 30, 60
Roughest Africa 86, **87**, 88, **89**, 90, 92, 125, 231, 232
Rowe, George 107, 118, **125**, 153, 169
Ruge, Billy 183
Rupert of Hee Haw 122, **123**, 124, **125**

Sailors, Beware! 194, 199, 200, **201**, **202**, 209, 231
Sampson, Teddie 13

Saps at Sea 223
Save the Ship 83, 84, 231
Saved from the Flames 47
The Sawmill 31, 171
Scorching Sands 90–92
Scram! 150
The Second Hundred Years 26, 36, 70, 187, 215, 216
Seeing the World 175, 181
Selznick Distributing Corporation 129, 139
Semon, Larry 5, 30–36, 43–45, 76, 79, 171, 231
Sennett, Mack 9, 20, 60, 68, 69, 167, 172
Seymour, Clarine 23, 24
The Sheik 55, 188
Shields, Sherbourne 171
Short Kilts 25, **126–128**
Short Orders 70, 80–83, 231
Should Husbands Pay? 172
Should Married Men Go Home? 25, 195
Should Men Walk Home? 173
Should Tall Men Marry? 209, **210**, 211, 212
The Show 34
Sitka, Emil 224
Skretvedt, Randy 40, 194, 204
Slappyhappy Sleuths 77
Sleeper, Martha 211
The Sleuth 155, **156**, 157, 158, 165, 232
Slipping Wives 184–188, 213, 231
Smith, Albert E. 30
Smith, Clifford 121
Smith, Hal 224
Smithy 109–111, 171, 197, 232
Snow, H.A. 86
The Snow Hawk 129, 151, **152**, 153
The Soilers 98, **99**, 100, **101**, 125
Sojin 194
Somewhere in Wrong 142–145
The Son of the Sheik 188
Sons of the Desert (film) 29, 219
Sons of the Desert (organization) 36
The Spoilers 98, 100
Spoor, George K. 38
The Stan Jefferson Trio **8**, 9
The Stan Laurel Collection 233
The Stan Laurel Collection Volume 2 233
Stanley, Forrest 188, 189
Stanley Comedies 10
Starvation Blues **171**
Sterling, Ford 13
Sterling, Merta 52
The Stern Brothers 11

Stevens, George 214
Stevenson, Charles 17, 18
Stevenson, Robert Louis 159, 162
Stone, Rob 5, 9, 12, 14, 16, 24, 31, 40, 47, 59, 68, 77, 93, 104, 108, 119, 132, 160, 172, 174, 188
The Strange Case of Dr. Jekyll and Mr. Hyde 159
Sugar Daddies 20, 118, 192, *212–215*, 216
Sweet, Harry 156, 164, 165
Swiss Miss 20, 44, 67, 137, 150, 187

Taylor, William Desmond 173S
Terry, Frank (Nat Clifford) 29, 171
That's My Wife 175, 176
Their First Mistake 219
Their Purple Moment 153, 188
Them Thar Hills 150
30 Years of Fun 43, 230
The Three Stooges 20, 72, 77, 94, 144, 173, 187, 224, 231
Tige *see* Pete the Pup
Tit for Tat 195
Todd, Thelma 113, 184, 192
Toto (Arnold Novello) 16, 17, 23
Towed in a Hole 219, 222
The Tramp 143, 144
Triple Trouble 94
Turpin, Ben 38, 150, 151, 230, 231
Twentieth Century–Fox 223, 224
Twice Two 146
Twins 145–147
Two Tars 20, 23, 147, 218, 230

Unaccustomed As We Are 28, 113, 114, 188, 218
Under Two Flags 63
Under Two Jags 59, *63–65*, 92, 185, 231
Unfriendly Enemies 169
Universal Studios 11, 17, 137, 142
Utopia see *Atoll K*

Valentino, Rudolph 54, 55, 56, 138, 188
Vaughn, Alberta **156**
Veidt, Conrad 43
Velez, Lupe 200, **201**
Verb, Boyd 172
Violent Is the Word for Curly 77
Vitagraph Company of America 30, 32, 37, 40, 76, 129
The Volga Boatman 196
Von Stroheim, Erich 97

Waite, Malcolm 194
Walker, H.M. "Beanie" 96, 121
Wandering Papas 170, 171
Way Out West 20, 44, 66, 81, 140, 190, 219
Wayne, John 215
We Faw Down 188, 217, 218, 230
The Weak End Party 44, 45, *50–52*
West of Hot Dog *139–142*, 232, 233
What's the World Coming To? 172
When Comedy Was King 43
When Knighthood Was in Flower 58
When Knights Were Cold 57, **58**, 59
White Wings *67–70*, 231, 232
The Whole Truth *92–94*, 232
Whose Zoo? 13, 14
Why Girls Love Sailors 179, *193–195*, 196, 200, 202
Weiss Brothers 69
West, Billy 52, 231
Wide Open Spaces *120–122*
Wife Tamers 172
Wild Bill Hiccough 120, 121
Wild Bill Hickok 121
Wild Poses 103, 136
Williamson, Robin E. 91
Willis, Leo 128
Winthrop, Joy 47
Wise Guys Prefer Brunettes 173
With Love and Hisses 110, *195*, *196*, **197**, 198, *199*, 200, 201
The Wizard of Oz 34
Wong, Anna May 194
Work 27
World of Laughter: The Motion Picture Comedy Short, 1910–1930 31
Wray, Fay 169

Yates, Hal 172
Yes, Yes, Nanette 169, 170
Young, Frank 115
Young, Noah 19, 20, 22, 29, 74, 170, 204
Youngson, Robert 43, 229, 230
Your Husband's Past 172
You're Darn Tootin' 18, 218, 230
Yukon Jake 151

Zeb vs. Paprika 92, 93, *111–113*, **114**, *115*, *116*, 117
Zev 112, 115

www.ingramcontent.com/pod-product-compliance
Ingram Content Group UK Ltd.
Pitfield, Milton Keynes, MK11 3LW, UK
UKHW041940140426
5217IPUK00014B/579